THE M. & E. HANDBOOK SERIES

COST ACCOUNTANCY

THE M. & E. HANDBOOK SERIES

COST ACCOUNTANCY

W. M. HARPER, A.C.W.A.

MACDONALD & EVANS LTD
8 John Street, London WC1N 2HY
1967

First published March 1967
Reprinted September 1967
Reprinted March 1969
Reprinted (with amendments) October 1969
Reprinted June 1972
Reprinted (with amendments) April 1973

ISBN: 0 7121 0311 2

Printed in Great Britain by Richard Clay (The Chaucer Press), Ltd., Bungay, Suffolk

GENERAL INTRODUCTION

The HANDBOOK Series of Study Notes

HANDBOOKS are a new form of printed study notes designed to help students to prepare and revise for professional and other examinations. The books are carefully programmed so as to be self-contained courses of tuition in the subjects they cover. For this purpose they comprise detailed notes, self-testing questions and hints on examination technique.

HANDBOOKS can be used on their own or in conjunction with recommended text-books. They are written by college lecturers, examiners, and others with wide experience of students' difficulties and requirements. At all stages the main objective of the authors has been to prepare students for the practical business of passing examinations.

P. W. D. Redmond
General Editor

NOTICE TO LECTURERS

Many lecturers are now using HANDBOOKS as working texts to save time otherwise wasted by students in protracted note-taking. The purpose of the series is to meet practical teaching requirements as far as possible, and lecturers are cordially invited to forward comments or criticisms to the Publishers for consideration.

AUTHOR'S PREFACE

IN this relatively short book I have attempted to summarise all the costing theory demanded by the major professional examining bodies for their papers on cost accountancy. This apparently ambitious task lies within the bounds of possibility only because cost accounting is essentially a practical technique and the theory is not particularly extensive. Students, therefore, should find this book a useful supplement to their studies, but I must, however, emphasise that it can only be a supplement—the various practical applications are unending, and anyone who knows nothing of these really knows nothing of cost accounting.

I hope, for this reason, that lecturers will find this book of value. It will enable them to devote most of their class time to developing the application of the theoretical concepts to different practical situations, and to discussing all the awkward complications that arise when trying to operate the simplest of theoretical systems in the real world of the shop-floor and the busy manager's office. At the same time the student can allow his imagination to dwell on the picture evoked by his lecturer without being distracted by the fear that he is failing to make a note of some necessary piece of theory.

1. Intermediate and final costing. The difference between intermediate and final costing, as defined by most examining bodies, is essentially one of degree, the final candidate being expected to have a deeper insight into topics than the intermediate candidate. In the text of this book I have made no distinction between these grades, though intermediate students would probably be wise to give priority to topics up to and including the Section on Simple Process Costing in Chapter XII and final students priority to subsequent topics.

2. Progress tests. The Progress Tests at the end of each chapter have been divided into two parts, *Principles* and *Practice.* The questions in the part on principles of costing can be answered from the text and the numbers in brackets after each question refer to the relevant paragraphs of the chapter. Full worked answers to the practical questions are provided in Appendix III.

3. Terminology. In this book many definitions have been taken from the *Terminology of Cost Accountancy*, January 1966, and my thanks are due to the Institute of Cost and Works Accountants for permission to use them. Where I have not given the Institute's definitions it is because when writing this book I wanted students to grasp concepts and gain insight into what "goes on," and in my experience definitions that are ideal for a practitioner who appreciates the full significance of each phrase are often only confusing to the student who lacks such appreciation. However, students should ultimately examine and learn the terminology given in the Institute of Cost and Works Accountants' publication on this topic, particularly those, of course, who are *I.C.W.A.* students.

Note to students studying for the examinations of the Institute of Cost and Works Accountants.

The variance analyses (cost and sales margin) given in this book are in accordance with the Institute's terminology except for the following minor differences:

INSTITUTE'S TERMINOLOGY	EQUIVALENT VARIANCES IN THIS BOOK
(i) Overhead expenditure variance	Fixed overhead expenditure variance + Variable overhead variance
(ii) Overhead efficiency variance	Variable overhead efficiency variance

The terminology does not distinguish between fixed and variable overhead variances (though this distinction is, of course, necessary to carry out the actual computations), nor does it analyse the sales margin quantity variance. Conversely, it analyses the overhead expenditure variance into price and utilisation variances which are not discussed in the book. These are simply the usual price and usage type variances applied to services.

4. Decimal currency. This book follows the recommendations of the various accountancy bodies and of the examining bodies responsible for National Further Education syllabuses and examinations, and gives decimal currency equivalents where appropriate. These are set out in the form advised by the Decimal Currency Board, as described in *Decimal Currency: Expressions of Amounts in printing, writing and in speech*, H.M.S.O., 1968.

5. Design of forms. The cost accountant uses internal forms almost exclusively, and consequently he should know something of the design of such forms. In this book, instead of giving a large number of form examples I have included a section on form design (in Appendix I) and illustrated only the more important of the forms discussed. This, I hope, will induce students to regard forms as things to be designed for the specific purpose they are to serve in an individual enterprise and not to be lavishly copied from a textbook.

6. Bibliography. For further study the student is referred to the following books:

For more detailed study of cost accounting:

H. J. Wheldon, *Cost Accounting and Costing Methods*, 11th ed. (Macdonald & Evans).
Buyers & Holmes, *Principles of Cost Accountancy* (Cassell).
R. Warwick Dobson, *An Introduction to Cost Accountancy* (Gee).

For a more detailed coverage of labour remuneration and incentives:

Institute of Cost and Works Accountants, *Employee Remuneration and Incentives* (Gee).

For more detailed coverage of standard costing and budgetary control:

J. Batty, *Standard Costing* (Macdonald & Evans).
Institute of Chartered Accountants in England and Wales, *Standard Costing*.

For the appreciation of presentation of information, scattergraph analysis, and other statistical techniques:

W. M. Harper, *Statistics* (Macdonald & Evans).

7. Acknowledgments. I gratefully acknowledge permission to quote from the past examination papers of the following bodies:

Association of Certified and Corporate Accountants (*A.C.C.A.*).
Chartered Institute of Secretaries (*C.I.S.*).
Corporation of Secretaries (*C. of S.*).
Institute of Chartered Accountants in England and Wales (*C.A.*).
Institute of Cost and Works Accountants (*I.C.W.A.*).
Royal Society of Arts (*R.S.A.*).

W.M.H.

December 1966, August 1969

CONTENTS

LIST OF FIGURES

PART ONE

FUNDAMENTALS

CHAPTER I

THE THEORY OF COSTING

INTRODUCTION

FOR study purposes the subject of cost accountancy can be broken down into a number of major topics. In this book each major topic has been made the subject of a *part.* In order to give the student a general pre-view of the subject the essence of each part, together with an outline of its contents, is here briefly summarised.

Part One: Fundamentals. In this part the fundamental concepts and principles of costing are outlined. Students approaching costing for the first time may find this a difficult or even, on the face of it, an inconsequential part; indeed, there is educational evidence that the importance of the foundations of a subject can be appreciated only after the "building," as it were, is virtually complete. However, it should be tackled first before passing on to the rest of the book, and then read again at the end, when the student may well gain more than he did at the first reading. Moreover, by doing this the student will to some extent have subjected himself to the valuable educational technique whereby the lecturer first tells the student what he *will* be telling him, then *tells* him and then tells him what he *has* told him.

Part Two: Cost Data. Before any cost methods or techniques can be examined it is necessary to be fully conversant with the different types of cost data. It must always be remembered that a cost statement can never be more accurate or reliable than the cost data upon which it is based. Appreciation of the sources of such data and the background from which they originate is a vital part of the cost accountant's know-how.

This part deals with this aspect of cost accountancy—cost data relating to materials, labour and expenses being dealt with in that order.

Part Three: Cost Ascertainment. Cost ascertainment is the historical function of cost accounting and involves finding out what the product cost. Traditionally the objective was to ascertain this cost after allowing for *all* costs, and so the technique of *total absorption costing* was employed. The objective of this technique is to absorb all costs, direct and indirect, into cost units. The charging of direct costs involves little technical difficulty; direct materials and direct labour are charged to cost units from the material and labour analyses respectively, and direct expenses rarely give any trouble. In the case of indirect costs (overheads), however, there is the problem of sharing these costs equitably between cost units, and this part opens with a chapter that considers this problem. Once this has been examined it is possible to see how cost figures relating to a single cost unit can be brought together in the form of a job cost. This in turn enables us to look at the book-keeping entries that will be needed in the Ledger. Next we will study the costing method employed when all the cost units are identical, before dealing finally with the rather special cases where waste, scrap, by- and joint products arise.

The student should appreciate that throughout this part we will be employing the total absorption technique: *i.e.* taking the *total* cost of running the enterprise and absorbing this entire cost into all the individual cost units so that every cost ultimately comes to rest in one or a number of these cost units. He should note the results given by this technique so as to be able to compare it subsequently with the marginal costing and standard costing techniques.

Part Four: Marginal Costs. In this part we will be concerned with techniques that are of particular importance in *decision-making*. When making decisions management initially want figures relating to possible future costs and incomes. This involves predicting costs, which in turn requires a thorough understanding of how costs behave. The first chapter, on break-even charts, therefore examines the principles that lie behind the behaviour and prediction of costs.

Management, however, also need these predicted costs to be put in a meaningful way. Essentially, when making a decision between a number of alternatives management is more concerned with the cost and income *differences* between alternatives rather than the absolute totals themselves. Costing that aims to exclude all costs which would be unchanged as the result of the decision made goes under the name of *marginal costing* and is the subject of the second chapter.

Part Five: Cost Planning and Control. Together with decision-making, *cost planning and control* is one of the two major functions of modern costing. Today industry is so complex that if management fails to plan costs and incomes it risks finding itself at the end of a trading period in an unexpectedly adverse position. *Planning* costs ensures that management start out in a favourable direction, but cost plans themselves are of little value unless management ensure the plans are kept to; *i.e.* unless they *control* costs.

This part opens with a brief outline of the theory of cost control, and then we examine cost planning based first on a period of time (budget) and then on a cost unit (standard cost). Next we consider the comparison of actual figures with planned figures and see how an analysis of all differences can be made so that management can pin-point exactly where the plan failed and the effect on profit of such failures. The effect of a standard cost system on the book-keeping is outlined, and in the final chapter the actual application of standard cost and budgetary control is discussed in the light of the other chapters.

Part Six: The Practice of Costing: In this last part a number of topics that relate mainly to the practical application of costing to enterprises are considered, including uniform costing and cost audits. The part concludes by emphasising that the theory of costing has no value without a keen appreciation of the practical circumstances in which it will be used, showing that costing can only be of real value when used as a down-to-earth pragmatic tool in the hands of an experienced and well-informed practitioner.

WHY COST?

1. Costing as a management service. It is the function of managers to manage those enterprises, or parts of enterprises, that are under their control. They can carry out this function effectively only if they have full information relating to all factors relevant to the area of their control. Among these factors are the following:

(*a*) Market, *e.g.* market potential, consumer requirements.
(*b*) Competitive position, *e.g.* competitors' prices and quality, plans of competitors.

(c) Economic environment, *e.g.* economic trends, availability of credit, tax laws.
(d) Personnel, *e.g.* skills, morale, union objectives.
(e) Production, *e.g.* processes, capacity, quality levels.
(f) Engineering, *e.g.* plant life, power requirements.
(g) Purchasing, *e.g.* material prices, quality, reliability of suppliers.
(h) Costs.

It is the purpose of costing to provide management with information relating to this last factor, costs.

Careful consideration of this concept of costing as a management service reveals that:

(a) Costs are prepared *for management* in order to *assist them to manage*. There is no virtue in preparing cost figures for their own sake.
(b) Cost is not the only factor managers must consider. They will not, therefore, run their enterprises or departments on a basis of cost figures only. Conversely, no good manager will attempt to manage without having the best cost information it is possible to obtain.

2. The objective of costing. Costing, then, aims at presenting managers with the cost information they need in order to manage effectively. More specifically, it is *information that indicates the economic implications and consequences of their decisions*. If a manager is, for example, considering the acceptance of a contract, he needs to know whether or not an adequate profit will arise from it—and if the contract is accepted, he will need to know how much profit he actually made (or lost) so that his future decisions can benefit from past experience. Similarly, when considering replacement of hand labour by a machine, the manager will need to know the probable savings or otherwise.

(However, the final decision may be made on other than economic grounds; for instance, the possibility of provoking a strike may be the determining factor.)

3. Money as a measure of economic performance. It is vitally important to appreciate that money has a double function in the running of modern enterprises:

(a) *It is an economic factor of production.* Money is *physically* as necessary as land, labour or materials. Without money (or credit, which is the same thing to a businessman) machines cannot be bought, debtors and stocks financed, nor taxes paid. In the same way as there are suppliers of materials there are suppliers of money—banks, finance institutions, shareholders and, of course, customers. A company can no more operate without money (or credit) than it can without any other economic factor of production.

(*b*) *It is a measure of economic performance.* Many management decisions hinge upon varying the proportions of the economic factors used, *e.g.* reducing labour hours by increasing machine hours, or reducing losses of material by improving storage equipment. Unfortunately usage of different economic factors cannot be directly compared; one cannot compare labour hours with machine hours, or hundredweights of material with feet of shelving. In order to render these things comparable they must be converted to a common measure, and *money* is the measure adopted. By converting the hours, hundredweights, etc., involved in various projects into money values (and, if need be, similarly converting the goods or services produced to money values) the projects can be compared with each other and the most economical one selected.

4. Financial, cost and management accounting. In modern business the three functions of financial, cost and management accounting are all carried out together and in many ways merge with each other. Hard and fast distinctions between these functions cannot be made, but in general their basic approaches can be outlined as follows:

(*a*) *Financial accounting.* This function treats money as an economic factor of production. Consequently cheques, notes, bank balances and overdrafts, debtors and creditors feature largely in this type of accounting. Indeed, the historical origin of financial accounting was literally "to account for" the money entrusted to the business.

(*b*) *Cost accounting.* This function treats money as a measure of economic performance. Here, then, the values of resources used are found and the techniques employed are all aimed at arranging money information in such a way that management is given as clear an indication as possible of their performance and the direction in which they must move in order to improve their economic efficiency.

(c) *Management accounting.* This function evolved out of cost accounting and the two are still closely interlinked. In management accounting, however, economic performance is not only measured but the whole of the enterprise is looked at as a single unit of business operating within an economic environment. In brief, management accounting involves advising management of the economic implications and consequences of their decisions. This, incidentally, leads to a close study of money as an economic resource and its sources of supply. Money also serves as a measure of economic performance to evaluate its use as an economic factor of production, *e.g.* the rate of return on capital employed.

BASIC COSTING CONCEPTS

5. What is a cost? A *cost* is the value of economic resources used as a result of producing or doing the thing costed. In a majority of cases the value of the economic resources used is the amount of money spent in acquiring or producing them, but this is not always so. For instance, if the market price of an article was £5 at the time of purchase and rose to £7 by the time it was actually used in production, then, strictly speaking, the cost is £7, since this is the *value* of the article used.

There are probably some people who would disagree with this definition of cost, and who would regard cost as simply what was paid for an economic resource. Yet clearly in the foregoing example, if the article was sold in its unmanufactured state for £6, then taking £5 as the cost means there is £1 profit. But this is not a measure of management's *manufacturing* performance (though it may be a good measure of their speculative performance). This simpler concept of cost relates really to measuring excess of income over expenditure, that is, we are back to the financial accounting concept of money as cash. In cost accounting one should, however, always bear in mind the ultimate need to consider economic values for measuring economic performance rather than cash expenditure.

Another example where cost does not equate to expectation is where the enterprise may own and use a block of land for which an annual rent of £500 could otherwise be obtained. This is the use value of the land and should, therefore, be regarded as its annual cost, since the enterprise is sacrificing the £500 in order to use the land. A cost relating to the *sacrifice* an enterprise makes, by use of some resource rather than the cash expenditure on that resource, is called an *opportunity cost.*

6. Cost = usage × price. Cost has been defined as "the value of economic resources used." Note that for each resource the "value" is always made up of two components: the quantity used of the resource and the price per unit. Cost, therefore, can be mathematically stated as:

$$Cost = Usage \times Price$$

This means that costing involves ascertaining both a usage figure and a price figure. Students will find this double-component feature arises throughout costing theory, and it is particularly significant in standard costing.

7. Profit appropriations excluded from costs. Profit appropriations are *not* regarded as costs. Thus dividends and taxes based on profits are not regarded as costs, although in decision-making it sometimes happens that different alternatives do not result in the same tax incidence (*e.g.* purchasing a second-hand machine means that the investment grant on a new machine is lost). In such cases the extra taxes payable must be regarded as costs of the various alternatives for the purpose of making the decision.

8. Cost units. We cannot have "costs" unless there are things being costed (such as pens, bridges, theatre performances, departments or factories) and when these are the things that the enterprise or department is set up to provide, then such "things" are termed "cost units." A *cost unit*, then, can be defined as a unit of quantity of produce, service or time in relation to which costs may be ascertained or expressed.

These cost units may be:

(*a*) Units of production, *e.g.* jobs, contracts, tons of material, gallons of liquid, books, pairs of shoes.
(*b*) Units of service, *e.g.* kilowatt-hours, cinema seats, passenger-miles, hospital operations, consulting hours.

NOTE: Students should learn and understand the definition of a cost unit, as the term is frequently used in this book. In most cases cost units are simply the individual items of production, and providing the student appreciates the wider meaning (*e.g.* service units) he may regard them as such for study purposes.

9. Cost centres. Costs can relate to things other than cost units. They can refer to individual parts of the enterprise. Such parts can range from an entire factory (in the case of a company with a group of factories) down to a single machine or a single salesman. Any part of an enterprise to which costs can be charged is called a *cost centre*. A cost centre can be:

(*a*) *Geographical*, *i.e.* an area such as a department, store-yard or sales area.
(*b*) *An item of equipment*, *e.g.* lathe, fork-lift truck, delivery vehicle.
(*c*) *A person*, *e.g.* salesman.

Charging costs to a cost centre simply involves charging to that centre those costs which relate to it. Thus a lathe will be charged with its costs of depreciation, maintenance, power and cleaning and also with a share of the rent, rates, heat and light costs of the enterprise. A salesman "cost centre" similarly will be charged with his salary, commission, expenses, entertainment, telephone, postage, samples, car costs (and the car itself may, of course, be a cost centre charged with depreciation, petrol, oil, maintenance, tyres, licence, insurance, etc.) and so on.

10. General costing principles. The following general costing principles should be observed:

(*a*) *Costs should be related as closely as possible to their causes*. A foreman's salary, for instance, cannot usually be pinned down to a single cost unit, but it should be so recorded that such a cost can be shared only among the cost units passing through that foreman's department and *not among any units remaining outside his department*. This relating of cost to cause, pinning the cost down so that it covers neither more nor less than the cost units or cost centres which caused it, is an important aspect of good costing. Grouping overheads into one single "general expenses" category is to be avoided if at all possible.

(*b*) *A cost is not charged until it is incurred*. This appears obvious, but is often forgotten. For instance, care should be taken that a cost unit is not charged with any selling costs while it is still in the factory, since units cannot incur selling costs until they are sold. Similarly, when the cost of lost units must be carried by good units such a charge cannot be imposed on units which have not passed the point of loss.

(*c*) *The "prudence" convention should be ignored.* One of the historical functions of financial accounting is to value assets conservatively in order to avoid the risk of paying dividends out of capital. This results in the "prudence" convention of financial accounting. This convention must be ignored in cost accounting, otherwise there is a danger that management appraisal of the profitability of projects may be vitiated. For instance, to fail to take advantage of a project which would in fact net £20,000 means that in effect the enterprise loses £20,000. Cost statements should as far as possible give the facts with no known bias. If a contingency needs to be taken into consideration it should be shown separately and distinctly.

(*d*) *Abnormal costs are excluded from costs.* Costing aims to provide information on economic performance to assist managers to manage. Abnormal costs, however, do not promote this object, since they do not relate to normal economic performance that management can influence but instead to infrequent accidents that cannot be controlled. Their presence in the costs, therefore, would tend to distort cost figures and mislead management as to their economic performance as managers under normal conditions. To charge gale damage costs (for instance) may result in a doubling of normal costs per unit, but such a figure gives production managers no real information as to their production efficiency. Abnormal costs are therefore excluded from costs.

(*e*) *Past costs are never charged to future periods.* There is often a temptation to charge past costs, or unrecovered costs, to a later period on the grounds that these costs have to be recovered somewhere, and since the past has gone they can be recovered only in future periods. This is quite wrong. Inclusion of past costs in future periods results in the distortion of the performance figures for those periods and gives rise to a risk of misleading management.

Care should be taken, however, in deciding whether a cost is "past" or not, a *past cost* being one from which no more benefit can be expected. If, however, the *benefit* of a particular cost comes in a later period, then such a cost is not a past cost and can, indeed must, be capitalised and charged in the period of benefit. (This is simply the old accountancy convention of charging expenditure to the period to which it relates.)

THE CLASSIFICATION OF COSTS

There are numerous methods of classifying costs; the method chosen is determined by the purpose which is to be achieved. In a well-organised system of cost accounting it should always be easy to reclassify costs when required, since it is rare (and inefficient) to prepare costs for one purpose only.

This section outlines the main forms of classification.

11. Direct and indirect costs. All costs fall into one of the two categories of direct and indirect costs.

(*a*) A *direct cost* may be defined as a cost that arises *solely* from the existence of whatever is being costed. With a direct cost there can be no suggestion of sharing the cost between the things being costed. If the individual "thing" being costed had not existed the cost would not have arisen at all.

(*b*) An *indirect cost* is simply a cost that is not direct, *i.e.* its existence does not depend solely on what is being costed. It therefore implies some element of sharing a cost that is common or jointly incurred by two or more things being costed. When the things being costed are cost units indirect costs can also be referred to as *overheads*.

This distinction between direct and indirect costs will be taken up again later (*see* VIII, **1–5**), but it should be noted in passing that the definitions refer to "whatever is being costed." If departments, sales areas or even customer classifications are being costed, then the definitions should be applied with these in mind. For example, a departmental manager's salary is a direct cost if the department is being costed, though indirect if costing the cost units in the department. However, the terms direct and indirect costs are used far more often in relation to the costing of cost units, and so, unless the context clearly indicates differently, they should be regarded as relating to cost units.

12. Fixed and variable costs. Costs can also be classified as either fixed or variable. A *fixed cost* is one that remains unchanged despite changes in activity, while a *variable cost* is one that varies in proportion to activity. (Activity is sometimes difficult to measure, but for the moment it may be equated to level of production.)

The importance of this classification lies in the fact that when the cost effect of small changes in activity is being studied attention need only be concentrated on the variable costs, since the fixed costs will remain the same for all the levels of activity under consideration. This concentration on the costs that change renders the relationship between activity changes and cost changes very much clearer.

This cost classification will be discussed in detail in Part Four, which deals with marginal costing. Here it is only necessary to note that:

(*a*) All costs can be ultimately (*i.e.* after any necessary analysis) placed in one or other of these two classifications, leaving no costs unclassified.

(*b*) Direct costs, by their very nature, must be variable, though indirect costs may be either fixed or variable.

13. Costs classified by nature. A further classification relates to the *nature* of the costs (*i.e.* what they are), the basic categories here being material, labour and expense. These three categories can be further broken down as required, *e.g.* material can be subdivided into raw materials, components and maintenance materials; labour into supervision, cleaning and clerical work; and expense into rent, power, depreciation, postage, etc.

14. Costs classified by function. Costs may also be classified according to the *function* to which they relate, typical categories being production, selling, distribution, administration, finance and research and development.

The category into which a given cost should be placed under this system of classification is sometimes uncertain. This is not particularly important: classification of costs by function is a traditional classification and is becoming less and less significant in modern costing, as the entire manufacturing process is rapidly becoming a single, integrated function. (For instance, if the sales manager insists on the factory placing an elaborate name plate on the product which acts mainly as a form of advertisement, is the cost of affixing this plate a production cost or a selling cost? The distinction is neither possible nor important.)

15. Costs classified by time. Finally, costs can obviously be classified according to the period in which either:

(*a*) the cost was incurred; or
(*b*) the benefit of the cost was obtained.

These periods are often the same, but may well differ, as, for example, when a sales department buys display equipment for use at an exhibition in a subsequent period.

16. Elements of costs. Traditionally the cost of a cost unit can be regarded as being built up of a number of elements of cost. Such a build-up can be shown diagrammatically as follows:

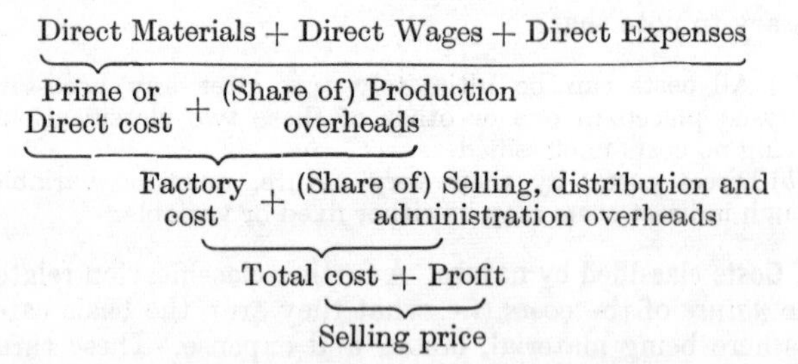

The definitions of these terms are as follows:

(*a*) *Direct materials.* Materials that actually become part of the cost unit.
(*b*) *Direct wages.* Wages paid to employees for the time they are engaged in working on the direct materials.
(*c*) *Direct expenses.* Expenses incurred specifically on behalf of the cost unit.
(*d*) *Production overheads.* Overheads incurred in production, *i.e.* generally speaking, overheads incurred within the four walls of the factory proper.
(*e*) *Selling overheads.* Overheads incurred in inducing customers to place orders.
(*f*) *Distribution overheads.* Overheads incurred in getting finished production from the factory to the customer. It includes warehouse, packing and transport costs.
(*g*) *Administration overheads.* Overheads incurred in managing the enterprise. It includes top management costs, accounts, legal and (usually) personnel department costs, audit fees and other such general enterprise costs.
(*h*) *Profit.* The difference between the selling price and the total cost.

NOTE: This profit is not quite the same as the accountant's profit (which means amount available for appropriation), since the total cost does *not* include an allowance for abnormal costs (*see* **10**(*d*)), unrecovered past period costs (**10**(*e*)), unabsorbed overheads (IX, **19**(*d*)), discounts (VIII, **11**), and interest (VIII, **12**).

These definitions represent the traditional concept of costs, and differ slightly from the more modern concept. For instance, a salesman's commission for selling a cost unit would be regarded as a selling overhead in the above definitions, though in modern costing it would be classed as a direct cost.

It should be appreciated that the above scheme relates only to costing cost units and that modern costing extends far beyond this traditional task.

APPLICATIONS OF COSTING

17. Cost ascertainment. Costs can be applied to ascertaining what it *did* cost to manufacture or sell a cost unit or to run a cost centre. This is the traditional application of costing and involves finding out just what direct material and direct labour (and possibly direct expenses) were used by whatever is being costed, and, if required, finding out what share of the overheads should be borne by it.

Any form of costing using past figures is termed *historical costing*.

18. Cost planning. Modern costing relates much more to the future than to the past, since management is better served if they are told what a thing *will* cost rather than what it *did* cost. Knowing in advance allows management to make different decisions; once the event is past they are powerless to alter it. Such costing is essentially cost planning and is dealt with in Part Five.

19. Cost control. Cost control is the application of costing to enable management to compare actual costs with planned costs and take any necessary corrective action. It is covered in the chapters relating to flexible budgets and standard costing.

20. Decision-making. Costing may also be applied to decision-making, where a single project must be selected from a group of alternatives. A limited survey of this application is given in the chapter on marginal costing. In practice, decision-making comes mainly within the field of management accounting.

21. Costing and price-fixing. The object of costing is *not* primarily to enable prices to be fixed. Costing relates to economic performance; it is not a sales office clerical procedure aimed at producing mathematically precise selling prices. Although the sales manager must have in mind cost figures in order to ensure that the price he is quoting will not result in the enterprise losing money, the following limitations to the use of costs for price-fixing should be remembered:

(*a*) Selling prices depend on supply and demand. They should therefore be based more on economic considerations (and particularly in relation to the prices of one's competitors) than on costs.

(*b*) Cost figures often imply a given activity level. If the actual level is different from this implied level, then the profits expected from using a simple "cost plus percentage profit" for the selling price may prove to be very much out of line with actual profits.

COSTING METHODS AND TECHNIQUES

22. Role of cost data. Costing is essentially the use of cost data to construct cost statements. Cost data in this context may be looked on as cost atoms, *i.e.* the smallest divisions of cost that exist. For instance, we may know that a tin of paint worth £2 was drawn from stock for general use in department A. There is no further breakdown of this £2 cost, and it is therefore similar to an atom. Clearly, in any cost office there will be a great many such "atoms." As the different combinations of chemical atoms in chemistry give different substances, so the different combinations of cost atoms give different kinds of cost statements.

Yet another way of looking at cost data is to consider them as building bricks. Such bricks can be used to construct "buildings" of quite different designs, *i.e.* used to construct quite different statements.

The important point to note here is that *the same cost data can be arranged and rearranged to give a number of quite different statements*, and that no one way is *the* only correct way.

23. Methods and techniques. The different ways of arranging cost data fall into two main categories: methods and techniques (*see* Fig. 1). Cost methods depend upon *the nature of production.* There are really only two basic ways, one where production results in cost units that are different from each other and the other where the cost units are all identical (*see* X and XII). Cost techniques, on the other hand, depend upon *the purpose for*

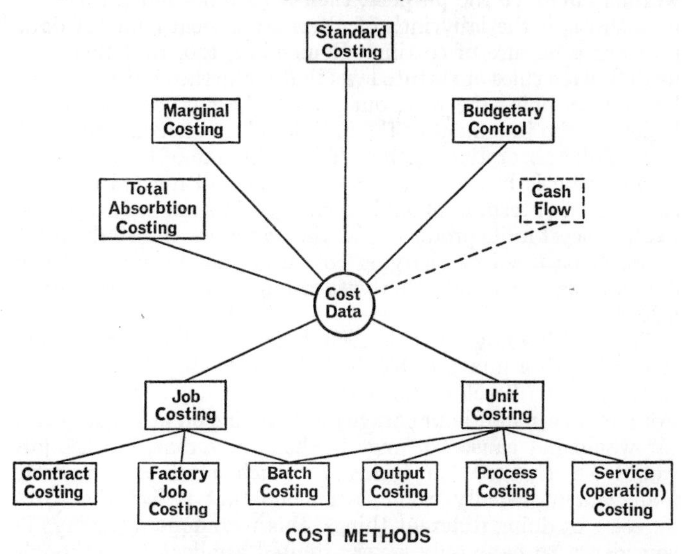

FIG. 1.—*Costing methods and techniques*

Cost methods depend upon the nature of production; cost techniques depend upon the purpose for which management require the information. (Cash flow is essentially a management accounting technique for decision-making and is not dealt with in this book.)

which management require the information. Management need information for a variety of purposes, such as control, decision-making, predicting profits and price determination, and the exact purpose determines the technique to be used. These techniques are outlined below and covered in Parts Three, Four and Five.

24. The basic principle of cost data arrangement. It must be emphasised at this point that all costing and all cost statements must always be prepared with the following question in mind:

for what purpose is the information required? This question lies at the heart of all costing, and every cost statement should be prepared with its particular purpose in the forefront of the cost accountant's mind. One is always faced in costing with the problem of choosing which pieces of data should be used, and if at every point one considers whether or not use of the data will help achieve the purpose, then it becomes much easier to pass through the labyrinth of alternative treatments of data that are a feature of costing. Remember, too, that there are no definitive rules or statute laws that make the choice for one; books may point the way, but always the final decision must be left to the judgment of the individual cost accountant.

25. Total absorption costing. The technique of total absorption costing is based on the concept that all normal costs of running an enterprise should be charged in some way or other to all the cost units produced, *i.e.* the cost units absorb the total costs. This involves charging cost units not only with their direct costs but in addition with a fair share of all the overheads.

The disadvantage of this technique is that cost units are charged with a mixture that includes costs they have specifically caused (direct costs) and costs they have not caused. For instance, a half-hour garage job changing oil in a customer's car would not cause a change in the garage rent, but the job would be charged something for such rent. As modern management usually want statements that reflect the *effect* on costs of doing different things, this technique nowadays is considered to have only a very limited application, although it is the traditional form of costing and until relatively recently was the only one employed by cost accountants.

26. Marginal costing. The marginal costing (or direct costing) technique is based on the principle that each cost unit should be charged only with those costs it individually and exclusively *causes* to be incurred. Since, it is argued, many costs in normal circumstances are incurred on a time basis and are not therefore dependent on the production of individual cost units for their amounts (*e.g.* rent, rates, audit fees), such costs are not charged to production at all. Cost units, therefore, will be charged with direct costs only.

This argument, however, can be pushed only so far. Although such costs are incurred on a time basis, the rate per week, month or year will depend upon the size of the building, audit and so on, which in turn will be determined by the anticipated production volume of cost units. There is therefore a link between the cost units and these time-based costs, and while charging direct costs only to cost units is valid in the short term, to continue such a practice in the long term may lead to unsound conclusions.

27. Budgets and standard costing. Budgets and standard costing are techniques which enable management to *plan and control* their economic activities. A budget is an economic plan for a given period of time, and a standard cost is a planned cost for a single cost unit. By carefully preparing such plans management ascertain what future economic practices are feasible possibilities. By then choosing one particular plan they know that attainment of the desired position depends solely upon the attainment of individual target figures within the plan. If actual detailed results are then compared with the detailed target figures it is possible to ascertain whether the plan is being achieved or not; and if not, where the plan is breaking down.

Knowing this, management can then concentrate its attention on overcoming such breakdowns and so improve the enterprise's chance of reaching its ultimate targets.

28. Methods and techniques are tools. Methods and techniques should be regarded as the tools of the cost accountant, and like any skilled man's tools, no attempt should be made to rank them in order of "superiority." All tools have their uses and for any given task the appropriate tool should be selected. Clearly, every tool will have its limitations, and it is a vital part of the cost accountant's skill to know when such limitations render a particular method or technique unsuitable.

It should be appreciated that just as a skilled man will often combine a number of tools to tackle a particular job, so the cost accountant may combine methods and techniques, *e.g.* standard costing, marginal costing and joint-product costing may be combined to give "standard marginal joint-product costing." Although this may appear confusing, if the basic principles of each method and technique are fully understood, then combining is only a matter of clear thought. Note, incidentally, that costing any cost unit involves the combination of at least *one method with one technique*, since a cost cannot be produced unless consideration is given both to the nature of the cost unit and the purpose for which the cost is required.

29. Economic terms involving costs. There are two terms used in economics that are rarely used in textbooks on costing but which should be noted by students to help them link economics and costing. These are:

(*a*) *Conversion cost*, which is the cost of converting raw materials to the finished state, or to the next stage of production. It includes direct wages, direct expenses and overheads.

(*b*) *Added value*, which is the market value of a product less the costs of bought-out materials and services. (In practice, usually the only important bought-out service is power.) The main difference between conversion cost and added value is that added value includes profit.

PROGRESS TEST 1

Principles

1. What is the purpose of costing? (1, 2)
2. Carefully distinguish between the two functions of money in modern business enterprises. (3)
3. What is an opportunity cost? (5)
4. Explain, giving the basic types met in practice:

(*a*) Cost units. (8)
(*b*) Cost centres. (9)

5. Write brief notes on:

(*a*) "Prudence" in costing. (10 (*c*))
(*b*) Abnormal costs. (10 (*d*))
(*c*) Past costs. (10 (*e*))

6. Distinguish carefully between:

(*a*) Direct and indirect costs. (11)
(*b*) Fixed and variable costs. (12)

7. What are the traditional elements of cost? (16)
8. What is historical costing? (17)
9. What determines the data and arrangement of a costing statement? (24)
10. What is the difference between total absorption costing and marginal costing? (25, 26)
11. What is the object of using budgets and standard costs? (27)

PART TWO

COST DATA

CHAPTER II

MATERIALS: PURCHASING, RECEIVING AND STOREKEEPING

PURCHASING

1. Importance of purchasing. Purchasing is important in manufacturing because:

(*a*) Usually more than 50% of the total product cost is materials. This means the buyer (purchasing officer) is in effect responsible for spending more of the enterprise's money than anyone else. An error on his part can be very expensive, if not disastrous.

(*b*) The purchase of sub-standard material can result in:

(*i*) high material wastage; or
(*ii*) seriously low product quality; or
(*iii*) expensive machine breakdowns.

Again the effect on profits could be disastrous.

(*c*) The choice of an unreliable supplier could result in the non-delivery of a vital material, with the result that the entire factory would be brought to a temporary stand-still. Loss of production in such circumstances can be very serious.

2. Initiating a purchase. Purchasing starts when someone in the organisation decides that they will be needing a particular material. The more usual persons concerned are:

(*a*) The storekeeper (or stores record clerk), who wishes to replenish low stocks.

(*b*) The production planner, who wishes to acquire materials for the manufacture of a new product.

(*c*) A departmental head (*e.g.* office manager, maintenance supervisor), who requires the material in the course of the running of the department.

3. Purchase requisition. Any person requiring materials raises a requisition requesting the purchasing department to purchase the wanted materials. This is called a *purchase requisition* (not to be confused with a materials requisition, *see* **20**).

* *Design:* Material description, specification and code number; quantity requested; last supplier and price; required delivery date; department requiring material.

Copies: Purchase office (original); stores or production planning (being advice from initiator to the other department); initiator (book). The important copy is, of course, the purchase office copy, which authorises the buyer to purchase the listed materials.

4. Selecting a supplier. On receipt of the purchase requisition the buyer selects a suitable supplier. This involves consulting purchase office records that detail the prices charged, and the reliability of the various suppliers in the past as well as published information. After selecting a supplier the buyer then issues a purchase order.

5. Purchase order. A *purchase order* is an order to a supplier for specified materials.

Purchase orders are very important, because they form the basis of a legal contract. It is essential, therefore, to:

(*a*) Specify carefully and unambiguously the exact materials and quantity required; (reference to a tender or a sample will make these items part of the purchase contract).

(*b*) Restrict authority to sign purchase orders to carefully selected responsible officials.

Design: Name and address of purchaser; name and address of supplier; description and specification of material; quantity ordered; price; discounts; delivery date and point of delivery; mode of transport.

Copies: Supplier (original); accounts; production planning and control; stores; receiving department; inspection; purchase office (book).

6. Progressing deliveries. The responsibility of the buying department does not end at the dispatch of the purchase order.

* Under *Design* only the data relevant to each specific form are listed. Common data, such as serial number and date, are assumed. Under *Copies* a possible distribution is suggested (*see* Appendix I on form design).

Deliveries must be watched, and it is often worth while, in fact, to check with a supplier a few days before expected delivery that delivery will be made on time. If such a check reveals delay, then at least management will learn of this delay some days earlier than they otherwise would.

In the event of a delivery hold-up the purchase office staff are the best people to deal with the offending supplier, since they alone have full knowledge of the background to the order.

The purchase office responsibility, therefore, does not end until the arrival of the material at least. Whether or not it extends to the receiving procedures depends upon the organisation of the individual enterprise.

RECEIPT OF MATERIALS

7. Receipt of materials: summary of procedure. Each stage in the physical intake of materials is recorded clerically.

Physical	*Clerical*
(*a*) Consignment arrives at factory.	Receipt given to carrier.
(*b*) Packages opened in receiving department.	Goods received note raised.
(*c*) Goods inspected.	Inspection note raised.
(*d*) Goods passed into store.	Goods received note copy signed by storekeeper.

8. Goods received note. A *goods received* (*G.R.*) *note* is a form recording all details relating to a receipt of materials. Raised when the packages are opened in the receiving department, it specifies the goods *actually received*. These are not necessarily the same as what the delivery note or purchase order state should have been received.

Design: Material description; quantity; supplier; mode of transport; condition of materials (damage, etc.); space for comments (*e.g.* Part delivery—3 out of 5 cases).

Copies: Accounts; purchase office; production planning and control; stores (on transfer of materials); receiving department (book copy).

9. Inspection note. Before leaving the receiving department the goods must be inspected and the results of the inspection stated on an *inspection note*. This note is often incorporated in the goods received note, particularly if no special technical knowledge is called for and the inspection is carried out by the receiving personnel at the time of unpacking.

Design: Material description and code number; quantity; number passed and number rejected; reasons for rejection; suggested disposal of rejects (*e.g.* return to supplier; negotiate reduced prices); comments.

Copies: as goods received note.

In the event of there being rejects it should be noted that these are best held in the receiving department until a decision as to their disposal is made. Only good items, therefore, are passed to stores.

10. Payment of supplier. The supplier's invoice should be checked before being paid. These checks cover the following points:

(*a*) Goods invoiced were the goods ordered—by comparing invoice with purchase order.
(*b*) Goods invoiced were received—by comparing invoice with goods received note.
(*c*) Invoice prices and discounts are correct—again by comparing invoice with purchase order.
(*d*) Multiplications and additions are correct—by recalculating.

Once these checks have been made and the accounts to be charged determined, the invoice should be *passed for payment* by some responsible official signing that he authorises the invoice to be paid. The invoice is then entered into the books of account.

This work is usually carried out in the buying department.

11. Invoice stamp. Invoices passing through the procedure have to be checked, analysed and also given a reference number. In order to ensure that nothing is overlooked, it is advisable to prepare a rubber stamp (or printed slip) which, when stamped on the invoices, allows data and initials to be entered in a systematic manner. This will show at a glance whether a particular entry or check has been made and who is responsible.

12. Returns to supplier. Materials to be returned are repacked in the receiving department and sent back to the supplier. A *debit note* is simultaneously raised and forwarded to the supplier charging him with the value of the returned materials. (Alternatively, the supplier is requested to send a *credit note* for such value.)

STOREKEEPING

The stores function in industry involves both keeping the store of materials and keeping the stores records. In some organisations these two aspects are merged, but they are better separated where practical, if for no other reason than that keeping a store is essentially a *physical* task, and keeping stores records is essentially a *clerical* task. This is *not* to suggest that storekeeping is simply labouring; on the contrary, it is much more skilled than stores recording.

In this book the two aspects are treated separately, and this section deals with keeping a store.

13. Objectives of good storekeeping. Good storekeeping involves storing materials so as to achieve the following objectives:

(*a*) Immediate *location* of required materials.
(*b*) Speedy *receipt and issue* of materials.
(*c*) Full *identification* of all materials at all times.
(*d*) Ability to give details on request of *quantities held* in store.
(*e*) Protection of materials against *deterioration* (*e.g.* from damp, crushing, evaporation).
(*f*) Protection of materials against *fire and theft*.
(*g*) Economical use of *storage space*.

These last three objectives relate primarily to factory administration and will not be considered further in this book.

14. Need for material codes. Material descriptions are often vague, *e.g.* "paper-clips," of which there are a number of different kinds, or they may be ambiguous as to their main word for the purpose of filing, *e.g.* should "step-ladders" be filed under "step" or "ladder"? Descriptions may also be very long. In order to avoid these disadvantages materials are coded. The purpose of coding may therefore be summarised as:

(*a*) To avoid ambiguity in description.
(*b*) To minimise length in description.

15. Principles of coding. The actual code itself is a matter of individual choice, although there are certain basic principles that require the code to be:

(*a*) *Exclusive*. Each code number should relate to one type of material, and one only. There must be no duplication.

(*b*) *Certain.* The code number must identify the material without any ambiguity or uncertainty whatsoever.
(*c*) *Elastic.* The code should be such that new materials can be added easily and logically.
(*d*) *Brief.* Large code numbers take longer to write and are more subject to errors. Numbers, therefore, should be as brief as possible without violating the other principles.
(*e*) *Mnemonic,* if possible (*i.e.* assisting the memory, such as M.S.B. for mild steel bar). Mnemonic codes are both easier to remember and less subject to error.

16. Classification of materials. Materials may be classified in the following groups:

(*a*) Raw materials: materials which are worked on in the course of manufacture (*e.g.* timber; sheet metal).
(*b*) Components: finished parts which are attached to the product during manufacture (*e.g.* instruments; locks).
(*c*) Consumable materials: materials used in running the factory generally (*e.g.* soap; cotton waste; brushes).
(*d*) Maintenance materials: materials required for the maintenance of plant and buildings (*e.g.* spare parts; door hinges).
(*e*) Tools: all forms of tools including jigs and fixtures.

Frequently separate stores are used for some or all of these groups (particularly tools, *see* **26**), though this is not essential.

17. Stores locations. Every bin, rack, drawer, tray or area of stores floor must be given a logical location number. Location of materials is vitally important, since expensive delay can result from a failure to locate required items.

18. Receipt of materials. On receipt into store of the materials and goods received note from the receiving department the code number should be checked, or a number allocated. The materials are then put in storage, the stores location being recorded on the goods received note. This note is then passed to the stores record office and the details thereon entered on the appropriate stores record card. The storekeeper will also record the location in his own files.

NOTE: Stores record cards are cards which record for each type of material all data relevant to the storing of that material (*see* III, **23**).

19. First-in, first-out storekeeping. Materials kept for any length of time often deteriorate. To avoid such deterioration storekeepers devise storing systems which enable them always to *issue the oldest stocks first*, *i.e.* the first stocks in are the first stocks out. This involves such techniques as stacking receipts at one end of a row and drawing issues from the other, or maintaining two bins for a single material, one for receipts and the other for issues. When the latter is empty it becomes receipts bin, and the other becomes the issue bin.

20. Issue of materials: materials requisition. Materials are usually issued against materials requisitions. A *materials requisition* is a document which authorises and records the issue of materials for use. Students should appreciate that this is a key document in nearly all costing systems. It is both:

(*a*) An authorisation.
(*b*) A record of usage.

Design: Material description and code number; quantity required; job or overhead account to be charged; department requisitioning. There should also be spaces to record price, value and stores record office action work (*e.g.* marked to show quantity issued recorded on stores record card).

Copies: Stores (original); person requisitioning (book).

There should be only two copies, the original being passed through all the appropriate departments. This is because information on the requisition may be amended (*e.g.* store may only make part issue for some reason), and if more than one copy is distributed it is possible for some copies to remain unamended and consequently carry incorrect data.

21. Issue of materials: bill of materials. Sometimes all the materials required for a specific order are listed on a single document by the production planning department and passed to the stores to serve in lieu of a material requisition. Such a document is termed a *bill of materials*, and has the following advantages:

(*a*) It reduces the number of pieces of paper.
(*b*) Exact quantities can be requisitioned.
(*c*) Risk of clerical errors is reduced.
(*d*) The storekeeper can be given advance warning of requirements.

22. Return of materials to store: materials returned note. Any materials returned to store should be accompanied by a *materials returned note*, which is, in effect, a "reverse" materials requisition, usually of virtually identical design to a materials requisition but coloured differently (generally red) to assist document identification.

23. Transfer of materials: materials transfer note. Any materials transferred from one job to another should be recorded on a *materials transfer note* and passed directly to the stores record office for pricing and forwarding to the cost office.

24. Bin cards. Storekeepers often need to know exactly what is in any specific bin (or rack) and to this end a *bin card* recording essential data relating to material in that bin is made out.

Design: Material description and code number; units; location; alternative locations of material; columns for receipts, issues and balances.

Note particularly when designing bin cards that:

(*a*) *Extra columns should be avoided*, if possible. Storekeepers, engaged in the physical movement of stores, rarely find it practical to record more than the essential minimum of data.

(*b*) Control data (re-order levels, etc., *see* III, 2–6) are rarely relevant, since individual material lines are often in more than one bin. A bin card, therefore, does not record the total of a material in the whole of the stores.

(*c*) The location should be given, as bin cards are occasionally removed for stocktaking purposes, and it is necessary to know the location to which they must be returned.

25. Choosing between central or departmental stores (main or sub-stores). Should a factory have a central (main) store or a number of departmental (sub) stores? In practice, both are usually necessary. A single *central store* has the following advantages:

(*a*) Smaller stocks are required. Numerous departmental stores inevitably leads to higher stock-holdings.
(*b*) Storekeeping staff can specialise.
(*c*) A smaller over-all storekeeping staff is probably required.
(*d*) Purchase requisitioning is minimised.

The following disadvantages must be considered:

(*a*) Small lots of material must be moved farther when issued to the more distant departments. This involves greater material handling costs and may also result in aggravating aisle overcrowding.

(*b*) It is not so convenient for people in these distant departments who need to draw materials.

26. Tool store. A tool store is different from most other stores insomuch that the tools it issues *must be returned.* To ensure no tools are lost it is necessary to devise a system that enables the holder of any given tool to be identified.

The following is an example of such a system:

(*a*) Each worker is given a specific number of metal discs bearing his clock number.
(*b*) A worker requiring a tool presents both a material requisition (authorising him to draw the tool) and one of his metal discs to be exchanged for the tool.
(*c*) The worker's disc is placed on a hook that specifically relates to the issued tool. Thus the holder of any tool is known.
(*d*) On return, the tool is replaced (or sent for repair or sharpening) and the disc returned to the worker.

It should be noted that *all* tools, including broken ones, must be returned to the store.

27. Costs of storage. The following costs are incurred in keeping materials in store, and the longer the materials are stored, the greater these costs become:

(*a*) *Capital costs.* The loss of return that could be obtained if the capital tied up in stock was employed elsewhere results in this cost being usually the highest one of all.
(*b*) *Space costs* (rent, heating, lighting, etc.).
(*c*) *Equipment costs* (bins, racks, material handling equipment, etc.).
(*d*) *Personnel costs* (storing, stocktaking, security, etc.).
(*e*) *Insurance.*
(*f*) *Deterioration.*
(*g*) *Obsolescence.* The higher the stock levels, the longer the time material is in stock, and so the greater the risk, and therefore ultimate cost of, obsolescence.

28. Annual stocktaking. The annual stocktaking involves ascertaining the physical quantities of stores of raw materials and stocks of work in progress and finished goods on hand at the end of the trading year. This method has serious disadvantages which continuous stocktaking (*see* III, **8**) avoids, but the following procedure indicates the main points to be considered if such a stocktaking is to be organised:

(*a*) The stocktaking should be organised well in advance to minimise production hold-ups.

(*b*) It should be designated as a major operation throughout the factory taking high priority over other activities.

(*c*) Either all production should be stopped or stock taken at weekend. It is rarely feasible to take stock while production continues.

(*d*) The factory and stores should be divided geographically into small sections and a responsible member of the stocktaking team made responsible for each individual section.

(*e*) It is usually found best for section stock-takers to take *all* stock of whatever kind found in their sections rather than allocate different categories of stock to different groups of stock-takers.

(*f*) Where possible, rough stock sheets for each section should be pre-written with material descriptions, code numbers and locations.

(*g*) Stock-takers should work in pairs—a clerk who fills in the rough stock sheets and a technical person who identifies materials and counts quantities. They should work strictly under their section supervisor.

(*h*) An effective method of marking items taken into stock should be arranged to avoid:

- (*i*) taking an item twice;
- (*ii*) omitting an item entirely.

(*i*) Care should be taken to ensure that the stock taken:

- (*i*) identifies materials not yet invoiced by suppliers to the enterprise so that an adjustment can be made;
- (*ii*) excludes finished goods already invoiced, though not dispatched to customers.

(*j*) Rough stock sheets should be collected and items collated on to final stock sheets. (It should be appreciated that the same type of material may be found in more than one place in the factory and therefore will appear on more than one rough stock sheet.)

(*k*) The final stock sheets should be checked against the stores record cards and discrepancies investigated. Such investigation may well reveal *stocktaking* errors.

(*l*) Final stock sheets should now be priced, extended (*i.e.* multiplied out) and added to give total stock values.

NOTE: On occasions bin cards can be used in lieu of rough stock sheets. These reduce the possibility of errors of description or code number, and also render collation easier.

PROGRESS TEST 2

Principles

1. Why is purchasing an important function? (1)
2. What details should be given on a purchase order and why are such details important? (5)
3. What is a G.R. note? (8)
4. Outline the procedure for paying a supplier. (10, 11)
5. (*a*) What is the value of a material code? (14)
   (*b*) What are the principles of coding? (15)
6. What documents will a storekeeper physically handling materials meet, and in what circumstances? (18, 20–22, 24)
7. What are the advantages and disadvantages of having a single central store? (25)
8. What are the costs of storage? (27)
9. Detail the steps taken in an annual stocktaking. (28)

CHAPTER III

MATERIALS: STORES CONTROL AND MATERIAL COSTING

STORES CONTROL

1. Need for stores control. There are two serious dangers which must be avoided when running a stores. These are:

(*a*) *Over-stocking.* The costs of storing were detailed in Chapter II (27), and if materials are overstocked such storage costs may significantly, or even disastrously, affect the profits.

(*b*) *Under-stocking.* Understocking leads inevitably to materials running out of stock at some time or other. The consequences of a "stockout" are:

(*i*) Wages and fixed costs incurred without any compensating output.
(*ii*) Loss of profits on lost sales.
(*iii*) Delivery delays, resulting in cancelled orders, loss of goodwill or even penalty payments.
(*iv*) Greatly increased procurement costs. In an emergency, prices and transport charges above normal must often be paid to obtain supplies quickly.
(*v*) Production disorganisation. Production must run smoothly to be efficient, and disorganisation results in unnecessary, though often hidden, costs.

When it is realised that a stores may carry hundreds of different materials, many of which individually would result in stopped production if they were not available, the need for effective control is self-evident.

2. Basis of stores control. Stores control is based on *predetermining for each item of material four critical levels: maximum, minimum, re-order level and re-order quantity.* By taking action on a basis of these levels each item of material will automatically be held within appropriate limits of control. Note, however, that such levels are not fixed once and for all; they must be adjusted if circumstances alter.

3. Maximum level. The *maximum level* of a given material is the maximum quantity that may be held in store. It is essentially an uppermost limit that the buyer must ensure is not exceeded (unless an excess is specifically authorised by higher management; for example, when unusually favourable purchasing conditions arise). It is set after consideration of:

(*a*) Rate of consumption.
(*b*) Risks of obsolescence.
(*c*) Risks of deterioration.
(*d*) Costs of storing above-normal stocks.
(*e*) Storage space available.

4. Minimum level. The *minimum level* is the lowest level to which stocks should fall. It is essentially a *buffer stock* that will not normally be touched. In the event of any item falling to its minimum level management is immediately alerted and the acquisition of new supplies given top priority. It is set after consideration of:

(*a*) Rate of consumption.
(*b*) The time required under top priority conditions to acquire enough supplies to avoid a production stoppage. (This is usually less than the normal delivery time, since small lots can be air-freighted, or one's own vehicle specifically sent to a supplier for the materials.)

5. Re-order level. The *re-order level* is the level at which a purchase requisition is made out (II, 3). By re-ordering when the stock falls to the re-order level, then, in the normal course of events *new supplies will be received just before the minimum level is reached*. It is set after consideration of:

(*a*) Rate of consumption.
(*b*) Minimum level.
(*c*) Delivery time, *i.e.* time normally taken from moment of raising purchase requisition to receipt of materials in store.
(*d*) Variations in delivery time. Excessive variation due to either unreliability of supplier or variable transport times may require a higher re-order level to avoid the minimum level being reached too frequently, with consequential expensive priority actions.

6. Re-order quantity. The *re-order quantity* is the quantity to be re-ordered in normal circumstances. By setting this level the buyer is saved the task of recalculating how much he should buy each time he orders. He may, of course, disregard this order quantity if he deems circumstances warrant it. It is set after consideration of:

(*a*) Rate of consumption.
(*b*) Cost of holding stock as against cost of purchasing, *i.e.* infrequent purchasing lowers purchasing costs but increases stock-holding costs, and vice versa. The quantity that minimises the sum of these costs is termed the *economic order quantity*.
(*c*) Bulk discounts.
(*d*) Transport costs (half a load involves virtually the same transport costs as a whole load).
(*e*) Obsolescence and deterioration risks.

7. Perpetual inventory. It should be clear from the above that in order to attain stores control it is essential to know the stock level of every item at all times. One method of ensuring that this information is available is by means of a *perpetual inventory*, *i.e.* the use of a record card for each item of stock that shows the balance in hand after each transaction. Usually this involves recording all receipts, issues and running balances on each card.

In addition to assisting management to control stores, a perpetual inventory enables management to ascertain stock *at any moment in time* without the bother or expense of a physical stocktaking. This is a considerable advantage; among other things it enables monthly final accounts to be prepared.

8. Continuous stocktaking. In any perpetual inventory system the recorded balances should agree with actual physical balances in the store. However, differences often arise due to:

(*a*) Clerical errors on the record card.
(*b*) Storekeepers' errors, clerical and physical (*e.g.* over-issue).
(*c*) Errors in procedure (*e.g.* failure to record returned material on a materials returned note).
(*d*) Unrecorded losses due to evaporation or breaking bulk.
(*e*) Pilferage and falsification of documents.

It is therefore, necessary to check the recorded against the actual balance. This is best done by checking a few items daily throughout the year. Such checking is termed *continuous stocktaking* and may be defined as "the continuous taking of stock, quantities counted being checked against the appropriate perpetual inventory balance figures."

9. Principles of continuous stocktaking. The following principles should be observed in continuous stocktaking:

(*a*) A few items should be checked each day.
(*b*) As with any normal audit check:

  (*i*) Checking should be made by staff unconnected with the keeping or recording of stores.
  (*ii*) There should be an element of surprise as regards the items checked on any day.

(*c*) All items should be checked at least once a year and certain items checked twice or more times.
(*d*) All discrepancies should be investigated and ultimately signed "noted" by an appropriate senior manager before being formally written off.

10. Advantages of continuous stocktaking over annual stocktaking. Continuous stocktaking has the following advantages over the annual stocktaking discussed in Chapter II (**28**):

(*a*) Regular skilled stocktakers may be employed. This improves the quality of the stocktaking.
(*b*) There is much more time to take stock. This also improves the quality of the stocktaking as well as allowing discrepancies to be more fully investigated.
(*c*) Competence and accuracy of storekeepers and stores clerks are appraised.
(*d*) Storekeepers are induced to maintain high work standards, as they never know just when a particular material will be checked.
(*e*) Stock deficiencies and losses are revealed sooner.
(*f*) Unauthorised changes in procedure are revealed.
(*g*) Production hold-ups are eliminated.

11. Objective of continuous stocktaking. It should be appreciated that the primary object of continuous stocktaking is not so much to bring records into line with actual stocks as *to confirm that the perpetual inventory system is functioning properly*. If only a few small errors are revealed by the check, then management will have confidence in the perpetual inventory figures, both as a method of control and a basis for valuing year-end stocks. On the other hand, too many errors would point to the unreliability of the perpetual inventory and the need for a thorough investigation of the system.

12. Using perpetual inventory balances for year-end figures. The perpetual inventory balance of any material may be used in lieu of a physical stocktaking for year-end figures if:

(*a*) The continuous stocktaking has confirmed the reliability of the system.
(*b*) The stock of that material has been checked at a relatively recent date.
(*c*) The value of that stock is not large in relation to the over-all stock.

NOTE: However, it is always advisable to check physically at the year end the stocks of any materials that have a very high turnover rate (*e.g.* wheat in a flour mill).

13. Materials control. The term *materials control* is sometimes used when discussing stores procedures. It should be noted, however, that materials control extends slightly beyond stores (or stock) control and includes in addition materials bought specifically for, and delivered directly to, individual jobs and departments.

PRICING STORES ISSUES

14. Basic problem of pricing stores issues. When pricing stores issues (*i.e.* charging out materials issued from store) there is always the problem as to whether the original purchase price or the immediate current price should be used. In times of rapidly increasing prices there is a danger that by using the original purchase price when costing a product the profit *from manufacturing* will be confused with the *paper profit arising from the increase in selling prices caused by the price rise of raw materials that the enterprise in fact bought at an earlier lower price.* If a radio is bought for £10 and the price then rises to £11, to sell it for £11 does not really bring in a £1 profit, since if the radio is to be replaced in stock this £1 cannot be distributed as a dividend. (This replacement involves no expansion, only a return to the original stock position.)

If, on the other hand, issues are priced at current (replacement) prices many people may argue this is not costing, since the original cost price is not being used.

This dilemma has led to a number of methods of pricing stores issues, all aimed at some form of compromise, the six most important being: FIFO; LIFO; simple average;

weighted average; replacement price; standard price. These six are discussed and illustrated below (**15–20** and *see* Fig. 2), all using the same basic data (given in Fig. 2).

15. FIFO (First in, first out). This method uses *the price of first batch received* for all issues until all units from this batch have been issued after which the price of the next batch received becomes the issue price. Upon that batch being fully issued the price of the next batch received is used, and so on.

Two points should be noted (*see* Fig. 2):

(*a*) The need to record units left in each batch after an issue.
(*b*) The balance cross-check: the 100 units left in stock at the end must comprise the last 80 received at £12·50 and the 20 remaining from the previous batch at £12, *i.e.*:

$$(80 \times £12{\cdot}50) + (20 \times £12)$$
$$= £1240 = \text{amount in the balance-value column.}$$

16. LIFO (Last in, first out). This method uses *the price of the last batch received* for all issues until all units from this batch have been issued, when the price of the previous batch received is used. Usually, however, a new delivery is received before the first batch is fully issued, in which case the new delivery price becomes the "last-in" price and is used for pricing issues until either the batch is exhausted or a new delivery received. In this case there are three points to be noted:

(*a*) The method can result in many batches being only partially "written off."
(*b*) This is a book-keeping method and must not be confused with the physical method of issue used by the storekeeper, who will always issue the oldest stock first (*see* II, **19**).
(*c*) The balance cross-check (*see* Fig. 2): the 100 units remaining in stock must now relate to the very first batch received and the value, therefore is:

$$100 \times £10{\cdot}25 = £1025 = \text{amount in balance-value column.}$$

17. Simple average. This method involves *adding the different prices and dividing by the number of different prices*. For instance, the simple average of the first two prices in Fig. 2 is:

$$(10{\cdot}25 + 12{\cdot}00) \div 2 = £11{\cdot}125$$

Issue price method	Date	RECEIPTS Quantity	Price £	Value £	ISSUES Quantity	Price £	Value £	BALANCE Quantity	Value £
FIFO	1/1	~~200~~ ~~100~~	10·25	2050				200	2050
	23/1	~~150~~ ~~120~~ 20	12·00	1800				350	3850
	4/2				100	**10·25**	**1025**	250	**2825**
	16/2				130[1]		**1385**	120	**1440**
	25/2	80	12·50	1000				200	**2440**
	4/3				100	**12·00**	**1200**	100	**1240**
LIFO	1/1	~~200~~ ~~120~~ 100	10·25	2050				200	2050
	23/1	~~150~~ ~~50~~	12·00	1800				350	3850
	4/2				100	**12·00**	**1200**	250	**2650**
	16/2				130[2]		**1420**	120	**1230**
	25/2	~~80~~	12·50	1000				200	**2230**
	4/3				100[3]		**1205**	100	**1025**
WEIGHTED AVERAGE	1/1	200	10·25	2050				200	2050
	23/1	150	12·00	1800				350	3850
	4/2				100	**11·00**	**1100**	250	**2750**
	16/2				130	**11·00**	**1430**	120	**1320**
	25/2	80	12·50	1000				200	**2320**
	4/3				100	**11·60**	**1160**	100	**1160**
REPLACE-MENT PRICE	1/1	200	10·25	2050				200	
	23/1	150	12·00	1800				350	
	4/2				100	**12·25**	**1225**	250	Not
	16/2				130	**12·50**	**1625**	120	used
	25/2	80	12·50	1000				200	
	4/3				100	**13·00**	**1300**	100	
STANDARD PRICE (£12)	1/1	200	*12*	*2400*[4]				200	*2400*
	23/1	150	*12*	*1800*[4]				350	*4200*
	4/2				100	*12*	*1200*	250	*3000*
	16/2				130	*12*	*1560*	120	*1440*
	25/2	80	*12*	960[4]				200	*2400*
	4/3				100	*12*	*1200*	100	*1200*

The five main methods of pricing stores issues are illustrated together, using the following data:

Date	*Units Purchased*	*Purchase Price*	*Units Issued*	*Market Price*
1/1	200	£10·25		£10·25
23/1	150	£12·00		£12·00
4/2			100	£12·25
16/2			130	£12·50
25/2	80	£12·50		£12·50
4/3			100	£13·00

(Standard Price = £12)

The figures in bold type indicate the differences in each method. Notice, also, that the crossed-out figures for FIFO and LIFO show old stock balances—remaining balances remaining uncrossed. For the Standard Price method, the unnecessary figures are italicised (*see* **20**).

1 Split issue: 100 at £10·25 + 30 at £12·00.
2 Split issue: 50 at £12·00 + 80 at £10·25.
3 Split issue: 80 at £12·50 + 20 at £10·25.
4 Gain or loss on purchasing written off in the accounts.

FIG. 2.—*Issue price methods.*

This is a crude and usually unsatisfactory method. If, for example, 1000 units were brought at £1 and 1 unit at £9 the whole 1001 units would be issued at an "average" price of £5 each!

This method is used only where the value of the issues is trivial.

18. Weighted average. This method *averages prices after weighting (i.e. multiplying) by their quantities.* Thus, the weighted average for the first two prices in Fig. 2 is:

$$\frac{(10{\cdot}25 \times 200) + (12 \times 150)}{350} = £11$$

Students are sometimes puzzled where there are units already in stock, but they need only remember that the average price at any time is simply the *balance-value* figure divided by the *balance-units* figure, *e.g.* in Fig. 2 after the February receipt there are 200 units, value £2320, in stock and the weighted average, therefore is:

$$\frac{£2320}{200} = £11{\cdot}60$$

NOTE: (*i*) Issue prices need only be computed on the *receipt* of new deliveries, not at the time of each issue as with FIFO and LIFO.

(*ii*) The balance cross-check: the 100 in stock in Fig. 2 is at the average price of £11·60, *i.e.* value is:

$100 \times £11{\cdot}60 = £1160$
$= $ amount in balance-value column.

19. Replacement price. This method simply uses *the current replacement price* to value issues.

NOTE: (*i*) The replacement price *at the time of each issue* must be found. This may involve considerable work.

(*ii*) The *balance-value* column cannot be used in the same way as in the methods described above (15–18); such use would quickly give rise to ridiculous figures.

20. Standard price. This method uses *the planned purchase price (standard price) for all valuations.*

NOTE: (*i*) Purchases are also valued at standard, the gain or loss following such a valuation being written-off in the accounts.

(*ii*) Since all quantities are valued at the same price, there is no need to record money figures at all (other than a single statement of the standard price). This means records can be kept in quantity only. (In Fig. 2 the unnecessary figures are italicised.)

(*iii*) Much less clerical work is required.

(*iv*) The value of the method is greatly improved if a complete system of standard costing is in operation (*see* Part Five).

21. Inflated price method. This is not a separate method of pricing, but one which must be used in conjunction with one

STORES RECORD CARD

Description: Moulding, Wood. Patt. 16 — Code No. 066-253

Size: 7/8" — Maximum: 100 — Re-order Level: 50

Units: 100 ft. — Minimum: 30 — Re-order Quantity: 40

Stores Locations: C/R19-20 — Stores Issue Price Method: FIFO

Date	Orders			Receipts				Issues				Balance	
1969	Supplier	P.O. No.	Quantity	G.R. No.	Quantity	Price	Value	Material Req. No.	Quantity	Price	Value	Quantity	Value
Jan. 5	A.R.B. Ltd.	921	~~100~~ 25										
" 19				6701	~~75~~ ~~65~~ ~~45~~ ~~25~~ 15	£1.50	£112.50					75	£112.50
" 20								L224	10	£1.50	£15.00	65	£97.50
" 24				6834	~~25~~ 20	£1.50	£37.50					90	£135.00
" 26								L281	20	£1.50	£30.00	70	£105.00
" 31								D40	20	£1.50	£30.00	50	£75.00
Feb. 1	A.R.B. Ltd.	1075	~~40~~ 20										
" 4								L369	10	£1.50	£15.00	40	£60.00
" 8				6993	20	£1.55	£31.00					60	£91.00
" 10								D92	20	£1.50	£30.00	40	£61.00

FIG. 3.—*Stores record card*

This typical stores record card shows the storekeeper's entries for January and February. Crossed-out figures indicate the progressive balance.

of the other methods. This method is used *where materials are subject to some loss in the stores* (*e.g.* evaporation), the issue price being inflated slightly to ensure that this loss is covered. For instance, if 1000 gallons of a liquid are delivered at £0·90 per gallon and a 10% loss due to evaporation is expected, then issues would amount to only 900 gallons. In order to recover the original cost of 1000 × £0·90 in the issue of this 900 gallons, the issue price must be:

$$\frac{1000 \times £0{\cdot}90}{900} = £1{\cdot}00 \text{ per gallon}$$

22. Base stock method. This is essentially a method of *valuing* stock. It assumes that the very first purchases were solely to provide a working buffer stock. Since in theory this "base stock" is never issued, it is always in stock, and therefore should *appear in every stocktaking at its original cost*. Excess stock above this base stock is, of course, valued on one of the bases discussed earlier.

23. Stores record cards. Owing to the close interconnection of all the material data discussed in this chapter, effectiveness of recording is maximised when all information relating to a single material is recorded on one document. Such a document is termed a *stores record card* (sometimes referred to as a stores ledger account) and an example of such a card is shown in Fig. 3.

A stores record card should therefore be made out for each material and kept in the stores record office.

COMPARISON OF THE COMMON METHODS OF PRICING STORES ISSUES

The advantages, disadvantages and effects of each of the six most common systems are analysed below.

24. FIFO.

(*a*) *Advantages.*

- (*i*) Realistic, *i.e.* assumes items are issued to shop-floor in order of receipt.
- (*ii*) Valuation of stock balance is a fair commercial valuation of stock.
- (*iii*) No profits or losses arise (*i.e.* value of issues after allowing for stock exactly equals cost of purchases).

(*b*) *Disadvantages.*

(*i*) Cumbersome.
(*ii*) Issue price may not reflect current economic value.

(*c*) *Effects on costs.* Lag behind current economic values.
(*d*) *Effect on stock valuation.* Value based on most recently acquired items.

25. LIFO.

(*a*) *Advantages.*

(*i*) Keeps value of issues close to current economic values.
(*ii*) Valuation of stock balance usually very conservative.
(*iii*) No profits or losses arise.

(*b*) *Disadvantages.*

(*i*) Cumbersome.
(*ii*) Not realistic, *i.e.* assumes physical issue principle to be opposite of that actually followed.
(*iii*) Valuation of stock balance may not be acceptable for income-tax purposes.
(*iv*) Should issues dip into "old stock" then they will be valued at out-of-date prices.

(*c*) *Effect on costs.* Very slight lag only behind current economic values.
(*d*) *Effect on stock valuation.* Completely out of line with current values.

26. Simple average.

(*a*) *Advantages.* Simple.
(*b*) *Disadvantages.*

(*i*) Misleading.
(*ii*) Profits and losses arise.
(*iii*) Can give very false issue and valuation figures.

(*c*) *Effect on costs and stock valuation.* May give rise to grossly false figures.

27. Weighted average.

(*a*) *Advantages.*

(*i*) Logical, *i.e.* assumes values of identical items will all be equal.

(*ii*) Since receipts are much less frequent than issues, not so cumbersome as LIFO or FIFO.
(*iii*) Damps down fluctuations in purchase price.
(*iv*) No profits or losses arise.

(*b*) *Disadvantages.*

(*i*) Issues may not be at current economic values.
(*ii*) Issue price is usually a fiction, *i.e.* never at any time existed in the market, *e.g.* the £11 in Fig. 2.
(*iii*) Issue price may run to a number of decimal places.

(*c*) *Effect on costs.* In between FIFO and LIFO.
(*d*) *Effect on stock valuation.* Usually satisfactory, though slightly out of date relative to FIFO.

28. Replacement price.

(*a*) *Advantages.*

(*i*) Issues are at current economic values.
(*ii*) Calculations are simple.

(*b*) *Disadvantages.*

(*i*) Difficult to be continually up-to-date with replacement prices.
(*ii*) Profits or losses arise.
(*iii*) Not a traditional "cost" price.

(*c*) *Effect on costs.* Costs are at current economic values.
(*d*) *Effect on stock valuation.* Valuation at current economic values, but can be used only with full understanding of replacement cost accounting.

29. Standard price.

(*a*) *Advantages.*

(*i*) Very simple to apply.
(*ii*) Provides a check on efficiency of purchasing department.
(*iii*) Eliminates price variations from costs, enabling satisfactory comparisons to be made.
(*iv*) Does not change over accounting period.

(*b*) *Disadvantages.*

(*i*) Require careful initial determination.
(*ii*) Profits and losses arise (under full standard costing this is not a disadvantage).
(*iii*) Issues may not be at current economic values.
(*iv*) Disregards price trends.

(c) *Effect on costs and stock valuation.* Standardised; not necessarily in line with current economic value or even past market values.

MATERIAL COSTING

Now that the various aspects of material procedure and pricing have been outlined it is possible to discuss the treatment of material costs.

30. Material costs: into store. The costing of materials delivered into store involves consideration of the following costs:

(a) *Invoice price.* The invoice price is the basic price at which materials are charged into store. (An invoice price is the net figure after the deduction of any trade or bulk discounts.)

(b) *Freight.* All costs of bringing the material to the factory should be added to the invoice price for charging to the materials.

(c) *Containers.* The cost of any *unreturnable* containers must also be added to the invoice price for charging to materials.

NOTE: However, if the containers are *returnable,* then their costs must not be added to the invoice price but charged instead to a Returnable Containers Account. (On returning the containers this account is, of course, credited with the appropriate amount.) If containers are *returnable but at a reduced value* the Returnable Containers Account is debited with this reduced value and the difference between this value and the full container charge added to the invoice price.

31. Cash discounts. Cash discounts (discounts allowed for prompt payment) are not normally deducted from the invoice price, since they are regarded *as a gain attributable to good financial management* rather than a reduction of material cost. It would, moreover, complicate the costing if ultimately a discount failed to be taken and the amount had to be written back, sometimes to materials already issued. However, a different view of cash discounts holds that they do represent a reduction of material cost and should be deducted from the invoice. If ultimately the discount is not taken it is not written

MATERIALS ANALYSIS												W/E 24/7/........
Requisition		Job No.					Process		Overhead Account No.			
Requisition No.	Total	425	426	443	452	454	A16	B52	101	102	103	104
7273	£3·40		£3·40									
7274	15·50					£15·50						
7275	0·90								£0·90			
7276	6·18	£6·18										
7277	0·75										£0·75	
7278	10·00						£5·00	£5·00				
Total £	941·28	31·05	116·50	93·00	144·33	371·41	60·10	54·98	31·29	14·00	23·30	1·11

FIG. 4.—*Materials analysis sheet*

This layout is most suitable for a materials analysis where the number of jobs and overhead accounts is small.

back to the material but regarded as *a loss due to poor financial management* and charged to financial overheads.

32. Material costs: out of store. The *materials requisition* is used to draw the materials from the store (*see* II, **20**) and the original copy passes through the following procedure:

(*a*) Initiated by foreman, who states material, quantity, job number or overhead account, and other minor details.
(*b*) Exchanged for material at store.
(*c*) Passed to stores record office where clerk:

(*i*) prices requisition from appropriate stores record card;
(*ii*) computes value of material drawn and enters on requisition;
(*iii*) enters quantity and value on stores record card.

(*d*) Passed to cost office, where cost clerk enters value on materials analysis sheet (*see* **33** below).

33. Materials analysis. A *materials analysis* is an analysis of materials drawn from stores to job numbers and overhead accounts. It ensures that all materials issued are charged to some part or other of the cost accounts and not overlooked.

In practice, the analysis can be carried out in various ways. However, for the purposes of illustration a materials analysis sheet suitable where the number of jobs and overhead accounts is small is given in Fig. 4.

It is important that the analysis does not omit any materials requisitions. To guard against this the serial numbers of all requisitions analysed should be checked to make certain none are missing. To ensure that all requisitions for the period have been received and none are still in the procedure "pipe line," the foremen's books of requisitions should be examined and the serial numbers of the last requisitions issued by them in the period noted. The materials analysis should not be completed until all requisitions up to and including these final ones have been received and entered.

34. Material cost book-keeping.

(*a*) *Materials into store.* The entry here is basically: Dr. Stores Account; Cr. Creditors Account, with cost of materials. Freight charges and containers may require minor additional entries.

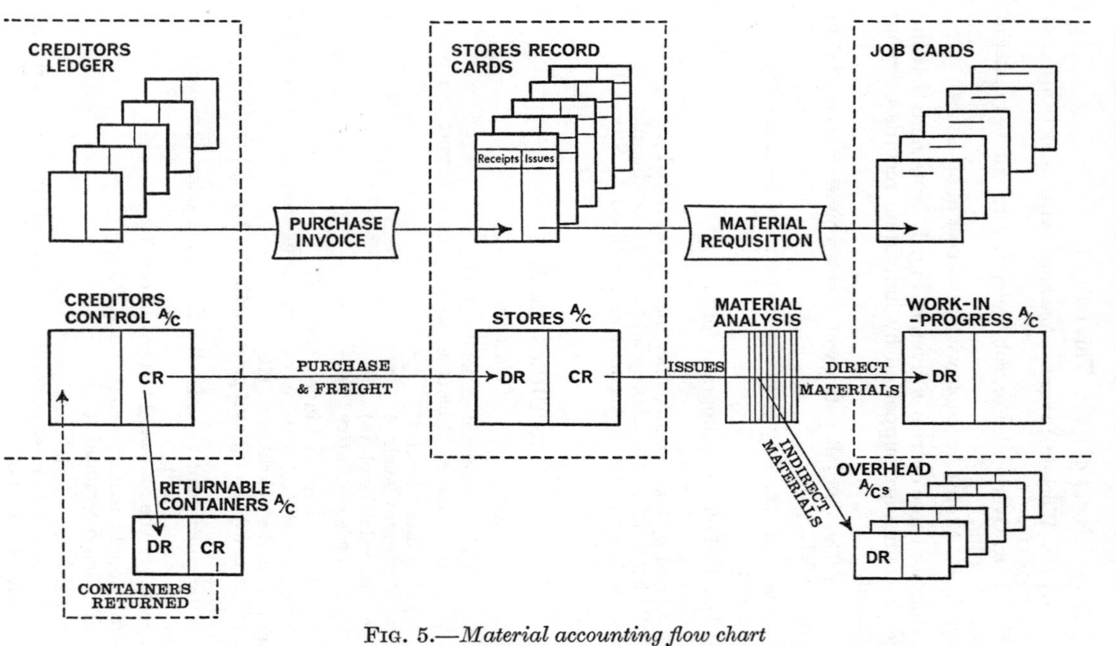

FIG. 5.—*Material accounting flow chart*

This chart shows the flow of data and the pattern of record-keeping necessary in material cost book-keeping.

(*b*) *Materials out of store.* This entry is:

(*i*) Dr. Work-in-Progress Account, with direct material costs.
(*ii*) Dr. Overheads Control Account, with indirect material costs.
(*iii*) Cr. Stores Account, with total cost of all issues.

A chart of these entries is given in Fig. 5. Note here that the ledger accounts are supported by individual records carrying the detail.

NOTE: The over-all pattern of cost accounting is covered in Chapter XI.

35. Stores losses. Any stores losses revealed by a stocktaking should be:

(*a*) Detailed on an appropriate form.
(*b*) Valued.
(*c*) Signed by a senior manager that he has noted the losses.
(*d*) Written off on the appropriate stores record cards.
(*e*) Credited to Stores Account and debited to Stores Losses Account.

PROGRESS TEST 3

Principles

1. Why is stores control important? (**1**)
2. What factors should be considered when determining:

(*a*) Maximum level, (**3**)
(*b*) Minimum level, (**4**)
(*c*) Re-order level, (**5**)
(*d*) Re-order quantity? (**6**)

3. What is a perpetual inventory? (**7**)
4. What are the advantages of continuous stocktaking over the normal annual stocktaking? (**10**)
5. What is (*a*) the *inflated price* method, (**21**) (*b*) the *base stock* method? (**22**)
6. What document records all information relating to an individual material? (**23**)
7. How are the following treated in costing:

(*a*) Bought material containers, (**30** (*c*))
(*b*) Cash discounts? (**31**)

8. What is a materials analysis? (**33**)
9. What is the difference between a bin card and a stores record card? (II, **24**, III, **23**)

Practice

(Answers to the practical questions in this and all other Progress Tests will be found in Appendix III.)

10. Briefly list the steps taken from reaching a re-order level to charging material to a job.

11. Two components, A and B, are used as follows:

Normal usage	50 per week each	
Minimum usage	25 ,, ,, ,,	
Maximum usage	75 ,, ,, ,,	
Re-order quantity	A: 300	B: 500
Re-order period	A: 4–6 weeks	B: 2–4 weeks

Calculate for each component:

(*a*) re-order level;
(*b*) minimum level;
(*c*) maximum level;
(*d*) average stock level.

Comment briefly on the difference in levels for the two components. (*I.C.W.A.*)

12. Suggest the lines along which a continuous stocktaking could be organised.

13. From the following data compute the value of the 20 units closing stock under (*a*) the FIFO method, (*b*) the LIFO method, and (*c*) the weighted average method:

Receipts:	1/6/...	40 units at £25 each.
	8/6/...	40 units at £30 each.
Issues:	2/6/...	30 units.
	9/6/...	30 units.

CHAPTER IV

LABOUR: LABOUR REMUNERATION

AFTER materials the next set of data relates to labour, and this chapter and the following two (V and VI) examine such data.

The first thing to be grasped in labour costing is the different methods of remunerating labour. Labour can be paid on a basis of time engaged, or work done, or a combination of both. Time engaged is the traditional basis: any scheme which incorporates work done is termed an incentive scheme. In this chapter the *mechanics* of the different methods are first examined and then the *application* of incentive schemes discussed.

METHODS OF REMUNERATION

There are three basic methods of labour remuneration: dayrate, piecework and premium bonus. These methods are explained below (**1–8**) and illustrated using the basic data given in **1**.

1. Dayrate (daywork; time rate). Under the *dayrate* method the employee is paid on a *basis of time engaged*. The formula is:

Hours worked × Rate per hour

Basic data:

Hourly rate	£0·50 per hr.
Agreed rate of production	100 units per hr.
Hours worked	8 hrs.
Units produced	1200 units.

∴ Dayrate earnings = 8 hrs at £0·50 = £4.

2. Dayrate: advantages and disadvantages. This method has its advantages and disadvantages.

(*a*) *Advantages:*

(*i*) Easy to compute and understand.
(*ii*) Avoids frequent complex negotiations inevitable with most incentive schemes.

(*b*) *Disadvantages:*

(*i*) No incentive for employee to do more than necessary. This means constant supervision may be required.
(*ii*) Efficient and inefficient employees are paid the same.
(*iii*) There is a direct incentive for employees to work slowly if uncompleted work results in overtime for them, since often employees wish to work overtime in order to increase their total weekly pay.

3. Circumstances under which dayrate is applicable. Dayrate is particularly suitable where:

(*a*) Quality is more important than production, *e.g.* tool-room work which involves expensive tools and where hurried workmanship can result in costly errors.
(*b*) Work is such that there is no basis for an incentive scheme, *e.g.* night-watchman.
(*c*) Rate of production is outside employee's control, *e.g.* oil-refinery operation.

4. High dayrate plan. The *high dayrate plan* is a dayrate variant that aims to avoid the complications and negotiations involved in incentive schemes and at the same time also avoid the lack of effort that usually accompanies dayrate work. Its main points are:

(*a*) All work is carefully studied and timed.
(*b*) On a basis of the timings, the work that can be expected from each worker when working at a steady rate is determined. This is usually much above that done under normal dayrate conditions.
(*c*) On engagement employees are told the work rate demanded and are offered a *dayrate wage well above average for the district*.

The effect of this plan is to attract employees who are prepared to make an extra effort in return for a substantially higher wage.

5. Piecework (P/W). Under the *piecework* method the employee is paid on a *basis of production*. The formula is:

$$\textit{Units produced} \times \textit{Rate per unit}$$

Sometimes each unit is given a "piecework hours" value. This use of "hours" is particularly applicable where units of production are varied. In these circumstances piecework earnings are the sum of all "piecework hours" earned multiplied by the rate per "piecework hour." It should be appreciated that "piecework hours" are in the nature of production "points" and are *not* the same as worked hours.

The basic figures (*see* 1) indicate management is prepared to pay £0·50 per 100 units produced.

∴ Piecework earnings = 1200 units at £0·50 per 100 = £6·00.

Alternatively, from the P/W hours aspect, the basic figures show management allow 0·01 hr per unit.

∴ P/W hrs earned = 0·01 × 1200 = 12 P/W hrs.
∴ Earnings = 12 P/W hrs at £0·50 hr = £6·00.

6. Piecework variants.

(*a*) *Piecework with guaranteed dayrate.* Under this method a dayrate is guaranteed, so that if at any time piecework earnings fall below the amount that would have been earned on dayrate, then the dayrate earnings are paid instead. This avoids an employee being poorly paid on account of low production which arose through no fault of the employee, *e.g.* poor materials. Virtually all modern piecework schemes carry a guaranteed dayrate.

(*b*) *Differential piecework.* In this type of scheme the piecework rate changes at different levels of efficiency, *e.g.* £0·05 a unit when efficiency is below 7 units an hour; £0·06 a unit when 7–10 units an hour; and £0·08 a unit when above 10 units an hour. The object is to provide a strong incentive to reach the maximum rate of production.

It should be appreciated that in such a scheme it is important to distinguish between paying the increased rate on *all* production or on only the *excess* production, *e.g.* if 11 units were produced under the above scheme, either the 11th unit *only* would be paid for at £0·08 or all 11, depending upon a more detailed definition of the scheme.

7. Premium bonus. Under the *premium bonus* method a time allowance (TA) for a job is given, the time taken (TT) is recorded, and *a bonus is paid on the basis of the time saved* (TS). It is important to remember that this method relates to *bonus*; the employee's basic pay is normal dayrate. The formula, therefore, for the employee's *total pay* is:

Dayrate wage + Bonus based on time saved

If the time taken exceeds the time allowed, then there is no time saved. There is, then, no bonus and dayrate only is paid for the time taken.

8. Formulae for premium bonus schemes. The formulae for the *bonuses earned* under the three most well-known schemes are as follows:

(*a*) Halsey: $Bonus = \frac{1}{2}\,\text{TS} \times dayrate$
(*b*) Halsey–Weir: $Bonus = \frac{1}{3}\,\text{TS} \times dayrate$
(*c*) Rowan: $Bonus = \frac{\text{TT}}{\text{TA}} \times \text{TS} \times dayrate$

EXAMPLE (Halsey):

Data: see **1**.

		Hours
Time allowed for 1200 units (TA)	$= \frac{1200}{100}$	= 12
Time taken (TT)		= 8
∴ Time saved (TS)		= 4

Method:

∴ Bonus $= \frac{1}{2} \times 4 \times £0{\cdot}50 = £1.$
∴ Total earnings = Dayrate wage + Bonus
$= [8 \times £0{\cdot}50] + £1 = £5.$

EXAMPLE (Rowan):

Data: As for Halsey.

Method:

Bonus $= \frac{8}{12} \times 4 \times £0{\cdot}50 = £1{\cdot}33.$

∴ Total earnings = Dayrate wage + Bonus = £4 + £1·33 = £5·33.

9. Setting time allowances. The following is a summary of the procedure adopted in setting time allowances:

(*a*) The work study department determine the length of time required by the average worker to do the job.
(*b*) Personal allowances are added to this time to give the expected time.
(*c*) The expected time is then increased by a set proportion laid down by management to give the *allowed time*. Such an increase is added so that employees who complete the job in the expected time earn a wage which is distinctly above the dayrate wage, a condition usually made necessary as a result of trade-union negotiations.

10. Graphing labour earning rates and unit costs. The different remuneration methods give quite different earning and unit cost patterns, as efficiency varies. For instance, under dayrate, earnings do not change with changing efficiency, so clearly the cost per unit is halved if efficiency doubles. Conversely, under piecework the unit cost remains constant, while earnings vary in proportion with efficiency. These effects can be graphed. Fig. 6(*a*) shows the earnings per hour and Fig. 6(*b*) the cost per 100 units for the three most usual methods of remuneration: dayrate, premium bonus (Halsey) and piecework (using data in **1**).

11. Labour remuneration and overheads. Under some schemes the labour cost per unit actually *increases* as efficiency improves. At first sight this may appear to involve management in a loss, but it should be realised that many factories have high fixed overheads, and a doubling of efficiency naturally halves the cost per unit of these costs. In consequence, the increased labour cost per unit is more than counterbalanced by this reduction in the fixed overhead cost per unit.

12. Overtime (O/T) premium. An *overtime premium* (or *penalty*) is an extra amount over and above dayrate earnings paid to an employee who works longer than a normal working day. It is almost invariably calculated as a percentage of the extra hours worked, usually 50%, called "time and a half," or 100%, called "double time."

For instance, if four hours overtime is worked at time and a half, a total of six hours (4 + 50% of 4) is paid, of which the payment for the *extra two hours* is called the overtime premium.

13. In lieu bonus. When it is desired to give an employee a bonus but the work is not suitable for an incentive scheme the management may make agreed payments in lieu of a normal bonus. Such a payment is termed an *in lieu bonus.* It is particularly made when an employee who is normally on bonus is temporarily transferred to non-bonus work.

14. Idle-time payments. If an employee on an incentive scheme is held up for any reason outside his control he records his "idle time" quite separately from his normal working time. He is then paid normal dayrate for such time plus, in some cases, an in lieu bonus. Obviously such "idle time" recording must be countersigned by some appropriate authority.

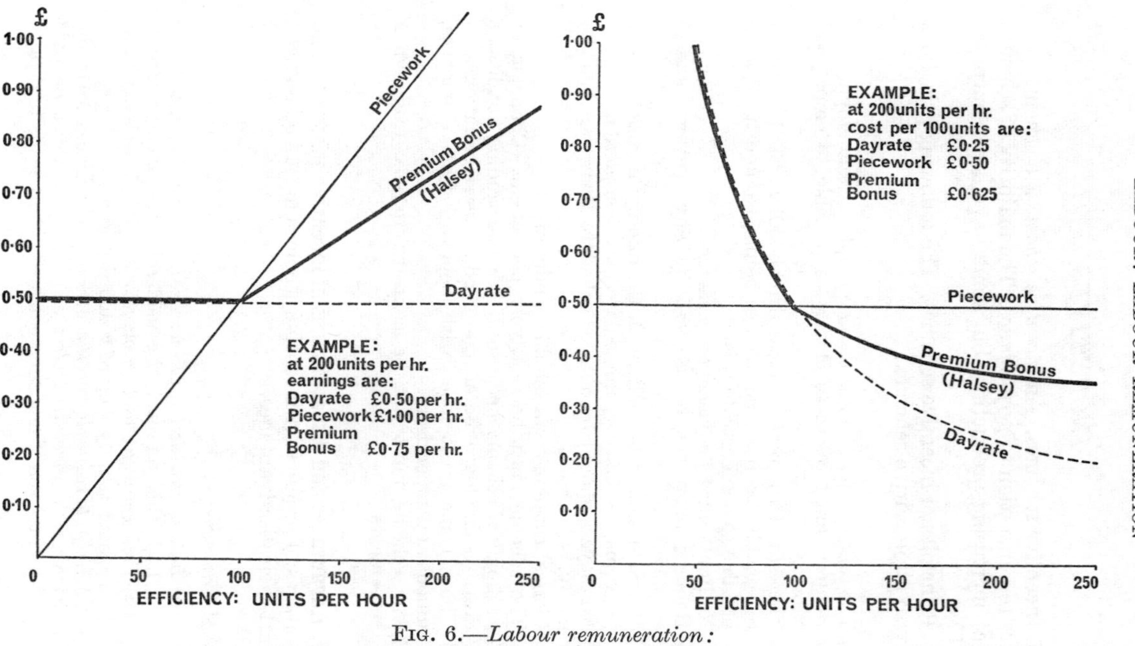

FIG. 6.—*Labour remuneration:*

(*a*) *Left:* Earnings per hour; (*b*) *Right:* Cost per 100 units. These graphs are based on a dayrate of £0·50 per hour and a normal production rate of 100 units per hour.

INCENTIVES

15. Incentive schemes. An *incentive scheme* is a scheme that relates remuneration to *performance*. The majority of schemes aim at increasing production, but some have other purposes (*see* **19**).

16. Principles of incentive schemes. The following principles apply to all incentive schemes:

(*a*) The scheme must be fair to both employer and employee.
(*b*) Bonuses must relate as closely as possible to employees' efforts.
(*c*) The standard performance demanded must be within reasonable reach of the average employee, and it must be possible to demonstrate this.
(*d*) No limits must be placed on earnings.
(*e*) Bonuses must not be affected by any matters outside employees' control.
(*f*) Payment should be made with the minimum of delay after performance—ideally, immediately on completion.
(*g*) Employees should be able to calculate their own bonuses easily.
(*h*) Clerical running costs should be minimised.
(*i*) The scheme must be relatively permanent. Changing or dropping a scheme because of adverse trading conditions destroys employee morale and good industrial relations.
(*j*) The scheme must meet with approval from employees, unions and supervisors.
(*k*) The scheme must not be contrary to any trade-union agreements.

17. Advantages and disadvantages of incentive schemes. The advantages of production incentive schemes must be balanced against their disadvantages.

(*a*) *Advantages:*

(*i*) *Rate of production is increased.* If fixed overheads are high, this can result in considerable cost saving per unit.
(*ii*) *Both employer and employees benefit.* Often customers benefit too, by way of reduced prices.
(*iii*) *Helps to reduce labour turnover* if good bonuses are made.
(*iv*) *Keeps management alert* as employees must be paid bonus even if management inefficiency leads to delays.

(*b*) *Disadvantages:*

(*i*) *Involves extra work* in setting time allowances and running scheme.

(*ii*) *May involve long, time-consuming negotiations* over rates.

(*iii*) *Difficult to include indirect labour.* If direct labour bonuses are high this may lead to resentment.

(*iv*) *Weak schemes cannot easily be withdrawn.* This may mean enterprise is saddled with an uneconomic scheme.

(*v*) *Scheme disputes may become source of friction.* This may result in low morale and costly strikes [including loss of contribution (*see* XV, 3)].

(*vi*) *Employees may devote their efforts to exploiting loopholes* rather than to improving performance.

(*vii*) *Production delays may prove very expensive*, since often in lieu bonuses (as well as dayrate wages) will have to be paid to waiting employees.

18. Setting up an incentive scheme. Setting up an incentive scheme requires considerable care. There are many dangers, most of which are hidden. Unfortunately management sometimes believe that an incentive scheme will solve most of their problems and hastily throw together a scheme that quickly doubles their problems, affixes a virtually permanent millstone round their necks and ends with a legacy of trouble and mistrust that may well outlive the enterprise.

When setting up an incentive scheme the following steps should be carefully taken:

(*a*) *Decide on the basis of payment.* This should relate to what management want from the scheme themselves. This often requires more thought than is initially apparent. For instance, a scheme generously rewarding a high *hourly* rate of production in a factory with high fixed overheads may prove expensive if employees earn so much in four days that they take the fifth day off.

(*b*) *Discuss the scheme with the foremen.* Remember that much of the day-to-day running will depend on them.

(*c*) *Discuss the scheme with the unions.* This is very necessary, since if they do not like it they can kill it.

(*d*) *Give the scheme a trial run in a small section of the factory.* This will enable minor unforeseen difficulties to be eliminated.

(*e*) *Initiate scheme with the maximum of explanation.*

(*f*) *Avoid paternalistic attitude.* Remember that management will probably gain more from the scheme than employees.

(*g*) *Resist rate changes.* Pressure quickly comes to change certain rates. Acquiescence may easily throw a scheme out of balance and result in a spiralling increase of all rates. (Incorrectly set rates must be amended, however.)

19. Schemes unrelated to increased production. Apart from increased production, incentive schemes may aim at:

(*a*) Improving quality.
(*b*) Reducing lateness and absenteeism.
(*c*) Improving safety and reducing accidents.
(*d*) Reducing waste of materials or services (*e.g.* heat, light, indirect labour).

20. Individual *v.* group incentive schemes. Under normal circumstances a scheme that rewards each employee on a basis of his own individual performance is better in all respects than one that rewards group performance. Individual incentive schemes, therefore, should normally be employed.

GROUP INCENTIVES

21. Circumstances requiring group incentives. Despite the usual superiority of an individual incentive scheme, group schemes should be employed in the following circumstances:

(*a*) *When work-force flexibility is required.* Some forms of work require employees to switch quickly from job to job so that the *individual's* performance cannot be measured, although the *group's* performance can.
(*b*) *When team-work is necessary*, *e.g.* in a coal-mine.
(*c*) *When production is on a continuous production-line basis*, so that extra production depends upon all employees increasing their speeds.

22. Determining group bonuses. The problem of rewarding effort under a group incentive scheme falls into two parts:

(*a*) Finding the *group* bonus. Methods for this include:

(*i*) *Group piecework.* A rate is paid to the group for each unit of production they produce.
(*ii*) *Saving on cost target.* The group is given a total expenditure allowance for each unit of production, and an agreed proportion of any saving on this allowance due to labour efficiency, reduction of waste or power, etc., is paid to the group.

(*iii*) *Payment on a points basis.* Points are awarded for production, quality, material saving, etc.

(*b*) *Sharing* the group bonus. The best basis for sharing a group bonus is one chosen by the group itself. To an outsider, the basis may appear unfair, but if members of the group are satisfied there is no justification for interfering.

23. Advantages and disadvantages of group incentive schemes. The advantages and disadvantages of group incentive schemes, compared with individual schemes, are as follows:

(*a*) *Advantages:*

(*i*) Improved co-operation.
(*ii*) Recording of labour times simplified.
(*iii*) Checking of completed production reduced and simplified.
(*iv*) Absenteeism is often reduced, as an absent member weakens a group and most employees do not like to "let down" their team.
(*v*) Indirect labour can often be included in the scheme by allocating such employees to groups.

(*b*) *Disadvantages:*

(*i*) Unfair to individuals. A hard-working member of a group is not rewarded in proportion to his efforts. This acts as a disincentive to extra effort by an individual.
(*ii*) Harder to obtain employees' acceptance of the scheme.
(*iii*) Usually requires a group leader. If such a leader does not emerge the performance of the group is often disappointing.
(*iv*) Apathy tends to dominate over enthusiasm, so that levels of performance rarely reach those found with individual incentive schemes.

Moreover, *as group size increases these disadvantages become more and more severe.*

24. Profit-sharing and co-ownership. Profit-sharing and co-ownership should be carefully distinguished. *Profit-sharing* is the payment to employees of a proportion of the company's trading profit; *co-ownership* relates to a scheme under which employees own shares in the company, the shares having been bought or given. The two terms tend to be linked, as companies that run these sort of schemes often give employees their share of the profits in the form of company shares.

Profit-sharing is rarely a good incentive. It complies with few of the principles of a good incentive scheme and suffers all the disadvantages of a group incentive. Moreover, it may be basically unsound, since it is management's responsibility to produce profits, and to pass on part of this responsibility to employees may represent a partial abdication by management. However, if given as a gesture of appreciation it may well improve morale.

Co-ownership clearly suffers the same disadvantages as profit-sharing, and in addition if the company runs into adverse trading conditions the employee may suffer a treble loss: his normal earnings, his dividend and the capital value of his shares.

Profit-sharing and co-ownership aim to make employees partners in the enterprise, but it may be that employees prefer to be well-paid, risk-free labour rather than risk-sharing partners.

DETERMINING DAYRATE

25. Wage levels. Wage levels in an organisation are determined by various economic factors including:

(*a*) Cost of living.
(*b*) Local supply of and demand for labour.
(*c*) Rates in local enterprises.
(*d*) Union strength in the industry.
(*e*) Ability of the organisation to pay high wage rates.

Where an organisation has high fixed costs (due, for example, to extensive mechanisation), then shop-floor employees are in a strong bargaining position, since management may be well prepared to pay high wage rates to gain even minor improvements in production efficiency.

26. Job evaluation. *Job evaluation* is a technique for determining the worth of each job relative to other jobs. The procedure is as follows:

(*a*) *Determine all the job factors involved* in the evaluation, *e.g.* training; experience; intelligence; responsibility; working conditions.
(*b*) *Determine a range of points for each factor*. Since some factors are more important than others, they will carry a higher range of points.

(c) Taking each job in turn, *decide on the points a job earns for each job factor*, and *total these points*.
(d) *Relate these points to a wage scale*, so that knowing the points value of any job, the appropriate wage rate can be read off.

A working sheet for job evaluation might appear thus:

Job factor	*Range of points*	*Job A*	*Job B*	*Job C*
Training	0–50	10	40	20
Experience	0–50	15	10	50
Intelligence	0–40	5	30	20
Responsibility	10–60	10	30	60
Working conditions	0–20	10	0	20
	TOTAL	50	110	170

If the wage scale in this particular factory ran from £0·20 to £1·00 per hr for a range of 40 to 200 points, then the following rates would be applicable:

Job A £0·25 per hr
Job B £0·55 per hr
Job C £0·85 per hr

In practice, other factors generally determine the actual wage rate paid, but a job-evaluated rate shows the level management should be endeavouring to achieve.

27. Merit rating. *Merit rating* is a technique for determining any addition that should be made to an individual's normal rate to reward him for above average service. It must be carefully distinguished from job evaluation. Job evaluation evaluates the *job* irrespective of who does it. Merit rating evaluates the *employee* doing the job.

To conduct a merit rating each employee is rated in respect of a number of personal attributes, such as initiative, reliability, attendance, punctuality, accuracy, thoroughness, safety, behaviour, co-operativeness, etc. He is often given points for each attribute and the total of his points related to some pre-determined scale which sets out the merit addition to be made to his rate of pay.

In addition to being used for determining merit payments, merit rating can be used for:

(a) Assisting promotion, demotion, transfer and discharge decisions.

(*b*) Guiding the employee interested in promotion and concerned with self-improvement.

(*c*) Assessing enterprise weak spots in personnel policy, selection and training.

PROGRESS TEST 4

Principles

1. What are the three basic methods of labour remuneration and how do they differ? **(1, 5, 7)**

2. If the wage cost per unit rose as the output per hour increased, need management necessarily be alarmed? **(11)**

3. How is overtime premium calculated? **(12)**

4. What is "in lieu bonus"? **(13)**

5. What are the principles of a good incentive scheme? **(16)**

6. What are the advantages and disadvantages of incentive schemes? **(17)**

7. How should an incentive scheme be set up? **(18)**

8. When should a group incentive scheme be employed? **(21)**

9. How can group bonuses be determined? **(22)**

10. What are the advantages and disadvantages of group bonus schemes? **(23)**

11. Distinguish between profit-sharing and co-ownership. **(24)**

12. What factors determine wage levels? **(25)**

13. How does one carry out:

(*a*) Job evaluation, **(26)**
(*b*) Merit rating? **(27)**

Practice

14. Jobs are issued to operative X, to make 189 units, and to operative Y, to make 204 units, for which a time allowance of 20 standard minutes and 15 standard minutes per unit respectively, is credited. For every hour saved, bonus is paid at 50% of the base rate, which is 50p per hour for both employees. The basic working week is 42 hours. Hours in excess are paid at time and a half.

X completes his units in 45 hours and Y completes his in 39 hours (but works a full week). Due to defective material, six of X's units and four of Y's units are subsequently scrapped, although all units produced are paid for.

You are required to calculate for each of X and Y:

(*a*) the amount of bonus payable;
(*b*) the total gross wage payable;
(*c*) the wages cost per good unit made.

(*I.C.W.A.* Adapted)

CHAPTER V

LABOUR: PAYROLL PROCEDURE

GATE TIMEKEEPING

1. Gate timekeeping. It is very important that the time an employee spends on the factory premises during any week is known. Employees on dayrate are obviously paid for all the hours they are on the premises, but even pieceworkers must record their hours, if only to be correctly paid for overtime. In practice, the actual hours spent on the premises by such workers is also needed to ensure regular and punctual attendance, for it is necessary to keep production not only at a high level but also flowing steadily. Irregular production by one man, high though his over-all production may be, leads to stresses at other parts of the production line which result in an unnecessary lowering of efficiency.

The recording of the time when employees enter and leave the premises is known as *gate timekeeping*.

2. Clock cards. In the past a variety of systems were used for gate timekeeping, but today the clock card is almost universal. A *clock card* is simply a stiff card that is inserted into a clock at the "gate" and the time of insertion stamped. Nowadays most "gate" clocks are situated in the employee's department. Each employee has his own clock card and he "clocks in" and "clocks out" every time he enters and leaves his department. Clock cards normally record clockings for a full week.

3. Clock numbers. On joining an enterprise an employee is given an individual *clock number* which is printed on his clock card. To avoid ambiguity, employees are identified in all enterprise procedures by their clock numbers.

4. Use of coloured inks. Time clocks can be adjusted to print in different colours at different times. If normal clocking times are printed black and non-normal times red (*e.g.* the colour changes to red immediately after the official starting time and remains red until leaving time), then an all-black card indicates that throughout the week normal hours were worked.

This means that a wages clerk need only look closely at *red* printings, since these alone will require an adjustment to be made to the employee's normal weekly pay. Overtime, of course, would always be shown in red.

5. Prevention of gate timekeeping frauds. Modern clocks assist in preventing the following two types of fraud:

(*a*) *Manipulating times.* To prevent employees clocking the current day's time in spaces relating to other days, the clocks print an indication of both the day and period (a.m. or p.m.). Also the design of many clocks and clock cards is such that it is virtually impossible to clock a time into the space of an earlier day.

(*b*) *Employees clocking unofficially.* Employees sometimes wish to clock the cards of their absent friends. Clocks therefore ring a bell when a clocking is made so that attention is drawn to such a clocking. Prevention of this kind of fraud, however, also depends upon close supervision, which may or may not exist.

WAGES OFFICE PROCEDURE

6. Payroll. A *payroll* (or *wage sheet*) is a list of all employees showing major details relating to their pay, particularly their gross pay, deductions and net pay (*see* Fig. 7, where the basic form of a payroll is included).

Preparation of the payroll falls into two parts:

(*a*) Computation of employees' gross wages.
(*b*) Computation of employees' net wages.

7. Computation of gross wages. The gross wage of each employee is computed by reference to the following documents:

(*a*) *Clock cards.* These are required, of course, for dayrate and premium bonus workers and also to compute overtime and minimum guaranteed wages for pieceworkers.
(*b*) *Piecework tickets.* These are tickets recording each pieceworker's production.

(c) *Job cards.* These are needed in order to compute premium bonuses, since bonuses depend upon total time spent on individual jobs.
(d) *Employee's record card.* This is a document recording remuneration details of the individual employee, *e.g.* rate of pay; insurance contribution; holidays taken or outstanding; PAYE code number and earnings summary.

8. Computation of net wages. From the individual's gross pay the following deductions are made:

(a) PAYE tax (this involves the entire PAYE recording procedure).
(b) Employee's insurance contribution.
(c) Employee's graduated pension contribution.
(d) Amounts for charities, social club contributions etc., that the employee has authorised in writing as regular deductions.

9. Payday procedure. The following is a typical payday procedure:

(a) *Cash is drawn from the bank.*

(i) The amount of cash drawn equates to the *net* wages, not the gross wages.
(ii) To ensure that the correct number of coins is obtained a *coin analysis* of the payroll is made to find the number required of each denomination, and the bank is informed in advance of collection.
(iii) To avoid wage robberies most up-to-date organisations engage special carriers using modern payroll protection devices to bring the wages from the bank.

(b) *The net wages are put into wage packets.*

(i) Usually two people work together on this, one counting the money out for each employee and the other checking it before putting it into the wage packet.
(ii) A *wage slip* is inserted with the cash giving pay details. This is often a carbon copy of the employee's line on the payroll.

(c) *The wage packets are distributed.*

(i) Employees must be correctly identified (by the foreman if need be) before the wage packet is handed over.

(*ii*) Unclaimed wage packets are held in the wages office until claimed by employee or someone holding his written authorisation to collect.

10. Prevention of payroll fraud. Payrolls are a favourite target for fraud. Prevention is helped by:

(*a*) Arranging for different clerks to carry out the different steps of computation, and on payday changing the clerks around yet again, so that no clerk who compiled the wages on any given wage sheet handles the wage packets relating to that sheet.
(*b*) Ensuring that each employee's insurance card and tax documents are in order. This prevents non-existent people being entered on the payroll.
(*c*) Insisting on overtime or loans being properly authorised before payment.
(*d*) Using "see-through" wage packets so that employees can check their wages before breaking the packet seal. (Too much blind trust should not be put in this device. It is not as foolproof as it might initially appear.)

11. Wages office reports. In addition to paying wages the wages office may prepare various reports such as:

(*a*) *Wages analysis report*, analysing wages by grades, age, sex or other classification of employee.
(*b*) *Timekeeping report*, detailing lateness and absenteeism.
(*c*) *Overtime report*, detailing overtime hours and premiums paid, together with reasons.
(*d*) *Labour turnover report*, measuring labour turnover (L.T.) so that the enterprise knows to what extent employees are being lost. One method of measure uses the following formula:

$$\text{L.T.} = \frac{\textit{No. of employees leaving who have to be replaced}}{\textit{Average number employed}}$$

A labour turnover report will include reasons for such turnover so that management can take action to reduce an unacceptable level.

PROGRESS TEST 5

Principles

1. Why is gate timekeeping required? **(1)**
2. What value have coloured inks in recording gate times? **(4)**
3. What are the main gate timekeeping frauds and what steps are taken to guard against them? **(5)**
4. What is a payroll? **(6)**
5. Why are job cards sometimes needed to compute an employee's gross pay? **(7)**
6. Outline a typical payday procedure. **(9)**
7. What steps are taken to guard against payroll frauds? **(10)**

CHAPTER VI

LABOUR: LABOUR COSTING

RECORDING LABOUR TIMES

1. Necessity for recording labour times. Labour is a major cost in most factories, and it is essential that a detailed analysis is made showing the production and activities on which the cost was incurred. Such an analysis can be made only if every employee records in detail his activities and the time he spends on each one.

2. Relationship to gate time. Clearly, the total employee time recorded on activities must equal the total gate time paid for (*see* V, **1**), and it is necessary to insert in the costing procedure a check that ensures those two totals do, in fact, agree.

3. Time sheets. The most common method of recording labour times is for each employee to fill in a *time sheet*, *i.e.* a sheet detailing the employee's activities and the time spent on each.

There are two kinds of time sheet:

(*a*) *Weekly time sheets.* These record the activities day by day of an employee for a complete week, each employee filling in one sheet a week. The *disadvantage* of weekly sheets is that since most employees do not start to fill them in until they are obliged to, *i.e.* at the very end of the week, the times spent earlier in the week on jobs have often been forgotten, and consequently the sheets are inaccurate. Sometimes, in fact, the job itself is forgotten and appears in the cost records as having been completed without the aid of any labour at all!

(*b*) *Daily time sheets.* These are similar to weekly time sheets, except that they are completed and sent to the cost office each day. The *disadvantage* of daily sheets is that they result in a considerable volume of paper—in the case of a small 100-man factory, for example, some 2,000 pieces per month. They do have the *advantage*, however, that the risk of times being forgotten or manipulated is considerably lessened.

4. Job cards. Another method of recording labour times is by means of *job cards.* A job card is a card made out *for each job*; unlike time sheets, which are made out for each employee. When an employee works on a job he records on the job card the time spent on that job.

There are two kinds of job card:

(*a*) *One card per complete job.* With this kind of job card the card travels round with the job and labour times are recorded upon it after each operation. This has the advantage that when the card reaches the cost office all labour times are listed, and the cost clerks have merely to insert the labour rates, multiply and add to obtain the full labour cost. It has, however, a serious disadvantage: until the job is fully completed none of the times are known in the cost office. As some jobs may be many weeks being completed, it is virtually impossible to reconcile labour time with gate times each week (*see* **2**).

(*b*) *One card per operation.* This method of recording means that a single job will have a number of job cards, one for each operation. This involves considerable paper work, but it does enable time bookings to reach the cost office quickly.

NOTE: Students should appreciate that no matter what method is used, there is always a possibility that in practice the times recorded are unreliable (*see* XXIII, **15**).

5. Time booking categories. Each employee must make sure that the total hours he books in a period is equal to the total hours he is paid for. Such time booked will be within one or a combination of the following categories:

(*a*) Production jobs, each with its own job number (*see* X, **1–3**).
(*b*) Process work (*see* XII, **6**).
(*c*) Overhead activities (*see* VIII, **7**(*f*)).
(*d*) Idle (waiting) time. If an employee has no work to do he must record the time he is "idle" and indicate the reason (*e.g.* breakdown; waiting for material, tools or instructions).

LABOUR COSTING

Having outlined various aspects of labour records and wages, it now remains to discuss the treatment of labour costs.

6. Wage analysis. A *wage analysis* is an analysis of the total gross wages on the payroll to cost activities, *i.e.* jobs and

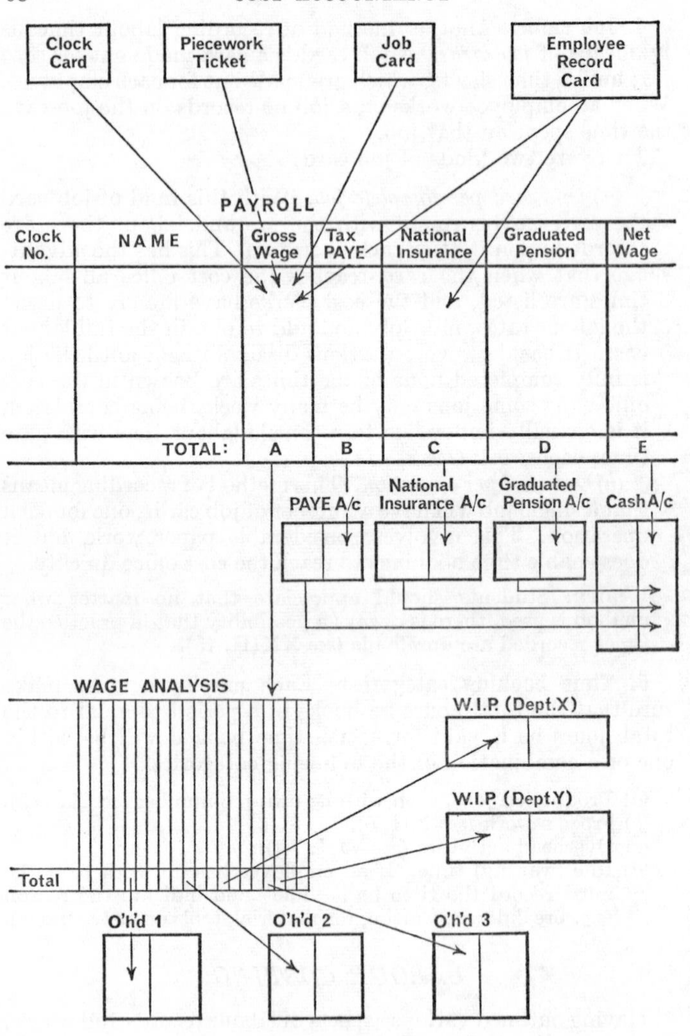

FIG. 7.—*Wage accounting chart*

This chart shows the procedures involved in accounting for wages paid.

overheads. Essentially the object is to examine each employee's gross wage and compute how much is chargeable to the individual jobs and overheads activities he was engaged upon. It is prepared by consulting the same sources of data that were used for preparing the payroll (*see* V, **7**), together with the labour time records discussed above. The basic design principle of a wage analysis is very similar to that of a materials analysis, *i.e.* employees' names and gross wages are listed vertically and the analysis of each employee's wage is entered into columns across the sheet (*cf.* Fig. 4).

7. Charging labour costs.

(*a*) *Direct labour.* This is charged in detail to the production the employee was engaged upon. In addition, the total direct labour cost of each department is debited to the individual departmental Work-in-Progress Account.
(*b*) *Indirect labour.* This is charged in detail to each individual overhead account.

8. Chart of wage accounts procedure. Fig. 7 shows a chart outlining the procedure involved in accounting for wages paid. It can be seen that after completion of the payroll the procedure is essentially:

(*a*) After analysis, *debit* the gross wages to the various Work-in-Progress and Overhead Accounts.
(*b*) *Credit:*

(*i*) Cash Account with the net wages.
(*ii*) The various liability accounts (PAYE etc.) with the deductions.

PROGRESS TEST 6

Principles

1. Distinguish between gate timekeeping and recording labour times. (V, **1**, VI, **1**).
2. What are the four documents that can be used to record labour times, and how do they differ from each other? (**3**, **4**)
3. What is a wage analysis? (**6**)

CHAPTER VII

DIRECT EXPENSES

1. Expenses. *Expenses* are costs which do not relate to either materials or labour. They include, therefore, such items as rent, rates, power, royalties, advertising, depreciation, printing, telephones, heating, lighting, sub-contracts, machine hire, freight, etc.

Very often selling and administration salaries are referred to as "expenses," though strictly speaking they are indirect labour costs. This view of salaries relates to the traditional costing approach, where the term "labour" was restricted to shop-floor activities.

2. Direct and indirect expenses. In Chapter I (**11**) a direct cost was defined as a cost that results solely from the existence of whatever is being costed. A *direct expense*, therefore, is an expense that results solely from the existence of whatever is being costed. An *indirect expense* is, of course, any expense that is not a direct expense. Indirect expenses are dealt with in the next chapter (VIII).

3. Types of cost unit direct expense. Cost unit direct expenses are relatively few, most expenses being indirect. However, the possibility of an expense being direct should always be kept in mind, and care taken not to form a habit of regarding all expenses as indirect.

The following are examples of cost unit direct expenses:

(*a*) *Royalties,* since royalties charged are based on a rate per unit.

(*b*) *Plant hire,* if the plant is hired solely in order to manufacture a specific cost unit.

(*c*) *Sub-contract or outside work,* if jobs are sent out for special processing, *e.g.* plating.

(*d*) *Salesmen's commissions,* since these are usually based on the sales value of units sold.

(*e*) *Freight,* if the goods are handled by an outside carrier whose charges can be related to individual units, *e.g.* rate per unit, or per pound weight.

4. Power, a direct or an indirect expense? In theory power is a direct expense, since it is an expense that can arise only from the existence of whatever is being costed; if the cost unit or centre is eliminated there is no use of power and therefore no cost. However, to measure its use as a direct expense would mean placing a meter on every machine and in every cost centre, and in the case of cost units, moreover, taking readings for every unit processed. This, of course, is not practical, and therefore for convenience power is treated as an indirect expense. (*See* VIII, **5** for other examples of direct costs being treated as indirect costs.)

PROGRESS TEST 7

Principles

1. What are expenses? (**1**)
2. How can a direct expense be distinguished from an indirect expense? (**2**)
3. In what circumstances would plant hire be a direct expense? (**3**)
4. Is power a direct or an indirect expense? (**4**)

CHAPTER VIII

OVERHEADS

WHAT ARE OVERHEADS?

1. Definition of overheads. In Chapter I (**11**) we said overheads were the same as indirect costs if cost units were being costed. *Overheads*, therefore, should be defined as costs which do not result solely from the existence of individual cost units.

Since in this context they are the same as indirect costs, they can also be defined as "the aggregate of indirect materials cost, indirect wages and indirect expense."

2. The border-line between direct costs and overheads. Although we have carefully distinguished between direct cost and overhead, in practice it is sometimes difficult to classify an individual cost. For example, a company may accept an order that requires a special tool. The tool is bought and used. Is the cost an overhead? If no other work will ever require the use of the tool, then clearly it is a direct cost to the order. If, on the other hand, the tool is to be used on future work the cost cannot really be said to result solely from the existence of the order, since future work would ultimately have given rise to the cost. In this case the cost is an overhead, and the current order should only bear a proportionate share of it. But sometimes it is very difficult to determine whether or not the tool will be of use in future work, and so it is virtually impossible to say whether or not the cost is truly an overhead.

3. Overheads that appear as direct costs. Sometimes what appears to be an indisputable direct cost turns out to be wholly or partially indirect. For instance, direct wages were earlier defined as wages paid to employees working on the direct materials (*see* I, **16**(*b*)). Now assume that 200,000 such hours were booked against the first of a group of aircraft. Clearly this particular aircraft would be charged with 200,000 hours' direct wages. However, it could almost certainly be argued that part of this total included time spent clearing up production queries that would never be incurred again and which would, in fact, benefit all future aircraft (*e.g.* minor blueprint errors). Such labour costs would be akin to design costs, which are, of course, overheads. Thus part of the wages paid for the 200,000 hours is overhead.

A similar case arises when a trainee works on a job. The labour cost here is partially a training cost. One way of dealing with this situation is to charge the job with the estimated direct wages which would otherwise have been incurred, and charge the balance of the trainee's wage to training overheads.

4. Effect of changes in cost analysis detail. If the cost unit is very large, say a new factory building, then many costs that are normally regarded as overheads become direct, *e.g.* supervision, site clerical labour, electricity, etc. However, if the cost accountant decides to cost each *part* of the building separately, then such costs become overheads to the individual parts.

Whether a cost is classified as direct or indirect, therefore, depends upon the extent of detail required in the cost analysis.

5. Minor direct costs treated as overheads. In practice, there are frequently a number of costs which are direct, but the amounts chargeable to the different cost units may be both small and difficult to ascertain. To avoid needless petty analysis such costs are treated as overheads. Examples of such costs are: sewing cotton; small nails and glue; material-handling labour; labour time spent on paperwork; power.

COLLECTION AND CLASSIFICATION OF OVERHEADS

6. Collection of overheads. It is part of the cost accountant's work to collect all the overheads. Most of these will come through to him as part of the routine, but he should know the source from which the overhead information is derived.

7. Sources of overhead data. The most important of these sources are:

(*a*) *Rent*—lease.

(*b*) *Rates*—local government assessment.

(*c*) *Fuel*—usage = opening stock + additions − closing stock.

NOTE: This formula, which gives the consumption over a period, is a useful one to remember, since it can often be applied in many other situations when no record of quantities used is made out at the time of use.

(*d*) *Office stationery*—supplier's invoice. Theoretically opening and closing stocks should be taken into account, but unless these change substantially, the extra work is not warranted.

(*e*) *Power and light*—meter readings will give the consumption, and this is then converted into cost by applying the electricity authority's rate.

NOTE

(*i*) Invoices are no use in this case, since they are generally quarterly, while most cost accounting periods are monthly.

(*ii*) Power and light are charged at different rates. They are on different circuits and each has its own meter.

(*f*) *Indirect wages*—time sheets.

(*g*) *Indirect materials*—materials requisitions.

(*h*) *Salaries*—salaries sheet.

(*i*) *Postage*—postage book.

(*j*) *Depreciation*—plant register (*see* **29**).

8. Classification of overheads. Overheads can be classified:

(*a*) By nature (*e.g.* materials; labour; depreciation; sales salaries).

(*b*) By cost centre (*e.g.* machine; department; sales area).

It is nearly always necessary to analyse overheads to both categories, and so all overheads are usually given a two-part code number, one part indicating the nature of the overhead and the other the cost centre where the overhead is incurred.

9. Standing order numbers. Overhead code numbers are sometimes called *standing order numbers.* They are given this name to contrast them with the normal works order numbers that identify the production passing through the factory. Use of this name facilitates shop-floor recordings, since all employees are told that all work times and materials drawn must be booked to order numbers, either normal works order numbers or standing order numbers.

OVERHEADS REQUIRING SPECIAL CONSIDERATION

10. Overtime premiums. When an employee works overtime his *normal* rate of pay is charged against all the work he does in that period, and the overtime *premium* (*see* IV, **12**) is segregated. This premium is then dealt with in one of the following two ways:

(*a*) *Charged to the cost unit.* If the overtime was worked at the customer's request, or would not otherwise have been worked but for the special needs of that particular job, then the premium is charged to the job.

(*b*) *Charged to overheads.* If, on the other hand, the employee worked overtime in order to help clear a backlog of orders, then obviously the job upon which he was engaged was one which just happened to be next in turn. Since the overtime was not worked solely because that job was in existence, but in order to aid production as a whole, then the premium is not a direct cost, but an overhead.

11. Cash discounts. These are generally excluded completely from the costs. In fact, as a general rule all financial costs are excluded from the costs. Actually this is only a traditional convention, and may well soon pass away.

12. Interest. Many years ago a controversy raged as to whether interest was a cost or a disguised form of profit appropriation. Today it is in the main accepted that interest:

(*a*) Should not be brought into the cost accounts.

(*b*) Should only be taken into cost computations if it is relevant to the problem in hand (*e.g.* when a comparison is to be made between the costs of carrying out an operation by hand or by machine. Clearly, the interest on the capital value of the machine must be taken into consideration to make the comparison valid.)

13. Notional charges. Sometimes an enterprise is able to avoid incurring a particular cost in the cost ledger, *e.g.* if the premises are owned by the enterprise there will be no rent. If in these sort of circumstances the cost accountant wants his costs to reflect the true economic position he will make a notional charge to his overheads for the missing item. Such a step is often taken where an enterprise owns some factories and rents others and wishes all its factory costs to be comparable (*see* XXIII, **4**).

NOTE: Cost book-keeping is dealt with later (*see* XI), but it should be mentioned here that to bring notional charges in the accounts, it is necessary to debit overheads with the charge and credit either the Financial or the Cost Profit and Loss Account.

14. Carriage inwards. This is not really an overhead at all, but is a cost that must be added to the purchase price of the goods (*see* III, **30**(*b*)).

15. Selling and distribution overheads. Selling and distribution costs have tended to be ignored in the past by cost accountants, but their increasing importance will bring them under more and more scrutiny. Even in companies that previously concentrated all their attention on production and relied, successfully, on their name to sell their output, selling (and often distribution) is quickly becoming a major function equalling that of production. From the point of view of importance, therefore, selling and distribution costs deserve as much attention as production costs. Unfortunately, selling costs cannot be so easily pinned down to cost units as can many shop-floor costs, and so cost analysis is restricted. However, cost control can be relatively thorough-going.

Some selling and distribution costs are direct: for example, sales commission and freight charges. Most, however, are indirect, as, for example:

(*a*) Selling (salesmen's salaries, showroom expenses, advertising).

(*b*) Distribution (vehicle costs, distribution salaries, depot costs).

As suggested above, these should be treated in all respects as thoroughly as factory overheads. The tendency to lump them together as a single item of overhead should be resisted in practice, while in theory such treatment is allowable only if it is fully appreciated that we are saying in effect: "all procedures relating to factory overheads will be repeated for selling and distribution overheads, and in order to avoid repetition of detail we are using the phrase 'selling and distribution overheads' to imply this."

DEPRECIATION AND OBSOLESCENCE

16. Depreciation. *Depreciation* is the loss in value of an asset due to wear and tear and deterioration. Usually the loss in value is due primarily to wear and tear, but an unused asset will lose value on account of deterioration.

17. Obsolescence. *Obsolescence* is the loss in value of an asset due to its supersession, *i.e.* the loss due to the development of a technically superior asset. There are degrees of obsolescence, since it is rare that the technical improvement is so dramatic that an existing asset is reduced to scrap value only.

The major problem with obsolescence is predicting its occurrence. Unfortunately it often occurs with very little warning (though past experience may give some guide to the type of equipment likely to become rapidly obsolete, *e.g.* computers, aircraft). This means, of course, that it is rarely possible to make any regular and realistic allowance for the future obsolescence of existing assets. To avoid being caught out some businessmen write down their equipment to scrap value as quickly as possible.

18. Depreciation and obsolescence. As obsolescence involves loss of asset value, it is often considered to be a part of depreciation, which is then defined as "loss of value due to effluxion of time," but as the loss of value is due to quite another reason than wear and tear and the circumstances are so very different, it is considered advisable to keep the two concepts quite separate.

19. Depreciation and obsolescence charges. The costs of asset depreciation and obsolescence are clearly chargeable to all production that makes use of such assets. Methods of making such charges fall into two groups:

(*a*) Methods based on the passing of *time*.
(*b*) Methods based on *production*.

Obsolescence charges should naturally be made on the basis of time, since an unused asset can be rendered just as obsolete as a well-used asset if a new development should emerge. However, as we have said, the life an asset will possess before becoming obsolete is rarely known, and such charges can, therefore, only involve inspired guesses.

On the other hand, depreciation charges can often be based on production, since wear and tear usually depends more on use than time.

NOTE: The traditional use of time as a basis for depreciation depended partially on the assumption that asset use would be constant (a rather doubtful assumption today, in view of modern machine diversification) and partially on the desire to incorporate some sort of charge for possible obsolescence.

It should be appreciated that charges are not made for *both* depreciation and obsolescence. The selection depends upon whether the asset will be obsolete before it is worn out, or vice versa. If this cannot be gauged, then the asset should be written down each year by an amount that reduces the asset value to one the management regard as realistic. This may result in fluctuating charges, but these are preferable to unnecessarily fast, or slow, asset write-downs.

20. Life of an asset. When discussing depreciation, reference is often made to the "life" of an asset. This life is often assumed to be its potential physical life. This is not always true; assets may well be used by the enterprise for a period less than their normal physical life (*e.g.* when bought for use on a particular contract only). To avoid error, therefore, the life of an asset should be regarded as *the length of time such an asset will be used.* It may be measured in years, production hours or units of production.

21. Revision of asset life. As time passes the original estimate of asset life may well be seen to be erroneous. In such a case the asset life should be revised and depreciation amounts adjusted accordingly. Although this may well cause some alteration of previously accepted figures, it is better to admit an error and minimise its effects than to ignore the error and allow some future period to carry large and inappropriate losses or gains.

NOTE. When revision is carried out:

(*i*) The problem of whether or not to charge depreciation where an asset is fully written-down disappears (since it cannot become fully written-down until its life is ended).
(*ii*) Any gains or losses due to incorrect charging in previous periods should be written off to profit and loss and *not* carried forward into future periods.

22. Asset cost. The full loss of value that must be accounted for by depreciation and obsolescence charges should be computed as follows:

$$\textit{Total loss in value} = \begin{matrix}\textit{Asset}\\ \textit{purchase}\\ \textit{price}\end{matrix} + \begin{matrix}\textit{Purchase and}\\ \textit{installation}\\ \textit{charges}\end{matrix} - \left(\begin{matrix}\textit{Scrap}\\ \textit{value}\end{matrix} - \begin{matrix}\textit{Dismantling}\\ \textit{and removal}\\ \textit{charges}\end{matrix}\right)$$

This over-all charge is normally simply referred to as "asset cost." A simple worked example is given in illustration.

EXAMPLE

Data:

Purchase price	£10,300
Freight and purchase costs	£80
Installation costs	£320
Scrap value	£800
Disposal costs	£100

Method:

Asset cost is, therefore:

$$£10{,}300 + £80 + £320 - £(800 - 100) = £10{,}000$$

23. Replacement value. Should depreciation rates for any given period be based on the original purchase cost of assets or upon current replacement prices? The answer to this question hinges upon whether the object of depreciation is to recover the cost of a capital outlay over the life of the asset, or to make an assessment of the true economic worth of the service given by the asset. In financial accounting one may well be primarily concerned with recovering the original cost, and therefore this figure will be used for calculating depreciation, but since the basic object of costing is to provide economic assessments, to adopt original cost in the depreciation calculations may well lead to serious error. However, study of the application of replacement costs is usually considered a management accounting topic, and so will not be further considered in this book.

24. Depreciation methods. The two most popular methods of charging depreciation are:

(*a*) *Straight line*, in which *equal amounts* of depreciation are charged each period throughout the life of the asset.

(*b*) *Reducing balance*, in which an *equal percentage* is applied each period to the written-down value of the asset at the beginning of the period to obtain the depreciation amount.

The straight-line method is usually preferred in cost accounting; since all periods benefit equally from the existence of the asset, it is felt that all should share the depreciation charge equally. If, however, one wishes to select a method that results in written-down values more closely equating to market values, then the reducing-balance method is usually chosen.

25. Straight-line depreciation. The formula for the straight-line depreciation charge is:

$$\frac{\textit{Asset cost}}{\textit{Life}}$$

Thus, if the asset cost is £10,000 and the asset life 10 years, the depreciation is:

$$\frac{10{,}000}{10} = \text{£}1000 \text{ per year}$$

26. Reducing-balance depreciation. The formula for the reducing-balance depreciation charge is:

$$\begin{matrix}\textit{Written-down value at} \\ \textit{beginning of period}\end{matrix} \times \textit{Fixed percentage}$$

This fixed percentage is the percentage which must be written off the written-down value each year so that ultimately the original total installed asset cost (A) is reduced to its net residual value (R) (*i.e.* scrap value less disposal costs) by the end of its life (n = life in years). This percentage can be found from the formula:

$$\textit{Percentage} = \left(1 - \sqrt[n]{\frac{R}{A}}\right) \times 100$$

EXAMPLE

Data: If A = £10,700, R = £700 and n = 10 years, then the fixed percentage is:

$$\left(1 - \sqrt[10]{\frac{700}{10{,}700}}\right) \times 100 \simeq 24\%$$

Method: Accordingly the depreciation charge for the first, say, three years is as follows:

	£
Original total installed asset cost	10,700
1st year's depreciation = 24% × £10,700	2,568
Reduced balance	8,132
2nd year's depreciation = 24% × £8,132	1,952
Reduced balance	6,180
3rd year's depreciation = 24% × £6,180	1,483
Reduced balance	4,697

In normal practice, rather than calculate the fixed percentage every time, an arbitrary percentage, determined by custom, is used.

27. Other depreciation methods. The other depreciation methods in use are listed with their formulae below.

Method	*Formula: Depreciation for period*
Production unit:	$\frac{\text{Asset cost}}{\text{Life (units of production)}} \times$ Units produced during period
Production hour:	$\frac{\text{Asset cost}}{\text{Life (production hours)}} \times$ Production hours for period
Repair reserve:	$\frac{\text{Asset cost + Estimated total maintenance costs during life}}{\text{Life}}$
Annuity:*	$\frac{\text{Asset cost + Total of all yearly interest charges to be charged on written-down value}}{\text{Life}}$
Sinking fund: *†	$\frac{\text{Asset cost − Total interest to be received from investment}}{\text{Life}}$
Endowment policy:†	Annual premium required to provide endowment at end of asset life equal to asset cost
Revaluation:	Difference between the value of the asset at the beginning of the year and its revalued value at the end of the year
Sum of the digits:	Asset cost $\times \frac{x}{y}$

In the last method, $\frac{x}{y}$ is computed as follows:

Let n = life of asset in years.
Then x is n for the 1st year,
$n - 1$ for the 2nd year,
$n - 2$ for the 3rd year, etc.
And y is the sum of the progression $1 + 2 + 3$, etc., up to n.

* These methods require the selection of an interest rate.

† These methods require the depreciation amount to be actually withdrawn in cash, which must then be used for buying an investment or paying a premium according to the method involved.

EXAMPLE: If life of asset is 5 years, then $y = 1 + 2 + 3 + 4 + 5 = 15$

$$\therefore \frac{x}{y} \text{ for the: 1st year} = \frac{5}{15}$$

$$\text{2nd year} = \frac{4}{15}$$

$$\text{3rd year} = \frac{3}{15}$$

$$\text{4th year} = \frac{2}{15}$$

$$\text{5th year} = \frac{1}{15}$$

28. Depreciation and maintenance. Clearly the loss in value due to wear and tear will depend very much on the extent to which the asset is maintained. Some assets, if well maintained, may last indefinitely and so carry virtually no depreciation charge, only an obsolescence charge. When setting depreciation charges in practice, therefore, this factor of maintenance should be considered and allowed for (as in the repair reserve method).

NOTE: The argument that the reducing-balance method over the years automatically gives reducing depreciation charges that just balance the increasing maintenance charges does not usually hold water in practice.

29. Plant register. It is important that all plant and equipment is recorded and any figures relating to such assets (*e.g.* purchase price; depreciation) shown in detail. Such a record is called a *plant register*, and usually consists of a sheet or card for each item of plant recording (where appropriate):

(*a*) *Single data*:

(*i*) Description of plant.
(*ii*) Supplier.
(*iii*) Date of purchase.
(*iv*) Purchase price.
(*v*) Installation costs.
(*vi*) Estimated life.
(*vii*) Estimated residual value.
(*viii*) Depreciation rate.

(*ix*) Plant identification number.
(*x*) Location.
(*xi*) Ancillary equipment (cross-referenced if such equipment is separately recorded in the plant register).
(*xii*) Technical and other important data.

(*b*) *Multiple data*: For each period:

(*i*) Depreciation.
(*ii*) Written-down value.
(*iii*) Maintenance costs.
(*iv*) Improvements and additions.
(*v*) Hours run.

Clearly the plant register totals should agree with the figures in the Plant and Equipment Accounts of the Ledger.

PROGRESS TEST 8

Principles

1. What are overheads? (**1**)
2. Why must one be careful when classifying direct costs and overheads? (**2–4**)
3. From what sources can the following charges be ascertained:

(*a*) Fuel,
(*b*) Power and light,
(*c*) Indirect wages and materials,
(*d*) Depreciation? (**7**)

4. What is the usual dual classification of overheads? (**8**)
5. How should overtime be charged in the costs? (**10**)
6. What are notional charges and why are they made? (**13**)
7. State whether selling and distribution costs are overheads or direct costs. (**15**)
8. Distinguish between depreciation and obsolescence. (**16–18**)
9. Should charges for depreciation and obsolescence be made on a basis of time or production? (**19**)
10. When considering depreciation charges, what is meant by:

(*a*) Asset life, (**20**)
(*b*) Asset cost? (**22**)

11. Give the advantages of periodically revising asset lives. (**21**)
12. Distinguish between the straight-line and the reducing-balance methods of depreciation. (**23**)
13. What are the different methods of depreciation? (**23, 27**)
14. What is a plant register and what details should be shown in such a register? (**29**)

Practice

15. How would you deal with the following costs in your cost accounts:

(*a*) wages paid to a departmental shop-steward engaged on union activities;
(*b*) experimental costs aimed at improving the surface quality of a product;
(*c*) wages paid to machine operators for idle time due to an area power cut;
(*d*) depreciation on a machine bought specifically and exclusively for a special contract?

PART THREE

COST ASCERTAINMENT

CHAPTER IX

ALLOCATION, APPORTIONMENT AND ABSORPTION OF OVERHEADS

INTRODUCTION

Overheads, by definition, cannot be charged direct to cost units, but must be shared equitably between them. Needless to say, cost accountants often have different opinions on what is equitable. Such differences of opinion are permissible, providing they are based on an intelligent understanding of the circumstances. Students must not, however, regard their right to disagree as a licence to hold views that are essentially rooted in ignorance.

For the purpose of exposition only the procedure for production overheads will be demonstrated. Non-production overheads will be briefly discussed later (*see* **23–25**), but, as was mentioned in Chapter VIII (**15**), strictly speaking, such overheads should have just as extensive a procedure as production overheads.

1. Allotment. *Allotment* is the charging of costs to cost units or cost centres. In this chapter we are concerned with allotting overheads.

2. Summary of overhead allotment procedure. The over-all overhead allotment procedure involves the following steps:

(*a*) Collection of overheads (*see* VIII, **6, 7**).

(*b*) Overhead analysis, to cost centres (*see* **3 – 12**):

- (*i*) Allocation of overheads to cost centres.
- (*ii*) Apportionment of overheads to cost centres.
- (*iii*) Allocation and apportionment of service cost centres' costs to production cost centres.

(*c*) Overhead absorption, into cost units (*see* **13 – 18**):

- (*i*) Computation of overhead absorption rates.
- (*ii*) Application of overhead absorption rates to cost units.

OVERHEAD ANALYSIS

3. Definition. An *overhead analysis* is an analysis that charges overheads to cost centres. It is essentially an analysis sheet listing the overheads vertically and the cost centres horizontally.

A complete worked example of an overhead analysis is shown in Fig. 8. Here the overheads are seen listed on the left-hand side together with the total amounts. These amounts are, of course, extracted from the cost records. In this example three service cost centres (Stores, Maintenance, and Production control and inspection) and two production cost centres (departments X and Y) have been assumed for the purpose of illustration.

When compiling an overhead analysis there are two ways of charging overheads to cost centres, *allocation* and *apportionment*. These two terms must be carefully distinguished (though students should be warned that some examiners do not make this distinction when setting papers).

4. Allocation. *Allocation* is charging to a cost centre those overheads that result *solely* from the existence of that cost centre. (Note the similarity to direct cost definition, *i.e.* if the overhead is a direct cost to the cost centre it is allocated).

Overheads should always be allocated if possible. However, allocation can be made only if the exact amount incurred is definitely known. This point should be clearly understood. An overhead cannot be allocated unless it meets both of the following conditions:

(*a*) *The cost centre must have caused the overhead to be incurred.* If an overhead would have been incurred anyway it cannot be allocated. Thus rent cannot normally be allocated, since rent is payable for the factory as a whole, and the existence or otherwise of an individual cost centre does not affect the amount.

(*b*) *The exact amount must be known.* If, as in the case of power for example, we know that a cost centre causes part of the total overhead cost, we cannot allocate that overhead unless we know exactly how much was incurred by the individual cost centre (*e.g.* by metering, which clearly is usually quite impractical).

In Fig. 8 only indirect materials and labour have been allocated (from the materials and wage analyses respectively). If, however, a plant register is kept along the lines indicated in VIII, **29**, then depreciation and possibly also machine insurance can be allocated.

5. Apportionment. *Apportionment* is charging to a cost centre a fair *share* of an overhead.

If an overhead cannot be allocated to cost centres it must be apportioned. This involves finding some basis, called the *basis of apportionment*, that will enable the overhead to be equitably shared between cost centres.

6. Bases of apportionment. The following are the most usual bases of apportionment and the overheads using them:

Basis	*Overheads apportioned on this basis*
Area	Rent, rates, heat and light, building depreciation
Number of employees	Personnel office, welfare, administration, canteen, supervision, time and wages offices, safety
Book value	Depreciation, insurance
Weight of materials	Materials handling, store-keeping
Space (volume)	Heating, building depreciation
Number of radiators	Heating
Direct (to cost centres) maintenance costs	Indirect maintenance costs
Technical estimate	Power, steam consumption

NOTE: A *technical estimate* is an estimate of usage made by a technically qualified person.

7. Choice of basis. Students will notice that some overheads in the above list can be apportioned on more than one basis. The choice of an appropriate basis is really a matter of judgment; it is necessary to ask oneself what factor is most closely related to a change in the overhead level. For example, "number of employees" is a good basis for apportioning time and wages office overheads, since the more employees there are in a cost centre, the more it will cost in clerical salaries and stationery to arrange their wage payments.

The choice of basis, therefore, is left to the judgment of the individual. He is not compelled, of course, to select one of the more conventional bases. If an unusual basis is more suitable it should be chosen and, indeed, the bases that can be devised are limited only by human ingenuity.

Overheads	Total	Apportionment			Stores		Maintenance		Production Control and Inspection		Production Dept. X		Production Dept. Y	
	£	Basis	Units	Rate Per Unit	Units	£	Units	£	Units	£	Units	£	Units	£
Rent	800	Area	80	£10	3	30	4	40	1	10	30	300	42	420
Indirect materials	174	*Allocation*				*11*		*25*		*44*		*31*		*63*
Indirect labour	5463	*Allocation*				*287*		*671*		*1660*		*1040*		*1805*
Factory admin. o'h'ds.	2184	No. Employees	546	£4	4	16	12	48	30	120	200	800	300	1200
Machine depreciation	440	Value £000's	40	£11	—	—	8	88	—	—	20	220	12	132
Power	550	kwh 000's	550	£1	—	—	20	20	—	—	320	320	210	210
Heat and light	80	Area	80	£1	3	3	4	4	1	1	30	30	42	42
Machine insurance	40	Value £000's	40	£1	—	—	8	8	—	—	20	20	12	12
Extraction (fumes) plant	120	No. of extraction points	40	£3	1	3	2	6	—	—	14	42	23	69
Total	9851					350		910		1835		2803		3953
Service Depts.														
Stores		No. of material requisitions	1750	£0·20		−350	175	35	—	—	1000	200	575	115
						Nil		945		1835		3003		4068
Maintenance		*Allocation*						*−630*		*10*		*190*		*430*
		Allocated wages	£630	£0·50 per £				−315	10	5	190	95	430	215
								Nil		1850		3288		4713
Production control and inspection		No. of employees	500	£3·70						−1850	200	740	300	1110
Total										*Nil*		£4028		£5823

FIG. 8.—*Overhead analysis*

The italicised figures are allocations, as opposed to apportionments. Total of X and Y = £4028 + £5823 = £9851, *i.e.* the grand total of all overheads. This cross-check proves the arithmetical accuracy of the analysis.

8. Illustrative example. Apportionments clearly depend on factory statistics, and in order that the student may be able to work through the overhead analysis given in Fig. 8 thoroughly, the statistics on which that analysis is based are given below.

FACTORY STATISTICS

	Total	*Stores*	*Maintenance*	*Prodn. control & insp.*	*Prodn. X*	*Prodn. Y*
Area ft^2 (000's)	80	3	4	1	30	42
Indirect material issues	£174	£11	£25	£44	£31	£63
Indirect labour bookings	£5463	£287	£671	£1660	£1040	£1805
Employees	546	4	12	30	200	300
Machine values	£40,000	—	£8000	—	£20,000	£12,000
Estimated kwh (000's)	550	—	20	—	320	210
Fume extraction points	40	1	2	—	14	23
Material requisitions issued	1750	—	175	—	1000	575
Maintenance labour bookings	£630	—	—	£10	£190	£430

9. Service cost centre costs. Once the overheads have been analysed to cost centres and totalled, the next step is to charge service cost centre costs to production cost centres. This is necessary since our ultimate object is to charge overheads to cost units, and as no cost units pass through service departments the costs of such departments must be charged to those cost centres where there are cost units, *i.e.* the production cost centres.

The method of analysing service cost centre costs is similar to that of the main analysis; where possible costs are allocated (*e.g.* wages of maintenance workers actually engaged in production cost centres), otherwise they are apportioned on some basis that reflects the work done by the service department for each of the production cost centres.

10. Service department charges illustrated. In Fig. 8 the first service department that must be charged out is Stores. A typical basis of apportionment for Stores, materials requisitions, has been selected and the £350 Stores cost charged in proportion to the number of requisitions used by each of the other cost centres.

In the case of Maintenance, £630 can be immediately allocated from the maintenance labour bookings. The balance of £315 must be apportioned on some basis that reflects the work done by Maintenance for other centres. Clearly, the maintenance labour bookings provide an excellent measure of work done by this centre, and the £315 is charged in proportion to the wages previously allocated. Since this allocation totalled £630, it can be seen that for every £1 maintenance wages allocated there must be £0·50 charged for apportionment of the remaining maintenance costs.

Finally, Production control and inspection overheads must be apportioned. A reasonable measure of the work done by this centre is the number of employees whose work is controlled and inspected. Since this centre only does work for the two production centres, the total overhead of £1850 must be shared on the basis of the total of 500 employees engaged in the two production centres. This gives a charge of £3·70 per employee (£1850 divided by 500).

11. Services working for other service departments. If a service department carries out work for a second service department, then clearly part of the former's costs are allotted to the latter department. Care should be taken, therefore, not to analyse the second department's costs until it has first been allotted its charges from all the other departments whose services it called upon (*e.g.* in Fig. 8 the Maintenance department is allotted its £35 share of stores costs before its own charges are analysed).

12. Reciprocal services. A problem arises when two or more service departments do work for each other. Thus if the departments are A and B, then until B's charge to A is known, A cannot allot any cost to B. But similarly until A's charge to B is known, B cannot allot that initial cost to A.

There are three methods of breaking this vicious circle which are explained below. Worked examples are given using the same basic data in illustration of each method.

(*a*) *Continuous allotment.* In this method the costs of the first service department are allotted in the normal way. This "closes off" the first department. However, subsequent allotment of the costs of other service departments results in new charges to the first department and so "re-opens" it. The total of these new charges is then allotted back to the other service departments in the same manner as the original costs. This in turn "re-opens" the other service departments. This process is continued until the amounts involved become insignificant.

NOTE: By deferring allotments to production cost centres until after the over-all cost for each service department has been found, some saving of time can be made. This has been done in the example below.

EXAMPLE

Data:

The overhead analysis prior to allotment of service cost centre costs shows the following overhead charges:

Service department A	£3200
,, ,, B	£4100
Production department 1	£8000
,, ,, 2	£6000

These overheads are to be apportioned as follows:

	To A	*To B*	*To Production 1*	*To Production 2*
Dept. A's costs	—	10%	50%	40%
,, B's ,,	50%	—	10%	40%

Method:

First compute the total overhead charge to each service department after service department allotments, and then go back and prepare a formal allotment allotting these totals.

Step	Dept. A	Dept. B	Dept. 1	Dept. 2
	£	£	£	£
Original allotments	3,200	4,100	Ignore initially	
Allot A (10% to B)	−3,200	320		
Allot B (50% to A)	2,210	−4,420		
Allot A	−2,210	221		
Allot B	110	−221		
Allot A	−110	11		
Allot B	6	−11		
Allot A	−6	1		
Allot B	0	−1		
∴ Gross cost centre overheads (add all allotments)	5,526	4,653		
Formal allotment:				
Original allotments	3,200	4,100	8,000	6,000
Allot A total	−5,526	553	2,763	2,210
Allot B total	2,326	−4,653	465	1,862
Total	*Nil*	*Nil*	£11,228	£10,072

(*All amounts rounded to the nearest* £)

(*b*) *Algebraic method.* Here the *total* service costs of each department are expressed as algebraic equations. The unknowns can then be found by either solving the simultaneous equations or by substitution, whichever is preferred.

EXAMPLE

Data: As in (*a*) continuous allotment.

Method:

Let a = *total* overhead charge to Dept. A after allotment from B.

Let b = *total* overhead charge to Dept. B after allotment from A.

so $a = 3200 + 0{\cdot}5\,b$

$$\therefore a - 0{\cdot}5\,b = 3200 \quad (1)$$

and $b = 4100 + 0{\cdot}1a$

$$\therefore b - 0{\cdot}1\,a = 4100 \quad (2)$$

$$\begin{aligned} \text{Solving: (1)} \times 2: &\quad 2{\cdot}0a - b = 6400 \\ \text{(2)} \times 1: &\quad -0{\cdot}1a + b = 4100 \\ \text{Add:} &\quad 1{\cdot}9a = 10{,}500 \\ &\quad \therefore a = £5526 \text{ (to nearest £)} \end{aligned}$$

Substituting in (2): $b - 0{\cdot}1 \times 5526 = 4100$

$$\therefore b = 4100 + 553 = £4653 \text{ (to nearest £)}$$

(Alternatively, using substitution, $a = 3200 + 0{\cdot}5b = 3200 + 0{\cdot}5\,(4100 + 0{\cdot}1a)$, and solve for a.)

Knowing these amounts, the formal allotment can be made as in the previous method, (*a*) continuous allotment.

(*c*) *Specified order of closing.* The order of closing departments is carefully determined so that the services that do the most work for other service departments are closed first. The departments are then closed off in this order in the normal manner, and return charges from other service departments *are not made.* Although this method gives a theoretically inaccurate result, it has the advantage of ease. Moreover, the word "accuracy" has little meaning within the context of apportionment so objections under this head tend to be pedantic (*see* **26**).

EXAMPLE

Data: As in (*a*) continuous allotment.

Method:

B, allotting 50% of its cost to A affects A more than A, allotting only 10% of its costs to B, affects B. Therefore, B is closed off first, and A's allotment to B omitted.

Step	*Dept. A*	*Dept. B*	*Dept. 1*	*Dept. 2*
Original allotment	3200	4100	8000	6000
Allot B	2050	−4100	410	1640
Allot A	−5250	—	2917*	2333*
Total	*Nil*	*Nil*	£11,327†	£9973†

* Since the 10% allotment to B is omitted, Depts. 1 and 2 must share all A's costs in the ratio of 50:40.

† Note that the relative error in this instance is only 1%.

OVERHEAD ABSORPTION METHODS

13. Absorption. Once overheads have been analysed to production cost centres they can be charged to cost units. In essence, the procedure is to take each centre and *share its overheads among all the cost units passing through that centre.* This procedure is clearly akin to apportionment, only in this case cost units are charged and not cost centres. The technical term for this is *absorption*, and can be defined as the charging of overheads to cost units.

14. Absorption steps. Two steps are taken in the absorption of overheads:

(*a*) *Computation of overhead absorption rate.*
(*b*) *Application of rate to cost units.*

15. Computation of overhead absorption rate. To compute the overhead rate some basis of absorption is first selected in a similar manner to the selection of an apportionment base (5, 6). The overhead rate is then found by means of the following formula:

$$\textit{Overhead absorption rate} = \frac{\textit{Total cost centre overheads}}{\textit{Total units of base used}}$$

Since there are a number of different bases that can be selected for absorption, in practice one comes across a number of different kinds of rates. The six most common rates have been listed below, together with their individual formulae and an illustrative example of the computation of the rates for a typical cost centre, 101.

Overhead rate		*Cost centre 101*	
Title	*Formula*	*Statistics*	*Rate*
Units of output	$\frac{\text{TCCO}}{\text{Units of output}}$	500 units	$\frac{£1000}{500} = £2$ per unit
Direct labour hr	$\frac{\text{TCCO}}{\text{Total direct labour hours worked o.a.p.}}$	2000 direct labour hrs	$\frac{£1000}{2000} =$ £0·50 per hr
Machine hr	$\frac{\text{TCCO}}{\text{Total machine hours engaged o.a.p.}}$	1600 machine hrs	$\frac{£1000}{1600} =$ £0·625 per hr
Wages percentage	$\frac{\text{TCCO}}{\text{Total direct wages paid o.a.p.}}$	£1000 direct wages	$\frac{£1000}{£1000} = 100\%$
Materials cost percentage	$\frac{\text{TCCO}}{\text{Total direct material used o.a.p.}}$	£3000 direct materials	$\frac{£1000}{£3000} = 33\frac{1}{3}\%$
Prime cost percentage	$\frac{\text{TCCO}}{\text{Total prime cost incurred o.a.p.}}$	£4000 prime cost	$\frac{£1000}{£4000} = 25\%$

TCCO = Total cost centre overheads. (TCCO charged to cost centre 101 in overhead analysis = £1000.)
o.a.p. = on all production, *i.e.* cost centre 101 production.

It is important to appreciate that only *one* rate will be computed for any single group of overheads. The table above shows the rates from which a selection can be made; it is not meant to suggest that all the rates given are to be computed simultaneously.

16. Applications of rate to cost units. Overheads are charged to individual cost units by simply multiplying the overhead rate by the units of the base that apply to each cost unit, *i.e.* the formula is:

Cost unit overheads = *Overhead rate* × *Units of base in cost unit*

The following example illustrates the application of the different overhead rates (computed in **15**) to a cost unit, Job X.

EXAMPLE

			£
Data:	Direct labour hours (which included 3 hrs' work on a machine)	4 hrs at £0·65 hr	2·60
		1 hr at £0·40 hr	0·40
		5 hrs	3·00
	Direct materials		12·00
		Prime cost	£15·00

Method:

OVERHEAD RATE		JOB X	
Title	*Rate*	*Units of base*	*Overhead charged*
			£
Units of output	£2 per unit	1 unit*	2·00
Direct labour hour	£0·50 per hr	5 hours	2·50
Machine hour	£0·625 per hr	3 hours	1·87½
Wages percentage	100%	£3·00 wages	3·00
Materials cost percentage	33⅓%	£12·00 materials	4·00
Prime cost percentage	25%	£15·00 prime cost	3·75

* In the case of this particular rate it must be assumed that all the cost units are identical units.

17. Choice of overhead rate. As with apportionment, absorption hinges on finding an appropriate basis for sharing the overheads. In the case of most overheads, *time* is the factor associated with cost units that is most closely related to a change in overhead level. It is logical, therefore, to charge those products that utilise factory facilities for the longest time with the largest share of the overheads, and so overheads are best absorbed on a time basis, *i.e.* using a direct labour hour, machine hour or wages percentage rate.

NOTE: It is sometimes said that what a factory really sells is its *time*, *i.e.* one buys essentially the time during which a factory is using its facilities to convert the raw materials to the finished product. (The cost of the raw materials is really only passed on from the supplier to the customer; it is quite possible for the customer to buy the raw materials himself and hand them to the manufacturer for processing.)

The following points should be noted in connection with the six methods of absorption:

(*a*) *Units of output*. This is the best of the rates, but unfortunately can be used only when all the cost units passing through the cost centre are *identical*.

(*b*) *Direct labour hour*. This is a good all-round rate. Students should use this rate in their answers unless there is a good reason for selecting a different one.

(*c*) *Machine hour*. When production is carried out on machines this rate is appropriate. Beware, however, of using this rate simply because most of the production is put on machines; using a machine hour rate in such circumstances would mean that any *non-machine* production would be charged no overheads at all. (For machine hour rates computed for *individual* machines, *see* **21**.)

(*d*) *Wages percentage rate*. This rate will give identical results to the direct labour hour rate if there is only one rate of pay in the cost centre. If otherwise, then overheads charged to cost units worked on by highly paid employees will exceed those charged to units involving lower-rated employees when times are the same. This is not strictly logical (since the overheads incurred per hour are the same whether the employee is highly-paid or otherwise), but as this method is clerically simpler than the direct labour hour method (for which direct labour hours must be separately recorded and added on job cards), it is a good practical rate.

(*e*) *Materials cost percentage rate*. Overheads are in no way related to the cost of material used. A large, expensive piece of material could be on the factory floor for only a few minutes, utilising virtually nothing of the factory facilities, and yet it would be given an overhead charge proportional to its material cost. This is clearly unsatisfactory, and students should almost always avoid its use.

(*f*) *Prime cost percentage rate*. Again overheads are not

often related to prime cost, and so usually this rate is quite unsuitable. One notable exception to this, however, arises with certain kinds of contract work when the rate is acceptable (*see* X, **5**(*d*)).

18. Combined rates. If a variety of activities are carried on in a single cost centre it may warrant the use of a combination of rates. For example, if both machine work and bench work are undertaken a machine hour rate could be used to absorb all machine costs and a direct labour rate to absorb other cost centre costs.

OVERHEAD ABSORPTION: GENERAL CONSIDERATIONS

19. Predetermined overhead rates.

(*a*) *Need for predetermined overhead rates.* So far we have used *actual* overheads when computing rates. In practice this can have two grave disadvantages:

(*i*) If jobbing work is done, use of actual overheads will result in delay, since the collection, analysis and absorption of actual overheads can be finalised only at the end of the costing period.

(*ii*) If work is seasonal, use of actual overheads results in fluctuating unit costs. Many costs are incurred regardless of the level of production (*e.g.* rent, salaries), and so when production is slack sharing these overheads between the few cost units produced results in a high cost per unit. Since any seasonal business expects the busy period to "carry" the slack, to charge slack-period production with the entire period fixed overheads gives no useful information.

In order to avoid these disadvantages, overhead rates are almost invariably calculated on a basis of future overheads (and, of course, future production). Such rates are called *predetermined overhead rates.*

(*b*) *Calculation of predetermined overhead rates.* These rates are calculated by the following formula:

$$\textit{Predetermined overhead rate} = \frac{\textit{Budgeted overheads for the next year}}{\textit{Budgeted units of base for the next year}}$$

(*c*) *Under- and over-absorption of overheads.* It is most unlikely that the actual overheads and units of base will exactly equal the budgeted amounts. Consequently, using predetermined overhead rates will result in actual production being charged somewhat more or less than the actual overheads incurred. The difference between the overheads charged and the overheads incurred is called *the under- (or over-) absorption of overheads.*

For example, assume:

Budgeted overheads	£15,000
Actual overheads	£15,160
Budgeted direct labour hours	10,000
Actual direct labour hours	9,820

$$\text{Predetermined overhead rate} = \frac{\pounds 15{,}000}{10{,}000} = \pounds 1{\cdot}50 \text{ per hour}$$

Therefore, since 9820 hours were worked, a total of £1·50 × 9820 = £14,730 would be charged to production. However, actual overheads were £15,160.

∴ *Under-absorption of overheads* = £15,160 − £14,730 = £430

In other words, £430 of the overheads incurred were not charged to production.

(*d*) *Disposal of under- and over-absorbed overheads.* Monthly under- or over-absorption can be disposed of in one of two ways:

(*i*) If seasonal, transfer to a Suspense Account. Over the year under- and over-absorptions should virtually cancel out. At the year end any balance should be transferred to the annual Profit and Loss Account.

(*ii*) If not seasonal, transfer at once to monthly Profit and Loss Account.

In *no* circumstances should any under- (or over-) absorption be included in the overheads of following periods (a basic costing principle, *see* I, **10**(*e*)).

NOTE: Sometimes "u/o" is used as an abbreviation for "under or over."

20. Budgeting the production level. In Chapter I (**10**(*d*)) it was explained that costing aimed at ascertaining *normal* production costs. For this reason the normal level of production should be budgeted when computing predetermined overhead rates unless there are very good reasons for doing otherwise.

21. Machine hour rates for individual machines. Since different machines usually differ considerably in their cost of operation, then if the machines in a cost centre are of various kinds a single machine hour rate for them all is often unsuitable. Rates, therefore, must be computed for individual machines (or sometimes small groups of machines). The formula for a machine hour rate remains unchanged by this (*i.e.* budgeted machine costs divided by budgeted machine hours), but as it is a favourite examination topic, we will look at the computation in more detail.

(*a*) First it should be appreciated that in order to compute a full machine hour rate we must treat the machine as a complete cost centre.

(*b*) Being a cost centre, the machine will automatically receive via the overhead analysis a share of the apportioned overheads: rates, heat and light, supervision, etc.

(*c*) Depreciation and maintenance can, of course, be *allocated* to the machine.

(*d*) The cost of any reserve (stand-by) equipment, such as spare motors or even a complete spare machine, should be included in the costs charged to the machine.

(*e*) Costs will be of two kinds:

(*i*) Fixed, *e.g.* depreciation, reserve equipment and apportioned overheads.

(*ii*) Variable, varying with running time, *e.g.* power and oils.

(*f*) The hours of actual production should be budgeted. *Only those hours when cost units are being produced* should be taken, since overheads can be absorbed into cost units only when the units are being worked upon. Any time spent in cleaning or warming up should not be included in the hours of production.

NOTE: Normal production hours do *not* have to relate to normal factory hours. Often machines are bought to be used for only a part of the normal working day. Their budgeted normal hours of production, therefore, relate only to that fraction of the day they are normally expected to produce. Idle facilities costs (*i.e.* the unabsorbed overhead arising from the machine being idle) arise only if the actual hours of production drop below this.

(*g*) The actual computation is best done as follows:

(*i*) The fixed costs should be budgeted for the full period.
(*ii*) Variable costs relating to *non-production* time (*e.g.* labour and power costs during warming-up, setting-up or cleaning) for the period should be added.
(*iii*) The total should be divided by the hours of production.
(*iv*) The normal variable cost per hour (*e.g.* power) should now be added to give the total machine hour rate.

(*h*) The labour cost per hour during hours of production may be included in, or omitted from, the rate as desired.

NOTE: If to be included, it may be easier to find the total wages paid to machine operators during the period and treat this as a fixed cost.

The calculation of a machine hour rate is illustrated in the following example.

EXAMPLE

Data:

Total machine cost to be depreciated (computed as in VIII, 22): £2300
Life: 10 years; straight line depreciation
Department overheads (p.a.): Rent £500
Heat and light £200
Supervision £1300
Areas: Department 7000 square feet
Machine 250 square feet
Number of machines in department: 26
Annual cost of reserve equipment for the machine: £15
Machine running time: 2000 hrs per annum
= 1800 hrs on production
200 hrs setting and adjusting
Power cost: £0·05 per hr running time
Labour: (*a*) when setting and adjusting, full-time attention
(*b*) when machine is producing, one man can look after three machines
Labour rate: £0·60 per hr

Method:

Yearly costs:

		£
Apportionment of rent and heating and lighting (on area)	$\frac{500 + 200}{7000} \times 250$	= 25
Apportionment of supervision (on machine numbers)	$\frac{1300}{26}$	= 50
Depreciation	(10% of £2300)	= 230
Reserve equipment		= 15
Power cost during setting and adjustment	200 × £0·05	= 10
Labour cost during setting and adjustment	200 × £0·60	= 120
Total		£450

Hourly costs:

		£
Yearly costs per hr	$\frac{£450}{1800}$	0·25
Power		0·05
Labour	$\frac{1}{3}$ × £0·60	0·20
Total machine hour rate (including labour)		£0·50

In this case, where the machine hour rate *includes* labour, the wages paid to such employees will not be analysed on the wage analysis to cost units, but to *machines*, to enable under- or over-recovery of machine costs to be computed.

22. Blanket overhead rate. A *blanket overhead rate* is a single overhead rate computed for the entire factory, *i.e.* total factory overheads divided by total units of base throughout factory.

Blanket overhead rates should never be used (other than in output costing, *see* XII, **1**), since cost units passing through centres with high overhead costs (*e.g.* machine shops) will be undercosted and those passing through low overhead centres (*e.g.* an assembly department) will be overcosted.

ABSORPTION OF NON-PRODUCTION OVERHEADS

23. Selling overheads. First of all it is important to appreciate that these overheads cannot be added to the factory overheads and absorbed in a single common rate, since this would result in charging cost units with selling overheads *before* these units had incurred any such costs. This is a breach of one of our fundamental costing principles (*see* I, **10**(*b*)).

Selling overheads vary by and large with the value of the item sold; the greater the value, the more one tends to spend to make a sale. Absorption, therefore, should be based on value, and it is often more convenient to use factory cost as a measure of value rather than selling price. The overhead rate can be computed as:

$$\textit{Selling overhead rate (factory cost percentage)} =$$

$$\frac{\textit{Total selling overheads}}{\textit{Total factory cost of all sales}} \times 100$$

By applying this percentage to the factory cost of individual cost units, the selling overheads applicable to each unit are found.

24. Distribution overheads. A distribution department is very similar to a production department from the point of view of costs. Thus there are direct materials (packing cases, wood-wool), direct labour (packers, van drivers), direct expenses (freight), departmental overheads (supervision, heat and light) and "machines" (vans, lorries, packing machines). It follows therefore that it should be treated in a similar way to a production department, with materials requisitions, time sheets and overheads absorbed by means of overhead absorption rates. The overhead rates for vans and lorries will be based on miles, tons, or hours, or a combination of these (*see* XII, **4**).

25. Administration overheads. These overheads are so divorced from both production and selling that any basis of absorption must necessarily be somewhat artificial. The following procedure, however, is suggested:

(*a*) *Before* making any overhead allotments of any kind examine each administration overhead in turn and, simply by the use of common sense, apportion it between production and selling.

(*b*) Incorporate these apportioned charges into the production and selling overheads respectively, and then compute absorption rates as usual.

NOTE: Factory administration overheads are best apportioned to cost centres on the basis of the number of employees.

26. Objections to overhead absorption. Students should be warned that nowadays many cost accountants regard overhead absorption as a discredited technique. Their objections are based on the fact that many overheads, such as rent and audit fees, are completely independent of whether an individual cost unit is made or not, and often even of the product line manufactured. The sharing out of such overheads among cost units does not therefore provide any useful information to management. Moreover, since such apportionments are very often arbitrary, different cost accountants often arrive at different cost unit costs, which indicates that such costs are hardly satisfactory bases for making intelligent management decisions.

PROGRESS TEST 9

Principles

1. Distinguish between allotment, allocation, apportionment and absorption. **(1, 4, 5, 13)**
2. What overheads would be apportioned on the basis of number of employees? **(6)**
3. Name three ways of allotting service costs to reciprocal services. **(12)**
4. What are the main absorption rates and which are the most satisfactory? **(15, 17)**
5. Why should overhead rates be pre-determined? **(19(*a*))**
6. How should one dispose of under- and over-absorbed overheads? **(19(*d*))**

Practice

7. XY Ltd. operates a factory whose annual budget shows the budgeted trading account for the year ending 30th November given overleaf:

	£	£	£	£
Selling value of goods produced				300,000
Production cost:				
Direct wages		70,000		
Direct material cost		90,000		
		——	160,000	
Indirect wages and supervision:				
Machine department X	3,800			
,, ,, Y	4,350			
Assembly department	4,125			
Packing department	2,300			
Maintenance department	2,250			
Stores	1,150			
General department	2,425			
	——	20,400		
Maintenance wages:				
Machine department X	1,000			
,, ,, Y	2,000			
Assembly department	500			
Packing department	500			
Maintenance department	500			
Stores	250			
General department	450			
	——	5,200		
Indirect materials:				
Machine department X	2,700			
,, ,, Y	3,600			
Assembly department	1,800			
Packing department	2,700			
Maintenance department	900			
Stores	675			
General department	400			
	——	12,775		
Power		6,000		
Rent and rates		8,000		
Lighting and heating		2,000		
Insurance		1,000		
Depreciation (20%)		20,000		
		——	75,375	
				235,375
			Budgeted factory profit	£64,625

The following operating information is also available:

Department	*Effective H.P.*	*Area occupied (sq ft)*	*Book value: machinery and equipment* £	*Productive capacity*		
				Direct labour		*Machine hours*
				Hours	*Cost* £	
Productive:						
Machine X	40	10,000	30,000	100,000	28,000	50,000
,, Y	40	7,500	40,000	75,000	21,000	60,000
Assembly	—	15,000	5,000	75,000	14,000	
Packing	10	7,500	5,000	50,000	7,000	
Service:						
Maintenance	10	3,000	15,000			
Stores	—	5,000	2,500			
General	—	2,000	2,500			
		50,000	100,000			

The general department consists of the factory manager, and general clerical and wages personnel.

(*a*) Prepare an overhead analysis sheet for the departments of the factory for the year ending 30th November. (Show clearly the bases of apportionment.)

(*b*) Calculate hourly cost rates of overhead absorption for each productive department. Ignore the apportionment of service department costs among service departments. (*I.C.W.A.*)

8. Department XYZ makes two products, Alpha and Beta. The departmental budgeted overheads for XYZ are £12,000, and the budgeted production is Alpha 2000 units, Beta 800 units. The estimated prime cost of Alpha and Beta was calculated thus:

	Alpha		*Beta*	
Material	24 lb of code 989 at £0·25 lb =	£6·00	15 lb of code 281 at £0·20 lb =	£3·00
Labour	5 hrs (of which 2 hrs are on a machine) at £0·40 hour =	£2·00	25 hrs (of which 10 hrs are on a machine) at £0·20 hr =	£5·00
Total		£8·00		£8·00

Calculate three different overhead recovery rates and show the overhead for 1 unit of Alpha and also 1 unit of Beta.

CHAPTER X

JOB COSTING

Job costing is the method of costing used when cost units can be separately identified and need to be costed individually. Its essential features are:

(*a*) Each job can be accurately identified.
(*b*) Direct costs are charged to individual jobs.

Many of the methods of charging costs to jobs have been explained in earlier chapters. Here we bring together and summarise these methods.

There are two main subdivisions of job-costing: *factory job costing* and *contract costing*. The difference is essentially only one of size, not of principle. Each is considered separately below.

NOTE: Job costing is a costing *method* and can therefore be combined with any of the cost techniques (*see* Fig. 1), but for the sake of illustration, it has been combined here with the total absorption cost technique.

FACTORY JOB COSTING

1. Definition. *Factory job costing* is the application of job costing to relatively small cost units. Being small, such cost units are generally worked on within the walls of a factory, but this may not always be the case, *e.g.* plumbing repairs in private households.

2. Preparation of a job cost. A job cost is prepared by bringing together all the costs involved in completing a job. The following steps are taken:

(*a*) During production:

(*i*) direct costs are charged to the job;
(*ii*) a share of the overheads of each cost centre that the job passes through is charged by means of overhead absorption rates.

(*b*) When the job is completed and put in the finished goods store it will not be valued at more than the sum of these two charges. This is the *factory*, or *works cost*.

(*c*) Later, when the job is sold and delivered:

(*i*) a share of the selling overheads is charged;
(*ii*) the cost of delivery is charged.

This now brings the cost up to the *total cost*. The difference between this and the selling price is the profit (or loss). If the selling price is fixed by adding to the cost a fixed percentage

Job 707:	*Usage*	*Price*	£	£
		£		
Direct materials: X 312	32 ft(a)	0·25 ft(b)	8·00	
P 99/8	44 lb(a)	0·62 lb(b)	27·28	35·28
Direct labour: Dept. 1	3 hr (c)	0·55 hr(d)	1·65	
	6 „(c)	0·40 „(d)	2·40	
„ 4	1½ „(c)	0·62 „(d)	0·93	
„ 6	8 „(c)	0·56 „(d)	4·48	9·46
Direct expenses: Royalty		0·50 unit(e)	0·50	
Plating charge (sub contract)	As invoice 913(f)	2·40 complete	2·40	2·90
Factory overheads: Dept. 1	9 Direct labour hr(c)	0·85 hr(g)	7·65	
„ 4	3 Machine hr(h)	1·25 „(i)	3·75	
„ 6	£4·48 Direct wages(j)	200%(k)	8·96	20·36
	Factory cost			68·00
Selling overheads: 20% factory cost			13·60	
Distribution costs (found from subsidiary job card prepared in the Distribution Dept.)			6·28	19·88
	Total Cost*			87·88
	Profit			12·12
	Selling price (taken from original sales quotation)			£100·00

* Administration overheads have already been apportioned to production, selling and distribution (*see* IX, **25**). Therefore no separate charge is shown here.

Sources of data:

(*a*) Materials requisition.
(*b*) Stores record card.
(*c*) Time sheets.
(*d*) Employee record card.
(*e*) Royalty agreement.
(*f*) Sub contractor's invoice.
(*g*) Direct labour hour overhead rate.
(*h*) Machine time sheet.
(*i*) Machine hour overhead rate.
(*j*) Department 6 direct labour cost entry on this cost card.
(*k*) Wages percentage overhead rate.

FIG. 9.—*Example of a job cost preparation*

The factory cost comprises direct costs plus a share of the overheads of each cost centre that the job passes through. Selling and distribution charges are added to make up the total cost.

or chosen amount for profit, then we refer to this as *cost-plus costing*.

These steps were listed in an earlier chapter (*see* I, **16**). A detailed example of a job cost preparation is given in Fig. 9.

3. Job card. Each job:

(*a*) is given a *job number* (or works order number) that identifies it from every other job, and

(*b*) has a card prepared for it that bears the job number and which is used to collect all the cost data relating to the job. Such a card is termed a *job card*.

JOB CARD

Description of Job.. Job No..............................

Customer.. Sales Order No..............................

Date of Despatch.. Order No. Date..............................

Direct Materials						Labour				Direct Wages		Factory O'h'ds	
Date	Req. No.	Description	Quantity	Price	Cost	Date	Dept.	Clock No.	Hrs.	Rate	Cost	O'h'd Rate	Cost
				Total £									
Direct Expenses:													
				Total £					Total £				

Comments:

Summary	
Direct Materials	
Direct Expenses	
Direct Labour	
Factory Overheads	
Factory Cost £	
Selling Overheads	
Distrib. costs—Dist. job card...	
Freight	
Total Cost £	
Profit	
Selling Price £	
Returnable containers, allowances, etc.:	

FIG. 10.—*Job card design*

This card is for a small job. Where jobs are large, usually only the analysis sheet totals are shown on the job card.

Job cards must be carefully designed so that they effectively and logically collect all the cost data involved. An example of a job card design is given in Fig. 10.

NOTE: Direct material and labour figures are taken from the costed materials requisitions and time sheets rather than the materials and wage analyses. This is because the card is for small jobs. When jobs are large the figures are taken from the analyses and the job card becomes in effect a summary sheet.

CONTRACT COSTING

4. Definition. *Contract costing* is the application of job costing to relatively large cost units, particularly units that take a considerable length of time to complete and are constructed away from the enterprise's premises (*e.g.* buildings, road construction and other civil engineering work).

5. Features of contract costing. Where contract work is carried out away from the enterprise's premises it generally shows the following features:

(*a*) Most of the materials are ordered specifically for contracts. They will, therefore, be charged direct from the supplier's invoices. Any materials drawn from a main store will be drawn on materials requisitions in the normal way.

(*b*) Most expenses are direct, *e.g.* electricity (meters will be installed on the site), insurance, telephone (the site will have its own telephones and, therefore, G.P.O. invoices), postages, sub-contracts, architects' fees, etc.

(*c*) Nearly all labour will be direct, even though it is a type of labour not usually regarded as direct, *e.g.* night-watchmen and site clerks.

(*d*) Nearly all overheads are head office costs. These obviously form only a small proportion of the total costs and as therefore errors of overhead absorption are not likely to be as serious as in other costing methods, only simple absorption methods are called for.

NOTE: Many head office costs will arise in preparing tenders and material procurement as well as labour administration. This means head office costs will tend to vary with the *prime cost* of contracts, and therefore the prime cost percentage absorption rate may well be the most appropriate.

(*e*) Plant and machinery may be charged to contracts in one of two ways:

(*i*) An hourly rate for each item of plant is calculated in a similar way to a machine hour rate (*see* IX, **21**) and contracts charged on a basis of hours of use.

(*ii*) If plant is at the contract sites for long periods of time contracts are charged with the full plant value on arrival and credited with the depreciated value on departure.

6. Architects' certificates. In the building trade progress payments are often made. Periodically the architect inspects the work and issues certificates to the contractor detailing work satisfactorily completed. It is important to note that these architects' certificates show the value of the work completed at *contract* price (*i.e.* "selling" price), not cost price. The contractor then submits to his customer invoices claiming these amounts as progress payments and encloses the certificates as evidence of work done.

7. Contract cost accounting: basic procedure. The basic procedure for costing contracts is to open a separate account for each contract, debit it with all contract costs and credit it with the contract price. This means each contract account becomes a small profit and loss account, the profit or loss being transferred to a Profits and Losses on Contracts Account.

A summary of the procedure for an individual contract is as follows:

(*a*) Open an account for the contract.
(*b*) Debit all contract direct costs (including cost of plant transferred to site if this method of charging plant is being used).
(*c*) Credit materials, plant and other items transferred *from* the contract.
(*d*) Debit head office overheads charged to the contract.
(*e*) Credit contract price.
(*f*) Transfer balance, profit or loss, to the Profits and Losses on Contracts Account.

8. Contract cost accounting: contracts uncompleted at end of a period. A complication arises if a contract is incomplete at the end of the trading period. In such circumstances only the first four items of the above procedure will be carried out:

(*a*)–(*d*) As in **7** above.

Then at the period end the procedure will be as follows:

(*e*) Mark off two blank spaces in the Contract Account.

(For reference purposes the first of these will be termed the P/L section and the second the Future section. The part of the account already containing the period costs will be referred to as the Current section.)

(*f*) Debit the Current section and credit the Future section with any accruals.

(*g*) Credit the Current section and debit the Future section with:

(*i*) prepayments;
(*ii*) stock on hand at site;
(*iii*) plant remaining on site at written-down values.

(*h*) Credit and close off the Current section with the balance now remaining (which must be the cost of work done) and *split this figure* into:

(*i*) cost of work done *and certified*, which is debited to the P/L section;
(*ii*) cost of work done and not yet certified, which is debited to the Future section.

(*i*) Credit the P/L section with the sales value of the work certified as shown on the certificates (the customer's personal account being debited).

(*j*) Complete the book-keeping as follows:

(*i*) Balance the P/L section to find profit to date.
(*ii*) Determine the profit to be taken (*see* **10**) and debit the P/L section with this figure, the Profits and Losses on Contracts Account being credited.
(*iii*) Debit the P/L section and credit the Future section with the remaining balance which is profit in suspense.

The P/L section is now closed and the Future section contains the opening figures for the new period. A worked example is given below.

EXAMPLE

Basic data:

(*i*) Details of Contract 158, for Customer ADE, begun during the year:

Item	£
Materials purchased and delivered to site	44,210
Materials issued from store	3,740
Materials returned to store	860
Site wages	14,400

Item	£
Site direct expenses	1,950
Plant sent to site	4,800
Plant returned from site	1,300
Architect's fees	2,000
Sub-contract work	6,800
Head office overheads charged ($12\frac{1}{2}$% of site wages)	

(*ii*) At the year end valuations were:

Item	£
Materials on site	1,240
Plant on site	2,050
Cost of work done but not yet certified (work in progress)	3,710
Prepayments	110
Accruals	370

(*iii*) During the year architects' certificates to the value of £81,000 were issued, and ADE made progress payments to this extent, less 10% retention monies (*see* **6, 9**).

Method: The letters in brackets in the Account refer to the steps detailed in **7**(*a*)–(*d*) and **8**(*e*)–(*f*).

Contract 158 A/c[a] *(Customer ADE)*
[*Current section*]

	£		£
Materials purchased[b]	44,210	Materials returned[c]	860
Materials in store[b]	3,740	Plant returned[c]	1,300
Site wages[b]	14,400	Prepayment c/d[g]	110
Site direct expenses[b]	1,950	Stock at site c/d[g]	1,240
Plant sent to site[b]	4,800	Plant at site c/d[g]	2,050
Architect's fees[b]	2,000	Cost of work certified c/d[h]	70,800*
Sub-contract work[b]	6,800	Work in progress c/d[h]	3,710
Head office overheads[d]	1,800		
Accruals c/d[f]	370		
	£80,070		£80,070

* After all the entries (*b*) to (*g*) have been made there is a debit balance of £74,510 on this part of the account. This balance represents the total cost of work done. Since the cost of work done and *not* certified is £3,710, then the cost of work certified is £74,510 less £3710 = £70,800.

[*Profit and loss section*]

	£		£
Cost of work certified b/d [h]	70,800	Work certified, ADE A/c [i]	81,000
P/L on Contracts, two-thirds profit [j]	6,800		
Profit in suspense c/d [j]	3,400		
	£81,000		£81,000

[*Future section*]

	£		£
Prepayment b/d [g]	110	Accruals b/d [f]	370
Stock at site b/d [g]	1,240	Profit in suspense b/d [j]	3,400
Plant at site b/d [g]	2,050		
Work in progress b/d [h]	3,710		

Customer ADE A/c (Contract 158)

Invoices and certificates, Contract 158 A/c [i]	£81,000	Cash, progress payment (less 10% retention)	£72,900

9. Retention monies. There is frequently a contract clause that entitles the customer to withhold payment of a proportion of the contract value (*e.g.* 10%) for a specified period after the end of the contract. During this period and before he is paid these retained moneys the contractor must make good all constructional defects that appear. The prudent contractor will therefore hold in suspense part of the contract profit and not transfer the amount to his Profit and Losses on Contracts Account until he has received all the retention monies. Any costs of remedying defects during the retention period would then be debited against this profit-in-suspense.

10. Profit taken on uncompleted contracts. It is unwise to take credit for the whole of the profit made on uncompleted contracts to the Profit and Losses on Contracts Account, since unforeseen and expensive difficulties and defects may well arise later in the contract.

How much profit, therefore, should be taken on uncompleted contracts depends on circumstances, particularly how near the contract is to completion. The likelihood of defects arising and even the possible insolvency of the customer are also factors to consider. The amount of profit that should be taken then is essentially a matter of judgment, and no sophisticated formula will ever enable an accountant to avoid the responsibility of making such judgment. Moreover, in view of the imponderables involved, a simple estimate that avoids the danger of spurious accuracy is to be preferred to any involved computations. For this reason it is suggested that the student should use *two-thirds as the proportion of profit to be taken* unless there are definite reasons for doing otherwise.

PROGRESS TEST 10

Principles

1. State two methods of charging plant to contracts. (5(*e*))
2. What are:

(*a*) Architects' certificates, (6) (*b*) Retention monies? (9)

3. Distinguish carefully between the three sections into which an uncompleted contract account divides at the end of a trading period. (8)

Practice

4. According to the factory job cost ledger, Job No. A 8473 has incurred the following prime costs:

Materials (Direct): 14 cwt 2 qr 12 lb at £2·37½ per cwt.
Wages (Direct): Department X 18 hours at 35p per hour.
Department Y 32 hours at 30p per hour.

Budgeted overhead for the year, based on normal capacity:

Variable overhead
Department X £6000 for 9000 direct labour hours.
Department Y £8000 for 10,000 direct labour hours.

Fixed overhead
Total budgeted direct labour hours for whole factory 22,000.
Total budgeted expenditure £16,500.

You are required to

(*a*) Calculate the cost of Job No. A 8473.
(*b*) Estimate the % of profit obtained if the price quoted to the customer was £150. (*A.C.C.A.* Adapted)

CHAPTER XI

COST ACCOUNTS

So far we have discussed costing with little reference to the actual accounting entries involved. In this chapter the over-all patterns on which cost accounts are based will be examined.

There are two basic types of cost accounting: *integral accounts* and *interlocking accounts*. They exist separately for purely historical reasons and not because their use depends upon different circumstances. Integral accounts evolved after and from interlocking accounts and is the better and more efficient system. However, interlocking accounts are still used in industry, and are still examined upon, and therefore both types are outlined here.

INTEGRAL ACCOUNTS

1. Definition. The term *integral accounts* relates to a single accounting system which contains both financial and cost accounts. In theory, all accounts are in a single ledger.

2. Chart of integral accounts. Fig. 11 shows a chart representing the essential accounting flow involved in a *system of integral accounts*. The following points should be noted:

(*a*) The accounts are usually drawn up on a monthly basis.

(*b*) The direct and indirect materials figures, and the direct and indirect wages figures, are abstracted from the materials and wage analyses respectively.

(*c*) The Overhead Control Account in this chart summarises what would in practice be a large number of separate overhead and departmental accounts (*see* **4**).

(*d*) Prepayments and accruals can be taken into consideration by the usual procedure of carrying them down, in this case in the Overhead Control Account.

(*e*) The debit in respect of overheads to the Work-in-Progress Account is the *absorbed* overheads and is found by multiplying the total units of base (*e.g.* direct labour hours) for the period by the overhead absorption rate. For instance, if 20,000 direct labour hours were booked to cost

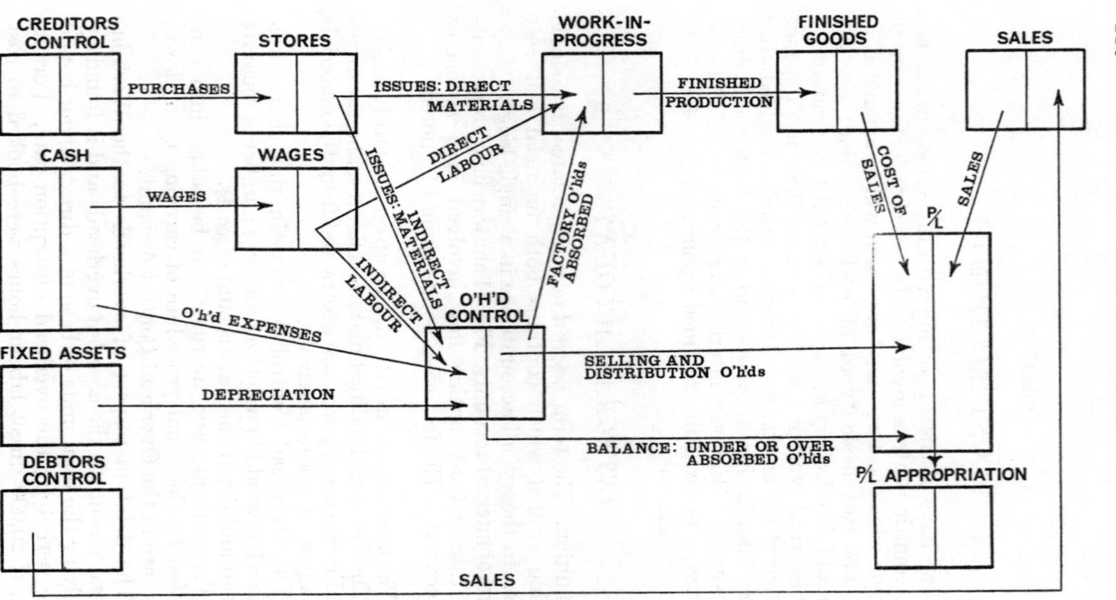

FIG. 11.—*Chart of accounting flow in an integral accounts system*

This is a single system containing both financial and cost accounts. The chart has been considerably simplified for purposes of clarity; *e.g.* in practice the Overhead Control Account would be split into many separate overhead and departmental accounts.

units and the overhead rate was £0·75 hour, then £15,000 would be debited to the Work-in-Progress Account for overheads.

(*f*) Selling and distribution overheads are *not* included in the charges to the Work-in-Progress Account (*see* IX, **23**). As these overheads are incurred at the time of sale and delivery, they are charged to the Profit and Loss Account in the same period as the sales to which they relate are credited.

(*g*) The final balance in the Overhead Control Account must be the under- or over-absorbed overheads (*see* IX, **19**(*c*)), and this, of course, is transferred to the Profit and Loss Account (unless the business is seasonal, *see* IX, **19**(*d*)).

(*h*) Often each department will have its own Work-in-Progress Account. If work passes from one department to another, then the cost of finished production credited to one Work-in-Progress Account is debited to the Work-in-Progress Account of the following department.

(*i*) The balance on the Profit and Loss Account (*i.e.* the profit or loss) must be transferred to a Profit and Loss Appropriation Account. If it were left as a balance on the Profit and Loss Account, then the "profit" of the following month would include the balance figure and would not show the separate period profit.

(*j*) The balances in the Stores Account, Work-in-Progress Account and the Finished Goods Account are all closing stock values. An analysis of these figures can always be found in the subsidiary records (*see* **3**).

(*k*) Under integral accounts the usual nominal accounts showing purchases, wages, expenses, etc. (all of which, the student will recollect, were always closed off to the Profit and Loss Account at the end of the period), *no longer exist*. The asset and liability accounts, however, remain and are in no way affected by the fact that they are part of an integral system.

3. Subsidiary records.

(*a*) *Stores*. All stores transactions are shown on *stores record cards* (*see* III, **23**), while the transaction *totals* are shown in the Stores Account. This means that the Stores Account is a control account for these stores record cards (*see* Fig. 5). The balance on the Stores Account, *i.e.* the stock value, represents the total of all the balances on the stores record cards.

(*b*) *Work in progress.* If jobbing work is being undertaken, then all costs of production are recorded on the *job cards.* As the Work-in-Progress Account is also charged with these production costs, it follows that the Work-in-Progress Account controls the job cards. Consequently the balance on this account equals the total costs recorded on those job cards that represent jobs still in progress. It also means that the credit to the Work-in-Progress Account for the production transferred to the Finished Goods Account can be found by totalling all job cards representing jobs completed during the accounting period.

(*c*) *Finished goods.* In the same way that the Stores Account controls the stores record cards, so the Finished Goods Account controls the *finished goods stock records,* and therefore the balance on this account represents the balances on all the record cards. Also the cost-of-sales figure credited to the Finished Goods Account can be found by using the finished goods stock record cards to price all items removed from the finished goods store.

4. Detailed overhead accounts. The Overhead Control Account shown in Fig. 11 is a very great simplification of the accounts used in practice, though a common enough account in examination questions concerned with cost accounting principles. This account represents not only individual overhead accounts but also the departmental accounts to which such overheads are charged from the overhead analysis (*see* Chapter IX).

5. Cost Control Account. In practice, it is generally found to be physically inconvenient to keep all the accounts in a single ledger. The Ledger is therefore physically divided into two, a Financial Ledger under the responsibility of the financial accountant and a Cost Ledger under the responsibility of the cost accountant. This does *not* affect the double entry given in Fig. 11, but in order to assist balancing, a Cost Control Account is opened up *in the Financial Ledger.* This control account is similar to any other control account (*e.g.* Creditors Control, or Debtors Control) in that:

(*a*) It records in total all amounts that enter into the Cost Ledger.

(*b*) It enables the Financial Ledger to be balanced independently of the Cost Ledger.
(*c*) The balance on the Cost Control Account must equal the net balance in the Cost Ledger as a whole.

6. Rules for operating a Cost Control Account. Although the operation of a Cost Control Account is identical to the operation of any other control account, it does sometimes appear more complicated. The student may therefore find the following rules helpful when operating a Cost Control Account. (These rules are illustrated in Fig. 12.)

(*a*) Establish a clear distinction between the Financial Ledger accounts and the Cost Ledger accounts. Students often find it useful to imagine the ledgers being divided by a distinct line. Which accounts are to be in which ledger is purely a matter of choice, although a division similar to that shown in Fig. 12 is usual.

(*b*) The double-entry shown earlier in Fig. 11 is adhered to without change, but in addition whenever the double-entry spans the two ledgers (and therefore crosses the dividing line) *the entry made in the Cost Ledger account is duplicated in the Cost Control Account.*

NOTE: This results in *all* entries within the Financial Ledger being balancing entries. Hence this ledger is self-balancing.

7. Financial and Cost Profit and Loss Accounts. In practice, there are often certain expenses which do not enter the cost accounts, *e.g.* cash discounts and interest. These expenses, therefore, must be recorded in the Financial Ledger. Before the profit on the Cost Profit and Loss Account can be transferred to the Appropriation Account such expenses have to be brought in. This is usually dealt with by transferring the cost profit to a Financial Profit and Loss Account in the Financial Ledger. These missing items are then incorporated into the cost profit and the resulting figure, *i.e.* the financial profit, transferred to the Appropriation Account. It is important to appreciate that *in integral accounts there is no contradiction between the cost profit and the financial profit*; reconciliation is unnecessary. The financial profit is simply the cost profit as transferred from the Cost Profit and Loss Account with a few small non-cost items incorporated.

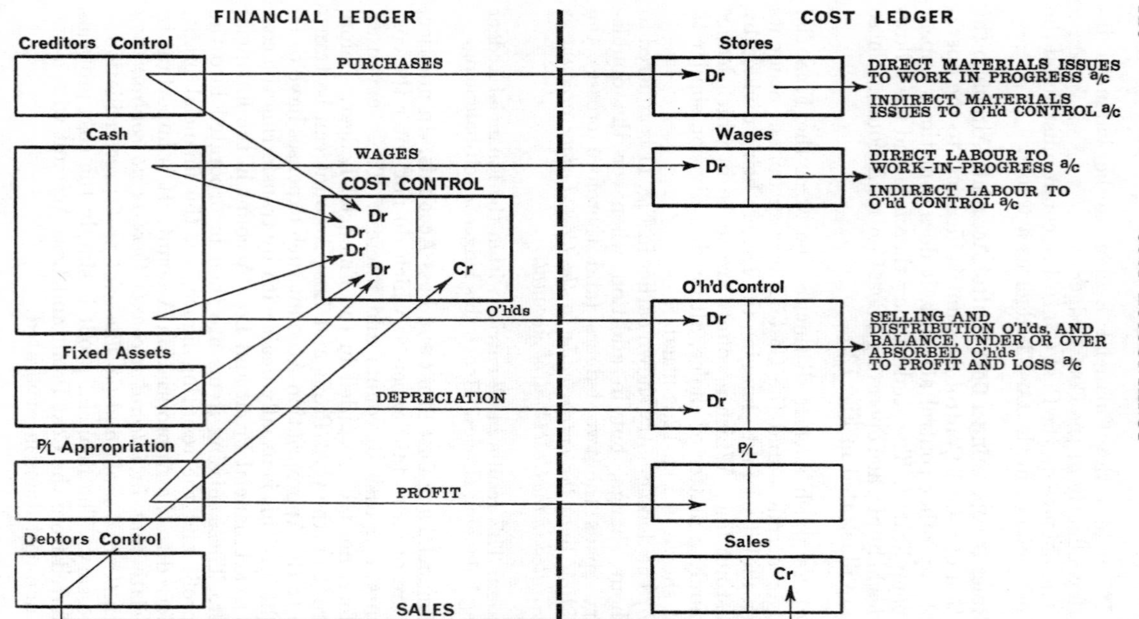

FIG. 12.—*Effect of including a Cost Control Account in an integral accounts system*

INTERLOCKING ACCOUNTS

8. Definition. *Interlocking accounts* is a system of cost accounting in which the cost accounts have no double-entry connection with the financial accounts, but use the same basic data. With interlocking accounts, therefore, the Cost Ledger is kept quite independently from the Financial Ledger, but since the basic data is the same, the two ledgers should be essentially in accord with each other. The pattern of interlocking accounts is shown in Fig. 13.

9. Features of interlocking accounts. Interlocking accounts display the following features (*see* Fig. 13):

(*a*) There are *no* double-entries that span the two ledgers.
(*b*) The Financial Ledger is the normal ledger one meets in book-keeping. The existence of the Cost Ledger in no way affects it.
(*c*) There is a Cost Control Account in the *Cost Ledger*, but it is not a true control account. It simply has the function of acting as a receptacle for those parts of the double-entries which would, in integral accounts, "cross the line" for entry into a financial account (*e.g.* cash, creditors), in other words, for disposing of the odds and ends of double-entries which in interlocking accounts lack a home. It is sometimes disrespectfully referred to as the "dustbin account."

NOTE: If the Cost Control Accounts in integral and interlocking accounts are compared it will be seen that:

(*i*) They are in opposite ledgers.
(*ii*) The entries are the same but appear on different sides of the accounts.

(*d*) The net profit on the Cost Profit and Loss Account should equal the net profit on the Financial Profit and Loss Account, *i.e.* the two accounts should independently give the same profit figure. However, if certain transactions are viewed differently by the financial accountant and the cost accountant (*e.g.* depreciation rates, stock valuations, exclusion of financial expenses from the costs), then *the two profits will not agree* and will need to be reconciled.

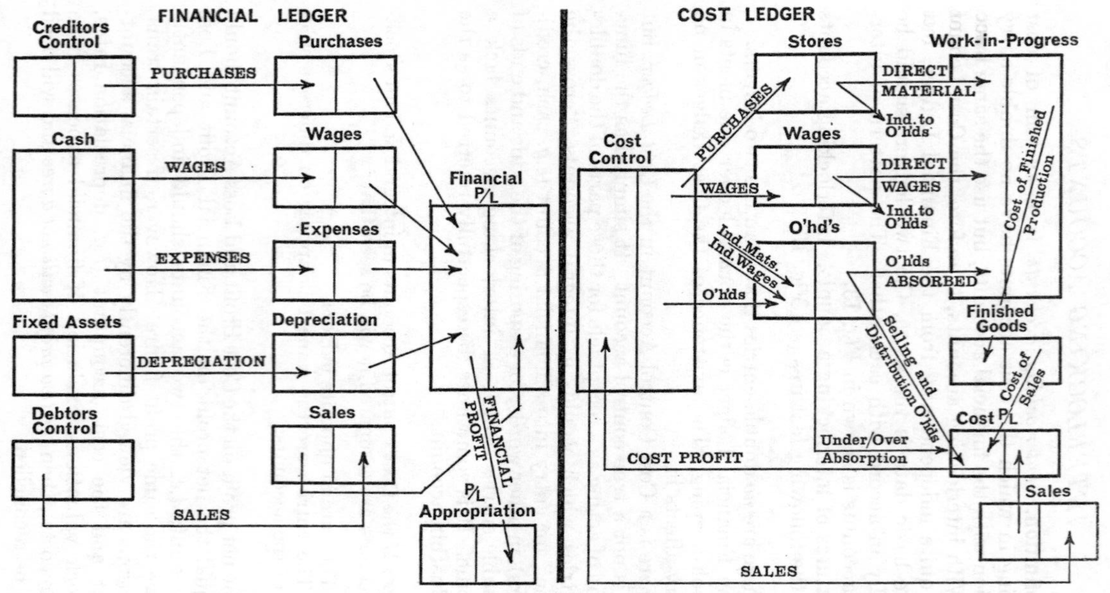

FIG. 13.—*Chart of accounting flow in an interlocking accounts system*

In this system the financial ledger is kept quite independently of the cost ledger. There are no double entries spanning the two ledgers and the Cost Control Account is no longer a true control account.

10. Reconciliation of financial and cost profits. To reconcile financial and cost profits in interlocking accounts:

(*a*) Start with the cost profit.
(*b*) Adjust for differing views:

(*i*) Ascertain all the points at which the financial accountant viewed a transaction or value differently from the cost accountant.
(*ii*) Compute for each point the money difference between the two views.
(*iii*) Ask yourself, "If the cost accountant had adopted the financial accountant's view, would the *cost* profit have been increased or decreased?" If increased, add the money difference, and vice versa.

(*c*) After taking into consideration all the points the resulting figure should be identical to the financial profit. If it is not, the two profits have not been reconciled and further differences must be sought.

EXAMPLE

Data:

Cost P/L Account	£12,800 profit
Financial P/L Account	£11,300 profit

In the Cost Ledger: a £5000 charge was made for depreciation, and the closing stock of raw materials valued at £23,600.

In the Financial Ledger: depreciation was £4400 and closing raw materials stock valued at £21,500.

Method of reconciliation:	£
Profit as per Cost P/L Account	12,800
Change if cost accountant had adopted financial accountant's depreciation charge	+ 600
	13,400
Change if cost accountant had adopted financial accountant's raw materials stock value	−2,100
Profit as per Financial P/L Account	£11,300

NOTE

(*i*) Change entries can be abbreviated to the name of the difference, *e.g.* "depreciation," "raw materials stock value."
(*ii*) Where there are more than two differences the layout is improved if all the additions are collected together and subtotalled, and similarly the subtractions.

PROGRESS TEST 11

Principles

1. Distinguish between integral and interlocking accounts. (1, 8)
2. What detailed records do the following accounts control:

(*a*) Stores, (*b*) Work-in-Progress (*c*) Finished Goods? (3)

3. Explain why the Cost and Financial Profit and Loss Accounts in integral accounts do not need to be reconciled. (7)

Practice

4. The Simplas ABC Co. Ltd. started the year with the following Trial Balance:

		£	£
Capital: Authorised and Issued:			
10,000 £1 Ord. Shares			10,000
Fixed assets		3,000	
Debtors		1,000	
Cost Control: Stores	£2,000		
Work in Progress	£2,000		
Finished Goods	£3,000		
		7,000	
Creditors			2,000
Bank		1,000	
		12,000	12,000

During January the following transactions took place:

	£
Raw materials purchases on credit	2000
Sales on credit	2500
General operating expenses (cash)	1000
Wages	1000
Discounts allowed	150
Discounts received	100
Creditors paid (cash)	1500
Payments by debtors (cash)	2000
Issues from Raw Materials Store	3000
Issues from Finished Goods Store	2000
Finished prod. transferred to Finished Goods Store	4000
Finished production kept in factory as an addition to fixed assets	500

Depreciation was taken at 1% for the month on fixed assets (no depreciation on the addition), and in the cost accounts £100 was charged to overheads for notional rent.

Prepare:

(*a*) All ledger accounts.
(*b*) Cost Profit and Loss Account.
(*c*) Financial Profit and Loss Account.
(*d*) The company Trial Balance as at the month end.

NOTE: The capital expenditure should be transferred to the financial accounts.

5. A company's Trading and Profit and Loss Account was as follows:

	£		£
Purchases	25,210	Sales: 50,000 units	
Less Closing stock	4,080	at £1·50 each	75,000
		Discounts received	260
	21,130	Profit on sale of land	2,340
Direct wages	10,500		
Work expenses	12,130		
Selling expenses	7,100		
Administration expenses	5,340		
Depreciation	1,100		
Net profit	20,300		
	77,600		77,600

The cost profit, however, was only £19,770. Reconcile the financial and cost profits, using the following information:

(*a*) Cost accounts value of closing stock: £4280.
(*b*) The works expenses in the cost accounts were taken as 100% direct wages.
(*c*) Selling and administration expenses were charged in the cost accounts at 10% of sales and £0·10 per unit respectively.
(*d*) Depreciation in the cost accounts was £800.

CHAPTER XII

UNIT COSTING

Unit costing is the method of costing used when the cost units are identical. Cost units that are identical should logically have identical costs, and this concept of equality of costs is the basic feature of unit costing. The basic computation in all unit costing will be, therefore:

$$\frac{\textit{Total cost}}{\textit{Number of units}}$$

There are three subdivisions of the method: output costing, operating costing and process costing. All three are examined in this chapter, although the last, process costing, is by far the most involved.

OUTPUT AND OPERATING COSTING

1. Output costing. *Output costing* is the form of unit costing used when the enterprise produces only one product, or essentially one product, since it may be in two or three grades. Enterprises using output costing include, therefore, dairies, quarries and cement works.

This is a very simple form of costing. Since there is only one product, there is no point in making involved calculations. Essentially, cost ascertainment will involve collecting and analysing all the costs and then dividing each cost by the total production to find the cost-per-unit (*see* Fig. 14). Figures for the previous period may be given for comparison.

In output costing work in progress is rarely introduced into the cost-per-unit calculations; with this sort of production it tends to be both constant (so cancelling itself out) and relatively insignificant.

2. Operating costing. *Operating costing* is the form of unit costing used when costing a service. This service may be sold by the enterprise, *e.g.* railways, or used within the enterprise, *e.g.* canteen, boiler house. It is clearly a common form of costing with local government authorities.

3. Operating cost units. A major problem that can arise in

KREEM DAIRY LTD. Cost Statement for quarter ending *31st March 1966* Total milk processed *876,950 gallons*			
Item of cost	*Cost*	*Cost per gallon*	
		This quarter	*Last quarter*
	£	*pence*	*pence*
Wages and salaries	23,606	2·7	2·5
Repairs, general	7,901	0·9	1·0
Steam	4,377	0·5	0·5
Rates	880	0·1	0·1
Foil and crown corks	3,522	0·4	0·4
Trade requisites	9,548	1·1	1·0
Electricity and water	3,495	0·4	0·4
Transport	5,265	0·6	0·6
Depreciation and interest	7,882	0·9	0·9
Other expenses	876	0·1	0·1
Total cost of dairy operation	£67,352	7·7*p*	7·5*p*
Materials	£441,121	50·3*p*	49·4*p*
Total cost	£508,473	58·0*p*	56·9*p*

FIG. 14.—*Output cost statement*

Since only one product is produced, it is necessary only to divide each cost by the total production to find the cost per unit.

operating costing is determining the cost units to be used. This involves finding some unit that will measure the amount of the service provided, *e.g.*:

Enterprise	*Unit*
Bus companies	Passenger-miles; seat-miles
Hospitals	Patient-days; operations
Electricity Boards	Kilowatt-hours
Boiler-houses	Pounds of steam raised
Canteens	Meals served; cups of tea sold
Road maintenance	Miles of road maintained
Transport departments	Ton-miles; miles travelled

Frequently costings are improved if two or more cost units are used simultaneously, and two sets of costs-per-unit figures computed.

4. Two-part units. Units such as passenger-miles and ton-miles are very useful measures. A ton-mile, for example, represents 1 ton carried for 1 mile. Thus, if 5 tons were carried 3 miles this would represent $5 \times 3 = 15$ ton-miles. Note that if a second similar load were carried there would be a total of $15 + 15 = 30$ ton-miles, *not* $(5 + 5) \times (3 + 3) = 60$ ton-miles.

5. Operating costing: method. Operating costing is similar to output costing. All the costs incurred during a period are collected and analysed and then expressed in terms of costs-per-unit.

A breakdown of costs between fixed and variable is of particular value in this type of costing, as it draws management's attention to the fixed cost to which they are committed regardless of the units of service ultimately given. It also indicates the additional cost involved in providing each additional unit of service—very useful information if the service tends to be utilised unevenly and there is unused off-peak capacity (*e.g.* buses and electricity generating stations).

SIMPLE PROCESS COSTING

6. Definition. *Process costing* is the form of unit costing used when cost units pass through processes. In this method the cost per unit is computed for each process the units pass through. It is a feature of process costing that *all* costs, direct and indirect, are charged to the process and then charged equally to cost units. The method is discussed below and illustrated with the same basic data throughout, unless otherwise stated (**7–22**).

7. Basic formula. As stated above, unit costing involves the division of all costs incurred during a period by the number of cost units and the cost-per-unit (CPU) is therefore:

$$\text{CPU} = \frac{\textit{Cost incurred during period}}{\textit{Number of units produced}}$$

For instance, where the total cost incurred was £5000 and 1000 units were produced the CPU would be £5.

8. Effective units. If some units are still in progress at the end of the period, then the number of units produced must include an allowance for these, since some of the costs were incurred in their partial production. This allowance is made by computing *effective units* where:

$$\textit{Effective units} = \textit{No. of units in progress} \times \%\ \textit{complete}$$

This is logical, since a cost that enables, say, two units to be each half completed may be regarded as the cost needed to complete fully one unit.

The basic formula now becomes:

$$\text{CPU} = \frac{\textit{Cost incurred during period}}{\textit{Units completed} + \textit{Effective units in-progress}}$$

Using the data given in **7**, assume that of the 1000 units, 600 are complete and 400 are in-progress and 50% complete.

Computations:

$$\text{Effective units in-progress} = 400 \times 50\% = 200$$

$$\therefore \text{Total effective production} = 600 + 200 = 800 \text{ units.}$$

$$\therefore \text{CPU} = \frac{5000}{800} = £6{\cdot}25$$

9. Cost elements. When we consider the degree of completion of any units in progress we may well find that the degree differs according to the cost element. To take a domestic example, if one is making a cake, then just before it is put in the oven the cake may well be complete as regards all materials, nearly complete as regards labour, but only just started as regards overheads since the oven heating costs will be the largest part of this element. In order to allow for this, then, it is necessary to treat cost elements separately and calculate a cost-per-unit figure for each element. Note that the resulting calculation gives the cost-per-unit for each element for a *complete* unit. This means that the *total* cost of a complete unit can be found by simply adding the separate element costs-per-unit.

For example, assume that the £5000 cost was made up of: materials £1000; labour £2500; overheads £1500. 600 units are complete and the 400 in progress are 75% complete in materials; 50% in labour and 25% in overheads. The CPU for each element can be computed as follows, using the formula in **8** above:

Cost element	£	*W.I.P. effective units*	*Total effective units produced*	*CPU* £
Materials	1000	400 × 75% = 300	+600 = 900	1·111
Labour	2500	400 × 50% = 200	+600 = 800	3·125
Overheads	1500	400 × 25% = 100	+600 = 700	2·143
Total	£5000			£6·379

10. Valuation of completed units and work in progress. The value of completed units is simply:

Number of completed units × *Total* CPU

From the figures given in **9** it can be seen that the value of the completed units = 600 × £6·379 = £3827 (to nearest £).

Work in progress can be easily valued by multiplying each element cost-per-unit by the number of *effective units* and then adding the products as follows:

		£
Materials:	300 effective units at £1·111 =	333·3
Labour:	200 ,, ,, at £3·125 =	625·0
Overheads:	100 ,, ,, at £2·143 =	214·3
Total W.I.P. value		£1173 (to nearest £)

11. Units transferred from a previous process. In process costing, units frequently pass through a number of processes in sequence. Consequently, many processes start with units from a previous process. Now it is a basic costing principle that cost units are transferred to later stages at their cumulative cost, and therefore these costs must be brought into the figures of the new process. It is convenient to treat such a cost as a separate cost element termed "previous process cost," the term "material" referring only to *material added to production during processing.*

"Previous process cost" is treated no differently from any other cost element. However, *its degree of completion is always 100%*, since it is that part of the unit cost relating to the cost of previous operations which, clearly, must be fully complete.

Assume now that *the 1000 units involved* (*see* **8** above) *were transferred from a previous process at a cost of £5 a unit.* This element will appear in the computations as follows:

1. *Cost element*	2. *Costs*	3. *Completed units*	*Work in progress* 4. *Units*	5. *% complete*	6. *Effective units*	7. *Total effective units*	8. *CPU*	9. *W.I.P. value*
	£						£	£
Previous process cost	5,000	600	400	100	400	1,000	5·000	2,000
Materials	1,000	600	400	75	300	900	1·111	333
Labour	2,500	600	400	50	200	800	3·125	625
Overheads	1,500	600	400	25	100	700	2·143	214
Total	£10,000						£11·379	£3,172

Check:

Value of 600 completed units
= 600 × £11·379 = £6827
Value of work in progress = £3172

£9999 total costs

NOTE: The £1 difference in the total costs is due to rounding. It is usual to adjust one of the valuations slightly to bring the total into line with the total costs. This aids subsequent double-entry.

12. The 9-by-4 layout. The layout of nine columns and four rows used above (**11**) has been devised for the solution of unit costing problems, and the student is advised to learn it thoroughly. Columns 2–5 show given data (the previous process cost will, of course, always be 100% complete as regards work in progress). Columns 6–9 are computed as follows:

Column 6 = column 4 × column 5
Column 7 = column 3 + column 6
Column 8 = column 2 ÷ column 7
Column 9 = column 6 × column 8

Note that column 3 records the total *completed* units, *i.e.* it will include units transferred to the next process and also any units completed but lost at the end of the process (*see* **16**).

13. Balancing the layout. The layout should always be balanced by ensuring that:

Total value of completed units + W.I.P. *value* =
Total cost of all elements (*column* 2)

This is a very useful cross-check to workings and was used in the computations in **11** above.

NORMAL LOSSES IN PROCESS

14. Costing principle regarding normal losses. It is a fundamental costing principle that the cost of normal losses should be borne by the good production. This is logical, since such losses are, in fact, one of the normal costs of production and therefore chargeable to whatever production emerges. Note, incidentally, that, among other things, losses can be due to evaporation, breakage or rejection on inspection.

15. Units lost at the beginning. If units are lost right at the beginning before any materials, labour or overheads have been incurred, then the 9-by-4 layout can be used as it stands without any adjustments.

For example, *100 units may be lost* at the very beginning of the process. Assume that *this results in only 500 good units now being completed.* This result will produce the following computations:

Cost element	*Costs*	*Completed units*	*Work in progress*			*Total effective units*	*CPU*	*W.I.P. value*
			Units	*% complete*	*Effective units*			
	£						£	£
Previous process cost	5,000	500	400	100	400	900	5·556	2,222
Materials	1,000	500	400	75	300	800	1·250	375
Labour	2,500	500	400	50	200	700	3·571	714
Overheads	1,500	500	400	25	100	600	2·500	250
Total	£10,000						£12·877	3,561

Check:

		£
Value of 500 completed units = 500 × £12·877	=	6,439
Value of work in progress	=	3,561
		£10,000

16. Units lost at the end. In unit costing it is vital to remember that costs must not be charged until they are incurred (*see* I, **10**(*b*)). This means that if units are lost at the end the cost of such losses can be charged only *to units which have reached the end*, *i.e.* completed units. The procedure then is:

(*a*) *Complete* 9-*by*-4 *layout as normal* remembering that column 3 shows completed units, *i.e.* total units completed, good and bad.

(*b*) Using the total cost-per-unit figure, find the cost value of the lost units.

(*c*) Divide this cost by the number of good, completed units. This gives the charge per good unit for the losses. Add this charge to the original cost-per-unit figure to give the final cost-per-unit of good production.

If, then, the 100 units were lost at the end the 9-by-4 layout would show the computations given below:

Cost element	*Costs*	*Completed units*	*Work in progress*			*Total effective units*	*CPU*	*W.I.P. value*
			Units	*% complete*	*Eff. units*			
	£						£	£
Previous process cost	5,000	600	400	100	400	1,000	5·000	2,000
Materials	1,000	600	400	75	300	900	1·111	333
Labour	2,500	600	400	50	200	800	3·125	625
Overheads	1,500	600	400	25	100	700	2·143	214
Total	£10,000						£11·379	£3,172

The 600 completed units comprise 500 good and 100 lost but completed units.

Cost value of 100 lost units $= 100 \times £11{\cdot}379 = £1138$

This cost shared between 500 good units $= \frac{£1138}{500} =$ £2·276

Final CPU £13·655

Check:

	£
Value of 500 completed good units $= 500 \times £13{\cdot}655 =$	6,828
Value of work in progress $=$	3,172
	£10,000

ABNORMAL LOSSES IN PROCESS

17. Treatment of abnormal losses. A further cost principle to be carefully observed is that only *normal* costs are to be charged to production. Consequently, any abnormal losses must be written off to Profit and Loss.

18. Ascertaining units lost that are to be regarded as abnormal. To ascertain how many lost units rank as abnormal losses:

(*a*) Predetermine a normal loss rate.
(*b*) Compute the normal loss for any given production.
(*c*) Then *Abnormal loss* = *Actual loss* − *Normal loss.* (Note that if the actual loss is *less* than the normal loss an "abnormal gain" is made.)

It is absolutely essential in this calculation to be quite clear as to where the physical point of rejection is, since *normal loss can only be computed on a basis of the number of units that pass that point.* For instance, if the normal loss rate is 10%, units are lost at the *end*, and a total of 500 units, good and bad, have reached the end, then the normal loss is 50 units. This figure is quite independent of the input, whether it was 1000 or 10,000. Similarly, if the loss occurred in the *middle* of the process and 800 units had reached this point, then the normal loss would be 80, regardless of how many either entered, completed, or remained in the process.

19. Valuing abnormal losses. When pricing abnormal losses it is important to remember that such losses must carry a share of the cost of *normal* losses.

To prove this, consider the following extreme example: 100 total units are completed; the actual loss is 99; the normal loss is 20%. The total good production, then, is only 1 unit, and the normal loss 20 units. Now if the abnormally lost units do not carry a share of the normal loss, then the 1 good unit will have to carry the whole cost of the 20 units normal loss, a cost "normally" shared between 80 units. This great burden is, then, clearly a non-normal charge arising on account of the abnormal loss. To keep the charge normal it is necessary to share the 20 units normal loss among *all 80 other units* so that the one good unit takes an eightieth part of the cost of the normal loss and the 79 abnormally lost units the remainder of the cost. In other words, abnormal losses must carry a share of the normal loss.

We can now give the procedure for valuing abnormal losses where such losses occur *at the end* of the process.

(*a*) Complete the 9-by-4 layout, remembering that column 3 includes *all* completed units: good units, normal loss and abnormal loss.

(*b*) Having done this:

(*i*) Compute the units of normal loss on the basis of this column 3 figure, *i.e.* col. 3 × normal loss rate.

(*ii*) Value the normal loss by multiplying these units by the initial cost-per-unit figure.

(*iii*) Divide this value by the total number of good and abnormal loss units to give a cost-of-normal-loss-per-unit figure (but *see* **21**(*c*)(*i*) *re* scrap value).

(*iv*) Add this figure to the initial total cost-per-unit figure to obtain the final cost-per-unit.

(*c*) Multiply the final cost-per-unit figure by the number of units of abnormal loss to obtain the value of the abnormal loss.

NOTE:

(*i*) The value of the good production is simply *good units* × *final* CPU.

(*ii*) The value of the work in progress is unaffected, since the loss costs are incurred at the end, *i.e.* they have not yet been incurred by work-in-progress units, and therefore such units must carry no charge for such losses.

(*iii*) The abnormal loss value is transferred to an Abnormal Loss Account.

(*iv*) The over-all formula for finding the final cost-per-unit figure to be applied to both good and abnormal loss units can be written:

$$\textit{Final CPU} = \textit{Initial CPU} + \frac{\textit{No. of completed units} \times \textit{Normal loss rate} \times \textit{Initial CPU}}{\textit{Good units completed} + \textit{Abnormal units lost}}$$

EXAMPLE

Using the computations given above (**16**), where the actual loss is 100 units, assume that we now have a predetermined *normal loss rate of* 6%. Since the total units completed of all kinds is still 600, and since the work in progress is unaffected by the losses, the 9-by-4 layout in **16** remains unaltered down to the initial total CPU of £11·379. The abnormal loss value is computed as follows:

The normal loss of 6% must relate to the total units passing the loss point (in this case the end), *i.e.* 600 units.

∴ Normal loss = 6% of 600 = 36 units.
The actual loss is 100 units.
∴ Abnormal loss = 100 − 36 = 64 units.
Cost of the normal loss is 36 × £11·379 = £410
This loss shared between remaining 564 units (*i.e.* good units + abnormal loss) $= \frac{410}{564} =$ £0·727

∴ Final CPU = £11·379 + £0·727 = £12·106
∴ Value of abnormal loss = 64 units × £12·106 = £775

Check:	£
Value of 500 completed good units = 500 × £12·106 =	6,053
Value of abnormal loss charged to Abnormal Loss A/c =	775
Value of work in progress =	3,172
	£10,000

OTHER CONSIDERATIONS IN PROCESS COSTING

20. Work in progress at the beginning. If there are units in-progress at the beginning of a period then:

(*a*) If the in-progress values are analysed to cost elements, simply add each in-progress element value to the element's period cost and proceed to the 9-by-4 layout using these totals in the cost column (*i.e.* column 2). No further adjustment or reference to the opening work in progress is necessary.

(*b*) If there is no analysis of in-progress values (although the percentage completion of each element must be given):

(*i*) Roughly draft the 9-by-4 layout. Any extra columns the student may desire to add later can then be inserted in the layout.

(*ii*) The opening number of units in-progress must be deducted from the number of completed units and the *net* figure inserted in the "Completed units" column (column 3).

(*iii*) For each element find the percentage to *complete* the opening in-progress units (*i.e.* 100 − percentage completed), multiply the number of in-progress units by this percentage to give the "effective units to complete", and add to the total effective units (column 7).

(*iv*) Find the element cost-per-unit in the normal way and multiply this by the "effective units to complete" figure, add these element products and also add the original opening in-progress value.

(*v*) Value the units transferred by adding the last value of step (*iv*) to:

(*Total transferred units* − *Opening units in-progress*) × *Total CPU*

The object of these five steps was first to compute how much it cost to complete the in-progress units and then, on the assumption that these units would be first out, adding this cost to the original in-progress value to find the total transferred cost of the in-progress units. Finally the remaining completed and transferred units are valued at the normal cost-per-unit figure.

21. Scrap. If scrap that has value arises in the course of processing, the following points should be considered:

(*a*) The value of the scrap should be shown as a deduction from the cost of the process.

(*b*) When abnormal losses are not involved the scrap value of any lost units is deducted from the cost of these units before dividing by the number of good units.

(*c*) When abnormal losses are involved:

(*i*) Subtract the scrap value of the *normal* loss units from the cost of these normal loss units before dividing by the total good and abnormal loss units.

(*ii*) Deduct the scrap value of the abnormal loss units from the cost of these abnormal loss units.

NOTE: If there is in fact an abnormal gain, then the scrap value of the units *not* scrapped must be deducted from the abnormal gain figure. This is necessary, since the initial apparent gain must be reduced to allow for the loss of scrap income that would otherwise have been received if the full normal loss had been suffered.

22. Units lost part-way through the process (*see* layout in Fig. 15). If units are lost part-way through a process, then the costs incurred relate only to partial completion. This means two complete sets of three columns need to be added to the 9-by-4 layout. These sets record normal and abnormal units lost and are both similar to the three work-in-progress columns (units lost; % complete; effective units lost). The effective units lost are added to the completed units (note that the lost units are *not* now completed units, so must not be included in this figure), and the effective work-in-progress units to obtain the total effective units figure (column 7). The layout is then completed, and after this the procedure continues:

(*a*) The work-in-progress and lost unit degrees of completion are compared to ascertain whether the work-in-progress units lie before or beyond the point of loss.

(*b*) The value of the *normal* loss is found by multiplying normal *effective* units lost by the relevant element costs-per-unit (column 8 of 9-by-4 layout) and totalling products.

(*c*) This loss value is divided equally between all good completed units, abnormal loss units and if, but only if, the work in progress lies beyond the point of loss, the work-in-progress units. (All units, not just effective units, are counted, since each unit passing the point of loss shares equally in this loss regardless of the degree of completion.) The resulting "cost-per-unit loss" figure is added to the total cost-per-unit (column 8) to give the final cost-per-unit figure. This figure is then used to value the completed good units.

(*d*) The value of the abnormal loss is found by multiplying the *effective* abnormal loss units by the relevant element costs-per-unit (column 8), totalling the products and adding a full "cost-per-unit loss" charge for each abnormal unit lost.

(*e*) Work-in-progress is valued as usual, but if it lies *beyond* the point of loss, then in addition each unit is given a full "cost-per-unit loss" charge.

For example, keeping the data used in previous computations above (*e.g.* in **19** and **16**), assume also that the lost units completion was: materials 50%, labour 25%, overheads 25% and the scrap value of lost units was £1 each.

A comparison of the completion figures of work in progress and lost units clearly indicates that the units in progress lie *beyond* the loss point.

Cost Element	Cost	Complete Units *	Work in progress			Normal Loss			Abnormal Loss			Total Effective units	CPU	Values		
			Units	%	Effective units	Units	%	Effective units	Units	%	Effective units			Normal loss	Abnormal loss	W.I.P
	£												£	£	£	£
Previous process cost	5000	500	400	100	400	60	100	60	40	100	40	1000	5·000	300	200	2000
Materials	1000	500	400	75	300	60	50	30	40	50	20	850	1·176	35	23	353
Labour	2500	500	400	50	200	60	25	15	40	25	10	725	3·448	52	34	690
Overheads	1500	500	400	25	100	60	25	15	40	25	10	625	2·400	36	24	240
	10,000												12·024	423	281	3283
Scrap: 100 units at £1	−100													−60	−40	
Total	£9900												12·024	363	241	3283
													0·386			
Final CPU £													12·410			
Charge for lost units: Abnormal loss 40 units at £0·386															15	
W.I.P. 400 units at £0·386																154
															£256	£3437

Normal loss of £363 shared equally between all units that passed the loss point, *i.e.* all units except normal loss units.

$$\therefore \text{ CPU loss } = \frac{363}{1000 - 60} = £0{\cdot}386$$

Check:		£
Value of completed units = 500 × £12·410	=	6205
Value of abnormal units transferred to Abnormal loss A/c	=	256
Value of work in progress	=	3437
		£9898
Total cost was		£9900

* If units are lost before completion, the costs incurred relate only to partial completion, so this column records *fully* completed units only. Extra columns are added to the 9-by-4 layout to record normal and abnormal units lost (*see* 22).

FIG. 15.—*Process cost computations: units lost part-way through the process*

∴ Normal loss = 6% of all units beyond loss point = 6% 1000 = 60 units.

∴ Abnormal loss = 100 − 60 = 40 units.

The layout and computations in this instance are shown in Fig. 15.

PROCESS COST BOOK-KEEPING

23. Basic form. Process cost book-keeping is virtually the same as that of job costing except for the following details:

(*a*) *A Process Account* (or number of such accounts) takes the place of the Work-in-Progress Account.
(*b*) To this Process Account are debited *all* materials and labour costs (direct and indirect) appertaining to the process, together with direct expenses and an allotment of overheads, *i.e.* the account is in fact a cost centre account and is charged with all direct cost-centre costs plus a share of the indirect costs.

The Process Account is, of course, credited with the value of completed units transferred, and the value of units in progress is carried down.

24. Units column. It is a feature of accounts relating to process costing that they show a column for units as well as value. The two unit columns (debit and credit) must balance.

25. Scrap. Scrap sales are usually credited to the Process Account. If, however, abnormal losses are computed, then only the sales of normal scrap are credited, the scrap sales of the abnormal loss being credited to the Abnormal Loss Account.

26. Abnormal Loss Account. The operation of this account is simply:

(*a*) Debit cost of abnormal loss (prior to scrap sales deduction).
(*b*) Credit scrap sales.
(*c*) Write off balance to Profit and Loss as an abnormal cost.

27. Process cost accounts illustrated. To illustrate process accounts, the process costs detailed in 22 and in Fig. 15 are shown as book-keeping entries below. It should be appreciated that the data in Fig. 15 appear in the form of practical working sheets, and the accounting entries given in the following example would be picked up from such sheets.

Process Account

	Units	£		Units	£
Transferred from previous process	1,000	5,000	Transferred to next process	500	6,205
Materials	—	1,000	Abnormal loss to Abnormal loss A/c	40	298*
Labour	—	2,500	Normal loss, scrap sales	60	60
Overheads	—	1,500	Work in progress *c/d*	400	3,437
	1,000	£10,000		1,000	£10,000
W.I.P. *b/d*	400	£3,437			

* This figure is the value of the abnormal units lost (£256) with their scrap sales value (£40) written back. In addition, a £2 adjustment to allow for rounding in the working sheet (Fig. 15) has been made.

Abnormal Loss Account

	Units	£		Units	£
Process Account, abnormal loss	40	298	Scrap sales, abnormal units	40	40
			Net loss to Profit and Loss A/c	—	258
	40	298		40	298

28. Abnormal gain. It should be remembered that in the case of abnormal gains the scrap sales value of the full normal loss is *still* credited to the Process Account, the difference between this and the actual scrap sales received being debited to the Abnormal Loss Account (which should now take the name Abnormal Gain Account).

For example, if the actual loss in the Process Account above (27) had only been 50 units, *i.e.* abnormal gain of 10 units, the book-keeping entries would have been:

(*a*) Dr. Cash Account 50 units at £1 £50
Dr. Abnormal Gain Account 10 units at £1 £10
(*i.e.* scrap value of the 10 units which were *not* scrapped)
Cr. Process Account 60 units at £1 £60
(*i.e.* scrap value of the normal loss)

(*b*) Dr. Process Account 10 units at £12* each £120
Cr. Abnormal Gain Account £120
Transfer if gain to Abnormal Gain Account

The Abnormal Gain Account would, therefore, ultimately appear so:

Abnormal Gain Account

	Units	£		*Units*	£
Process A/c, units not lost	10	10	Process A/c, cost of units gained at £12*	10	120
Net gain to Profit and Loss A/c		110			
	10	£120		10	£120

* This value is assumed since the change in the number of lost units changes all the figures in Fig. 15. (Note, for example, that there are now 550 completed units, and that columns for computing effective abnormal loss units are not needed since the 10 units abnormal gain are fully completed, not partially completed.)

PROGRESS TEST 12

Principles

1. Distinguish carefully between output, operating and process costing. (**1, 2, 6**)

2. Give examples of operating cost units. (**3**)

3. What entries are found in an Abnormal Gain Account? (**28**)

Practice

4. A product passes through two processes, A and B, in turn. From the following information compute the cost per unit of the good finished production:

	A	*B*
Material input	£5,221	Output from A
Process labour and overheads	£4,650	£10,480
Good units produced	2,247	1,802
Units scrapped (and scrap values)	360 at £1·50 each	445 at £2 each

5. The following figures relate to a single industrial process:

Quantity of work in process at commencement: 8000 units
Costs of work in process at commencement:

Material:	£29,600
Wages:	£6,600
Overhead:	£5,800

During the period under review, a further 32,000 units were introduced, and the additional costs were:

material: £112,400; wages: £33,400; overhead: £30,200.

At the end of the period, 28,000 units were fully processed, and 12,000 units remained in process. This closing stock was complete as regards material cost, and one-third complete as regards wages and overhead.

Using the average method of valuation, tabulate these production and cost figures to give quantities, unit values, and total values for completed output, and for each of the three elements comprising the closing work in process.

Attention should be paid to the form of presentation.

(*I.C.W.A.*)

6. Using the information given in question 5 above, recompute the cost per unit of the completed units and the value of the closing work in process if 8000 units are lost at the end of the process.

CHAPTER XIII

WASTE, SCRAP, BY- AND JOINT PRODUCTS

Waste, scrap, by- and joint products: these are terms of classification of materials unavoidably produced in manufacturing that rise in an ascending sequence from waste with no value to joint products with considerable value. There are no sharp distinctions between these categories: they shade imperceptibly into each other. What is called scrap in one factory is called a by-product in another. This means that there can be no hard-and-fast rules regarding the treatment accorded to each category. Common sense and a due regard for the circumstances are what are required, and the student should keep this in mind.

WASTE AND SCRAP

1. Waste. *Waste* is material arising in production that has little or no value. Usually waste is physically disposed of in the easiest and cheapest manner consistent with legal requirements. For example, gas produced in the refining of petroleum is burnt, and many liquid wastes are poured into adjacent rivers. If the waste has any sale value at all, then the small amount received is simply rated as "other income." There are no cost records in connection with waste.

2. Scrap. *Scrap* is material that can no longer be used for its original purpose, *e.g.* off-cuts or broken parts.

Any scrap may be dealt with by one of the following three methods:

(*a*) Sales of scrap are simply treated as "other income."
(*b*) Sales of scrap are credited to work in progress or the overheads of the department incurring the scrap.
(*c*) If the scrap is kept for an alternative use, then again work in progress or department overheads is credited and the stores debited with the *re-use price*, *i.e.* the worth of the scrap in its new capacity. The deposit of the scrap in the store is recorded by means of a materials returned note, and a scrap stores record card is subsequently raised.

NOTE: If the job (or product) on which the scrap arose can be identified then work in progress and the job are credited. If not, overheads are credited.

3. Spoilage. Spoiled work is a form of scrap and may be so treated. However, if circumstances warrant, the following more detailed treatment may be used:

(*a*) The spoiled work is costed up to the point of rejection. The Work-in-Progress Account is credited with this cost and a Spoilage Account debited.
(*b*) The Spoilage Account is credited with any sales of spoiled materials.
(*c*) The balance in the Spoilage Account is transferred to overheads, or alternatively, written off to Profit and Loss.

4. Rectification. If the spoiled work is to be rectified its cost is transferred to a Rectification Account instead of a Spoilage Account. This Rectification Account is then debited with all costs of rectification and credited with the normal cost value of the rectified work. Any balance is then transferred to overheads or written off to Profit and Loss.

Alternatively, rectification costs can simply be regarded as normal costs of production and debited directly to the Work-in-Progress Account.

BY- AND JOINT PRODUCTS

5. By-products: definition. A *by-product* is any product of value that is produced *incidentally* to the main product. For example, basic slag, a useful fertiliser, is obtained in the process of converting iron into steel.

6. By-products: cost treatment. There are four basic cost treatments of by-products:

(*a*) *Regard as other income.* This method is convenient if the value is small.
(*b*) *By-product value deducted from joint cost.* Here the sales value of the by-product is deducted from the joint cost of producing both main and by-product. The resulting figure is then termed the "main product cost."
(*c*) *By-product sales added to the main product sales.* In this method the combined sales figure for all products is computed and the total costs then deducted, the difference

being the combined profit or loss on operation. This approach is based on the view that since it is physically impossible to produce one product without the other, then accounting statements must reflect this by producing *combined* figures.

(*d*) *By-product is treated as if it were a joint product.*

7. Joint products: definition. *Joint products* are products which by the very nature of the production process cannot be produced separately, and which have equal economic importance. Joint costs are a particular feature of the butchery industry.

8. Joint products: cost treatment. The joint costs incurred in connection with joint products can be dealt with by either of the following two methods, as the examples show:

(*a*) *Apportionment on a physical units basis.* In this method the output relating to all the joint products is measured in some common physical unit (*e.g.* tons, gallons) and the joint costs apportioned in proportion to these outputs.

EXAMPLE

Data: 100 tons of Z is processed to give 70 tons of A and 30 tons of B. Total joint cost (*i.e.* process costs and cost of 100 tons of Z) = £900

Selling prices: A £12 per ton; B £8 per ton.

Method of apportionment (physical units basis):

	Total	*A*		*B*	
Sales	£1080	70 tons at £12 =	£840	30 tons at £8 =	£240
Joint cost	£900	$\frac{70}{100} \times 900$ =	£630	$\frac{30}{100} \times 900$ =	£270
Profit	£180		£210	*Loss*	£30

(*b*) *Apportionment on a sales value basis.* Here the *sales values* of the joint products are used to apportion joint costs. Note that the basis is sales value, *not* selling prices. Use of selling prices results in completely invalid apportionments.

EXAMPLE

Data: As in **8**(*a*) above.

Method of apportionment (sales value basis):

	Total	*A*	*B*
Sales	£1080	70 tons at £12 = £840	30 tons at £8 = £240
Joint cost	£900	$\frac{840}{1080} \times 900$ = £700	$\frac{240}{1080} \times 900$ = £200
Profit	£180	£140	£40

SUBSEQUENT PROCESSES AND COSTS

9. Meaning of "subsequent." It is important to appreciate that the methods discussed relating to by- and joint products relate *only to those parts of production where the products are being treated jointly.* Once a product separates out and becomes independent, it is treated by the usual cost methods. The point of separation is called the *split-off point* and all events that come after the split-off point are termed *subsequent* events. Thus the terms *subsequent processes* and *subsequent costs* relate to processes and costs that come after the split-off point. Events prior to split-off are termed "joint."

10. Subsequent costs. It is very necessary when preparing by-product and joint-product cost statements to ensure that all subsequent costs are charged strictly to the appropriate product, and not regarded as joint. For example, where the by-product value is to be deducted from the joint cost (*see* **6**(*b*) above) the subsequent costs of the by-product must first be deducted from the by-product sales value before attempting to deduct the sales value from the joint cost, *e.g.*:

	£	£
Joint cost		5000
Less by-product value *i.e.:*		
By-product sales	1000	
Less by-product subsequent costs	−200	−800
Main product cost		£4200

Similarly, joint product "apportionment of joint costs on a sales value basis" requires the sales values of joint products to be reduced by all subsequent costs before they are used for apportionment purposes.

11. Selling and distribution costs. It should be noted and remembered that selling and distribution costs are virtually always subsequent costs.

PROGRESS TEST 13

Principles

1. Distinguish between waste, scrap, by-products and joint products. (**1, 2, 5, 7**)
2. How could spoiled work subsequently rectified be dealt with in the cost accounts? (**4**)
3. Give the four methods of cost treatment for by-products. (**6**)
4. What are the two main methods of cost treatment for joint products? (**8**)
5. What are subsequent costs and why are they important? (**10**)

Practice

6. From the following information, find the profit made by each product, apportioning joint costs on a sales value basis:

	A	*B*
Sales	£38,000	£42,000
Selling costs	£5,000	£20,000

Joint costs: Materials £31,200, Process costs £13,800.

PART FOUR

MARGINAL COSTS

CHAPTER XIV

BREAK-EVEN CHARTS

Our attention now turns to decision-making. This involves *predicting* costs, and since all successful prediction depends upon understanding how the thing predicted behaves, we must first make a close study of how costs behave.

On examining cost behaviour one immediate fact is noticed: almost invariably, in any business, an increase in activity will lead to an increase in costs, *i.e.* activity and costs are related. In the absence of actual data one might expect the relationship to be rather loose and of little constancy. In fact, for most practical purposes, providing we remain within the normal range of activity, it is very close; statistically we would say there is a high correlation between the variables.

In this chapter this relationship and its importance in costing is examined.

THEORY OF BREAK-EVEN CHARTS

1. Fixed and variable costs. When relating costs to activity it is clear that it would be extremely useful to be able to classify all costs in the following two categories:

(*a*) *Fixed costs*, which are costs that remain unchanged regardless of changes in the level of activity (*e.g.* debenture interest, rent, rates, audit fees).

NOTE: Students are apt to assume fixed costs are unchangeable. This is wrong. Fixed costs can and often do change (*e.g.* audit fees increase), but such changes are due to *other* causes than changes in activity.

(*b*) *Variable costs*, which are costs that vary in direct proportion to the level of activity (*e.g.* direct materials, direct labour, power).

In practice, it *is* possible to make such a segregation of costs (*see* **5–8** below), and the rest of this section will assume this and develop the important theoretical consequences that follow such a segregation.

2. Graphing costs and income. If *all* costs can be segregated into fixed and variable, then:

$$\textit{Total cost} = \textit{Fixed cost} + \textit{Variable cost}$$

Graphing this equation, costs against activity, the fixed cost curve will show as a horizontal line at a height equal to the fixed cost and the total cost curve as a straight upward-sloping line starting from the fixed cost curve at nil activity (since at nil activity the variable costs must by definition be nil and the total cost, therefore, equal to the fixed cost).

If a third curve representing the income received (sales) at the different activity levels is added, the graph then shows the corresponding profit or loss levels. The sales curve will, of course, start at the origin of the graph, since nil activity leads to nil income.

Such a graph is shown in Fig. 16 and is called a *break-even (B/E) chart*. It should be appreciated that it assumes production and sales are matched, *i.e.* there is no build-up or run-down of stocks. The break-even charts in Figs. 16 and 18–21 are all based on the following data: At 100% activity: Sales £200,000; Fixed costs £90,000 (includes £30,000 depreciation); Variable costs £50,000.

3. Features of a break-even chart. The following features of a break-even chart should be carefully noted (*see* Fig. 16.):

(*a*) *Costs and income.* The total cost, together with the income, can be directly read off the chart for any chosen level of activity.

(*b*) *Profits and losses.* Since the difference between the total cost of operating and the resulting income is the profit (or loss), then the gap between the total cost line and the income line at any level of activity measures the profit (loss) at that level.

(*c*) *Break-even point.* When the income line crosses the total cost line income and total costs are equal then neither a profit nor a loss is made, *i.e.* the enterprise *breaks even.* This point is called the break-even point, and is usually measured in terms of activity (*e.g.* break-even point of Fig. 16 = 60% activity).

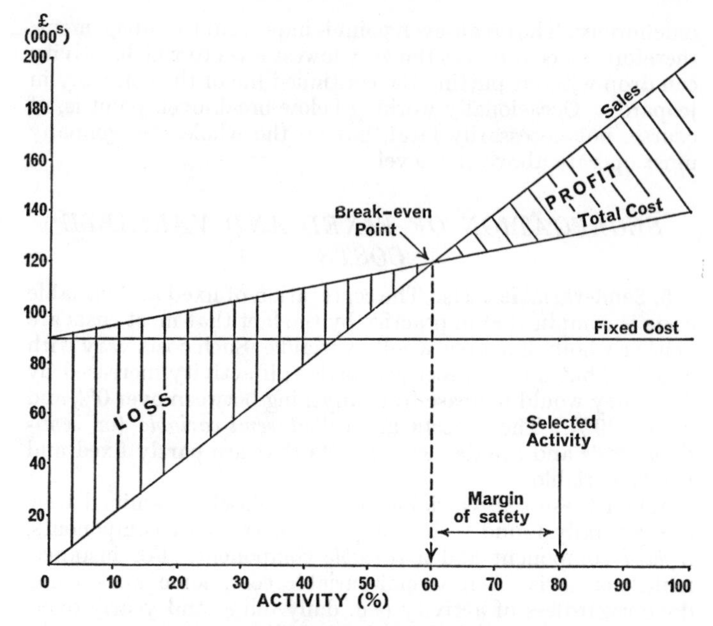

FIG. 16.—*Traditional break-even chart*

Break-even point is measured in terms of activity. This chart shows that if the selected activity is 80%, then:

Expected sales	£160,000
Expected total cost	£130,000
Expected profit	£30,000
Margin of safety	20%

The following data are used in Fig. 16 and in Figs. 18–21:

At 100% activity: Sales £200,000
Fixed costs £90,000 (includes £30,000 depreciation)
Variable costs £50,000

(*d*) *Margin of safety.* This is simply the difference between the break-even point and any activity selected for consideration.

4. The importance of the break-even point. If a company is continually making losses, no matter how small, then its life is definitely limited. On the other hand, if it is making profits, no matter how small, then theoretically it can continue indefinitely. The break-even point is important to management, therefore, since it marks the very lowest level to which activity can drop without putting the continued life of the company in jeopardy. Occasionally working below break-even point is, of course, not necessarily fatal, but on the whole the company must operate above this level.

SEGREGATION OF FIXED AND VARIABLE COSTS

5. Semi-variable costs. The segregation of fixed and variable costs is complicated in practice by the fact that most costs are neither wholly fixed nor wholly variable. Such costs vary with activity, but not in direct proportion; if activity increased by 20% they would increase from anything between over 0% and under 20%. These costs are called *semi-variable* (or *semi-fixed*) *costs* and are defined as costs that are partly fixed and partly variable.

When these semi-variable costs are closely examined they are generally found to be composed of two cost components, a *fixed* component and a *variable* component. For instance, maintenance is often a semi-variable cost, some work being done regardless of activity (*e.g.* daily oiling and yearly overhauls) and other work depending wholly on the extent of the activity (*e.g.* 1000-mile services for vehicles, and breakdowns due to worn-out parts). The former costs are clearly fixed and the latter variable.

If, then, the semi-variable costs can be broken down into these two components, the fixed component can be added to the ordinary fixed costs, and the variable component to the ordinary variable costs. This will eliminate the semi-variables and allow us to proceed on a basis of fixed and variable costs only.

6. Analysis of total cost. In practice, it is virtually impossible to segregate the fixed and variable costs by simple inspection (as was suggested in maintenance above). Such segregation must be done statistically. The following is a simple method of segregation (*see* Fig. 17):

(*a*) Prepare a graph with axes for activity (horizontal) and costs (vertical).

(*b*) Take the figures from a number of past periods and for each period plot the activity and costs as a single point.

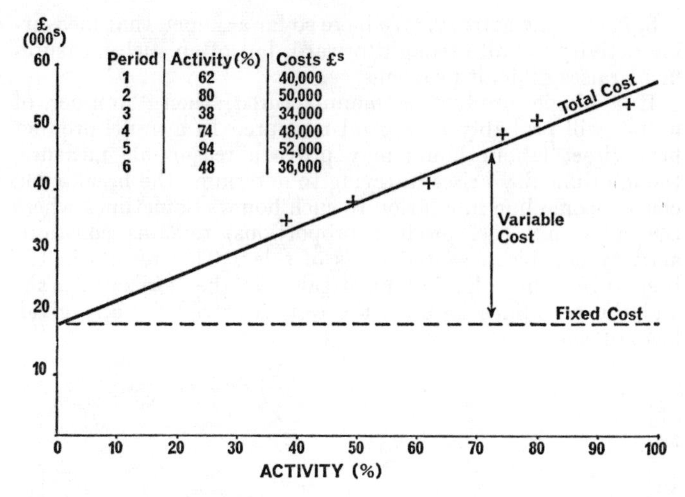

FIG. 17.—*Segregation of fixed and variable costs by scattergraph*

Activity and costs for each period are plotted as single points. The "line of best fit" is the total cost curve. The point where it cuts the cost axis gives the fixed cost.

This graph shows that the fixed cost is approximately £18,000 and the variable cost is £380 per 1% of activity.

(*c*) Draw the "line of best fit" through the points and extend it to the cost axis. This is the *total cost line.*

(*d*) The point where the total cost line cuts the cost axis gives the *fixed cost.*

(*e*) The *variable cost* at any level of activity is given by the difference between the fixed cost and the total cost line.

NOTE: Students who have studied statistics may have realised that we have been constructing a scattergraph and that, indeed, the whole object has been to find the regression line of costs on activity (*see* Chapters XVI and XVII, *Statistics,* W. M. Harper, Macdonald & Evans).

7. Analysis of individual costs. Unfortunately this method gives no indication as to the extent to which *individual* costs are fixed and variable. However, by applying the above procedure to each cost in turn, the fixed and variable values of each cost can be found. This analysis of individual costs is essential if costs are to be controlled (*see* XVII, **18**).

8. Measuring activity. We have so far assumed that measuring activity is quite straightforward, but often such measurement raises difficult problems.

If a single product is manufactured, then "number of units" will probably be a good measure. In a multi-product firm direct labour hours may prove a reasonable measure, though difficulty arises in trying to determine the break-even chart income line in relation to such hours. Sometimes where the sales mix (*i.e.* product proportions) remains constant, activity can be measured in £s of sales. This results in the break-even chart having £s of sales on the horizontal axis, and the cost lines indicate the *costs* involved for any given level of *sales*.

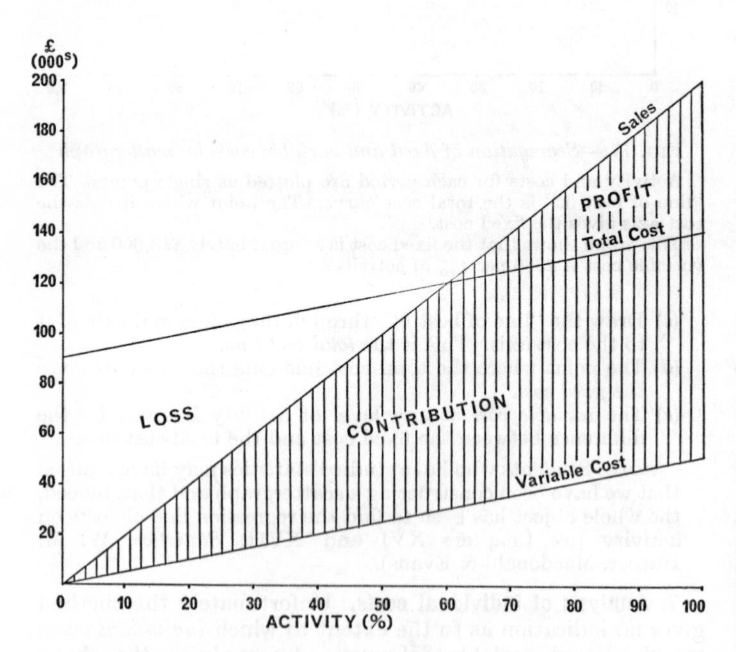

FIG. 18.—*Break-even chart with variable costs at base*

Here the variable cost curve is drawn first. This is an important improvement on the traditional break-even chart shown in Fig. 16, since it provides a direct measure of contribution (*see* XV, 3).

In the case of service enterprises, activity can often be measured by the units selected as being appropriate cost units for the enterprise (XII, 3).

BREAK-EVEN CHART VARIANTS

So far we have only examined the break-even chart in its traditional form. In this section we look briefly at a few break-even chart variants.

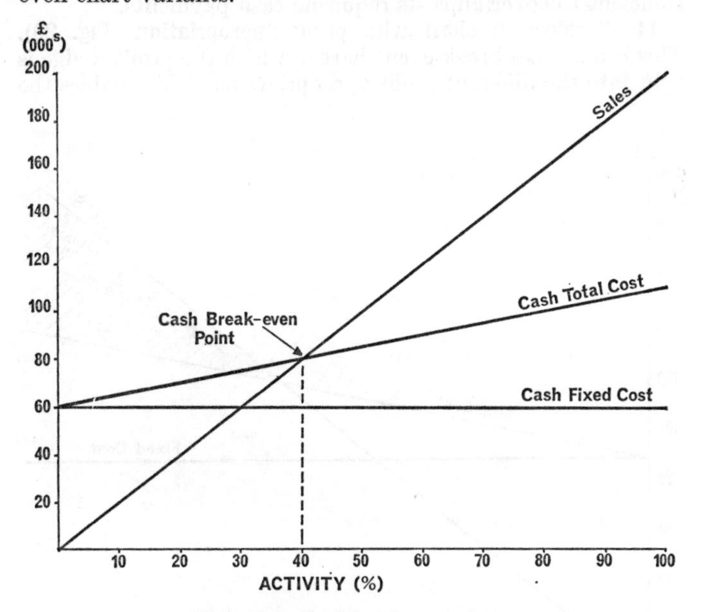

FIG. 19.—*Cash break-even chart*

In this type of break-even chart book charges are ignored, eliminating depreciation and lowering fixed costs. This chart shows that if activity reaches 40%, then enough cash will be received from sales to cover all *cash* costs; this excludes credit considerations, however.

9. Break-even chart: variable costs at base (Fig. 18). Break-even charts can be drawn showing the variable cost and its relation to activity first, and then adding the fixed cost to give the total cost curve. This really is a better form of chart, since it shows as much as the traditional form, and in addition the gap between the variable cost and income curves is a direct measure of contribution (*see* XV, 3).

10. Cash break-even chart (**Fig. 19**). Here only *cash* costs and income are graphed; book charges are ignored. The major effect of this is to eliminate depreciation, which results in a reduction of the fixed (and therefore, total) costs. On such a chart the cash break-even point measures the level of activity required to ensure that the cash received from income is sufficient to cover all costs requiring cash payments.

11. Break-even chart with profit appropriation (**Fig. 20**). This is a normal break-even chart in which the profit wedge is split into the different profit appropriations. This enables the

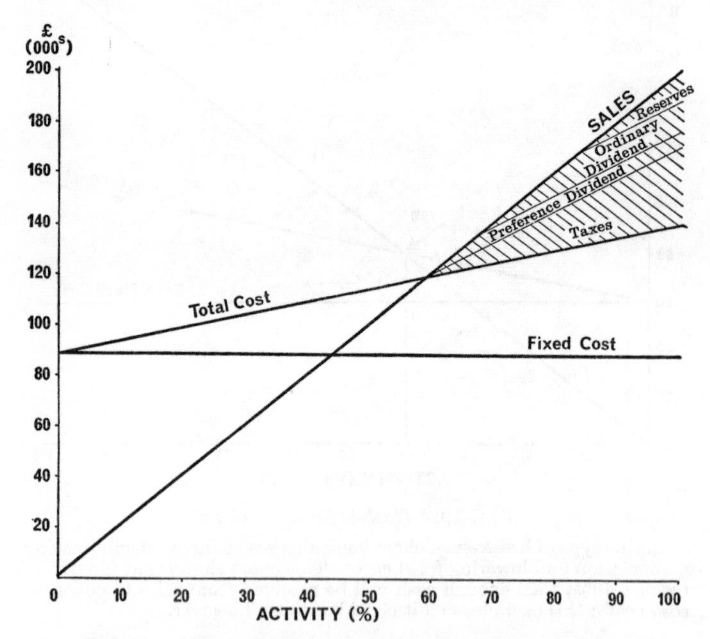

FIG. 20.—*Break-even chart with profit appropriation*

Dividing profit into its different appropriations enables the activity required to attain any selected appropriation result to be read off the chart directly. For purposes of illustration, it is assumed that taxes are £0·50 in the £ (average); Preference Shares are £75,000 at 8%; Ordinary Dividend is 20% maximum on £60,000.

activity required to attain any selected appropriation result to be read off the chart directly (*e.g.* increase in reserves of £4500 after payment of 20% ordinary dividend requires activity of 90%).

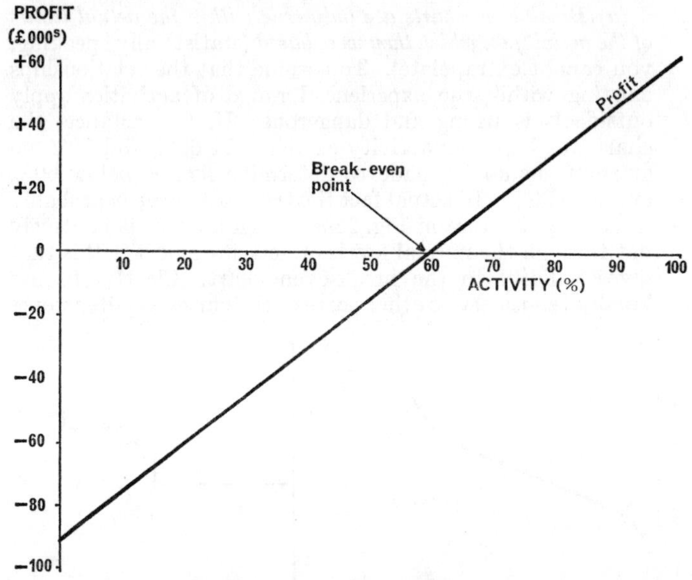

FIG. 21.—*Profit graph*

Profit is plotted directly against activity. At nil activity, therefore, loss equals the fixed cost.

12. Profit graph (Fig. 21). Profit cannot be read *directly* off a break-even chart—it is necessary to deduct the total cost reading from the income reading. A profit graph overcomes this by plotting the profit directly against activity. This means that at nil activity a loss equal to the fixed cost will be suffered (£90,000), and at break-even (*i.e.* nil profit) the profit curve will cut the activity axis (60%).

VALIDITY OF BREAK-EVEN CHARTS

13. Validity of break-even charts. As can be seen, the break-even chart is a useful tool for relating costs and profits to activity, but it does have certain limitations that must always be borne in mind. In practice, before jumping to any conclusions, the validity of any individual chart should be considered in the light of the following considerations:

(a) *Break-even charts are only true within the actual limits of the activity on which they were based* (statistically speaking, you cannot extrapolate). To assume that the relationships existing within the experienced range of activities apply outside it is wrong and dangerous. If, for instance, the chart was based on activity extremes of 60% and 90% no attempt should be made to determine figures below 60% or above 90%. In actual fact the true cost curve is probably something like that in Fig. 22(*a*). Such a curve is relatively flat through the normal levels of activity and it is this that gives validity to the break-even chart. Clearly, to use break-even theory at other parts of the curve is quite wrong.

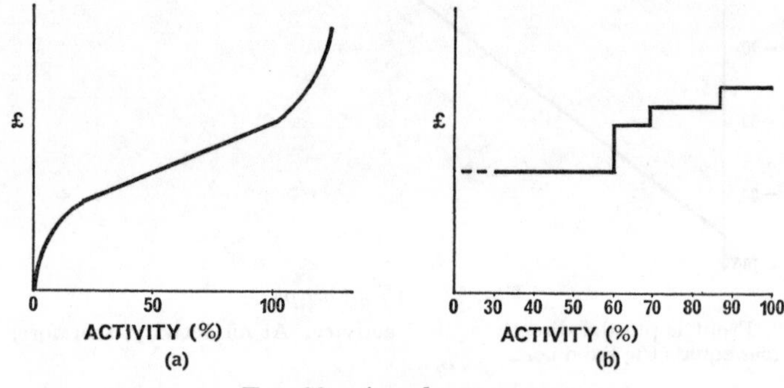

FIG. 22—*Actual cost curves*

In (*a*) the true *total cost curve* is relatively flat only through normal levels of activity. It would be wrong to apply break-even theory outside the normal levels of activity.

In (*b*) a single *fixed cost curve* is seen to increase in steps, as the fixed cost changes at particular activity levels.

(*b*) *Fixed costs may change at different levels of activity.* For up to 80% activity, for instance, one storekeeper in a small company may suffice, but above that level he may need a full-time assistant. The wages of the assistant will therefore increase the fixed cost total.

It should be noted that such fixed costs tend to increase in steps, *i.e.* the increase takes place with a sudden jump at a critical activity level (*see* Fig. 22(*b*)).

(*c*) *Variable costs may not give a straight-line chart.* Attempts to sell more units may well entail transporting the extra units over longer distances to reach more distant markets. Thus distribution costs may increase at a *faster* rate than activity. Overtime and bulk discounts, too, have the effect of putting kinks in the cost line so that the angle of the slope changes. (These factors should not be over-estimated, however. In practice, within the normal range of activities, they are frequently of only slight significance.)

(*d*) *The income curve may bend a little.* It may be necessary to give extra discounts in order to sell extra units, and this will reduce the slope of the income curve at the higher sales level.

(*e*) *The relevant time span affects the chart.* If the chart is based on short-term considerations, then many costs will be fixed that, in a longer time context, would vary to some extent. For instance, if only the next day is being considered, even direct labour becomes a fixed cost, since men cannot be put off (or on) at such short notice. Conversely, a twenty-year time span means even debenture interest may become a variable cost (*i.e.* increased activity: increased loan required). This all means, of course, that different break-even charts are needed when different time spans are under consideration.

(*f*) *Managerial decisions can alter the fixed and variable balance.* Management can, at any time, interchange fixed and variable costs. For instance, they can replace a small labour team, a variable cost, by an automatic machine having mainly fixed costs. This means a break-even chart can be completely out-dated by a management decision, and so usually it is necessary to prepare a new chart every time break-even figures are required.

PROGRESS TEST 14

Principles

1. Define fixed and variable costs. (**1**)
2. How can fixed and variable costs be segregated? (**6, 7**)
3. What are:

   (*a*) Cash break-even charts, (**10**)
   (*b*) Profit graphs? (**12**)

4. A well-known writer commenting on the break-even chart said, "It (the break-even chart) must be applied with an intelligent discrimination, with an adequate grasp of the assumptions underlying the technique and of the limitations surrounding its practical application." Expand on this statement, giving illustrations of the points which the writer had in mind. (13)

(A.C.C.A.)

Practice

5. From the following profit and loss statement, construct a break-even chart and determine:

(*a*) The break-even point.
(*b*) The margin of safety.
(*c*) The sales necessary to obtain a profit of £10,000.

		£	£
Sales			84,000
Costs:	Variable	56,000	
	Fixed	24,000	80,000
	Profit		£4,000

CHAPTER XV

MARGINAL COSTS

Using the knowledge of fixed and variable costs gained in the previous chapter, we are now able to examine marginal costs.

MARGINAL COSTS AND BREAK-EVEN CHART THEORY

1. Definition. A *marginal cost* is the variable cost incurred as a result of undertaking a specified activity. It is clearly comprised in the main of direct materials costs, direct labour costs and direct expenses. Variable overheads are also part of the marginal cost, but these tend to be of much less importance. It should be appreciated, therefore, that marginal costs and direct costs are virtually the same thing and, indeed, in England the terms *marginal costing* and *direct costing* are often regarded as interchangeable.

Economists define marginal cost as the additional cost of producing one additional unit, but manufacturers are usually more interested in the additional cost of a *block* of units, and so cost accountants often give the term this meaning. In practice, the distinction is of little importance, since in most cases the economist's "marginal cost" multiplied by the number of units in the block equals the cost accountant's "marginal cost."

2. Marginal cost per unit. A vitally important feature of marginal cost theory is that *the marginal cost per unit remains unchanged regardless of the level of activity.* A moment's thought shows this is fairly obvious: the marginal cost of a unit of production will involve the direct material, labour and expense to make that unit, and since each unit will require the same material, labour and expense for its production, then these costs will remain the same regardless of the number of units produced.

For example, if a desk needed £5 of material and £3 of labour for its construction, then a second desk would also need £5 of material and £3 of labour, *i.e.* the marginal cost of

£8 per unit would remain unchanged. (It is assumed that material and labour are the only marginal costs here.)

3. Contribution. *Contribution* is the difference between sales and the marginal cost of sales. Like marginal cost per unit, *the contribution per unit remains unchanged regardless of the level of activity.* This follows from the fact that within a normal range of activity the selling price per unit does not alter and since the marginal cost per unit does not alter either, then the difference, the contribution per unit, also remains unchanged. (Selling prices tend to remain steady, since the normal variations in activity of a single business will not significantly alter the balance of supply and demand.)

4. Contribution and profit. If we assume the desk above has a selling price of £12, then since its marginal cost is £8, there is a contribution of £4. This means that every time we make and sell a desk we receive £12 from the customer, pay £8 for the material and labour and have £4 over. This £4 is not, of course, profit, since the fixed costs remain to be paid. Indeed, until we have sufficient bundles of £4 to pay all these fixed costs there can be no profit. For instance, if the fixed costs are £400, then we need to make and sell 100 desks before we have enough £4 bundles to pay the fixed costs. Note that:

(*a*) At this level we break-even and this, then, must be the break-even point.

(*b*) If we make and sell one desk more the £4 contribution received is no longer required for the fixed costs, and is therefore all profit.

This means that *above the break-even point all the contribution is profit.*

5. P/V ratio. It should be appreciated that sales and contribution are in direct proportion to each other, *i.e.* if the sales increase by 20%, then the contribution increases by 20%, etc. For instance, if we sell 10 desks our sales are £120 and our contribution is £40. Increase sales by 20% (*i.e.* 2 desks) and our contribution rises to £48, *i.e.* by 20%.

Since sales and contribution are always in direct proportion then dividing one by the other will always give the same figure, *e.g.* contribution divided by sales in the above examples gives:

$$\frac{4}{12}; \frac{40}{120}; \frac{48}{144}; \text{ all of which cancel down to } \tfrac{1}{3}.$$

This fraction is called the *P/V ratio* and can always be calculated so:

$$P/V\ ratio = \frac{Contribution}{Sales}$$

This ratio is useful inasmuch as it enables the contribution to be quickly calculated from any given level of sales (or vice versa), since the formula can be turned round to *contribution = sales × P/V ratio* (*e.g.* given a sales figure of £180, the contribution will be £180 × $\frac{1}{3}$ = £60).

6. Break-even chart mathematics. The break-even chart shows graphically the relationship between fixed costs, variable (marginal) costs, profits, losses, the break-even point and activity. These relationships can also be shown mathematically through a series of equations such as the following, where *C = contribution*, *F = fixed cost* and *B/E = break-even*:

(*a*) $Sales - Marginal\ cost\ of\ sales = C$

(*b*) $Profit\ (loss) = C - F$

(*c*) B/E (measured in units of production) $= \dfrac{F}{C\ per\ unit}$

(*d*) B/E (measured in £s) $= F \times \dfrac{Sales}{C} = \left(F \times \dfrac{1}{P/V\ ratio}\right)$

(*e*) $P/V\ ratio = \dfrac{C}{Sales}$

Given sufficient data, use of the above formulae will enable any missing figures to be found.

EXAMPLE 1.

Data:

B/E = 1000 units
Sales = 1500 units at £6 each
Fixed cost = £2000

Find the marginal cost per unit and the profit (using formulae (*c*) and (*b*) above).

Method:

$$\text{B/E (units)} = \frac{\text{F}}{\text{C}\ per\ unit}$$

$$\therefore\ 1000 = \frac{2000}{\text{C}\ per\ unit}$$

$$\therefore\ \text{C}\ per\ unit = \frac{2000}{1000} = £2$$

And since selling price is £6, the marginal cost per unit must be:

$$6 - 2 = \underline{\underline{£4}}$$

Also total contribution must be 1500 × £2 = £3000

$$\therefore \textit{Profit} = C - F$$
$$= 3000 - 2000 = \underline{\underline{£1000}}$$

EXAMPLE 2.

Data:

Fixed cost = £4000
Profit = £1000
Break-even is at £20,000

Find sales and marginal cost of sales (using formulae (*b*), (*d*) and (*a*) above).

Method:

$$\textit{Profit} = C - F$$
$$\therefore 1000 = C - 4000$$
$$\therefore C = £5000$$

$$\text{And B/E} = F \times \frac{\textit{Sales}}{C}$$

$$\therefore 20{,}000 = 4000 \times \frac{\textit{Sales}}{5000} = \frac{4}{5}\,\textit{Sales}$$

$$\therefore \textit{Sales} = \frac{5}{4} \times 20{,}000 = \underline{\underline{£25{,}000}}$$

$$\text{Also } \textit{Sales} - \textit{Marginal cost of sales} = C$$
$$\therefore 25{,}000 - \textit{Marginal cost of sales} = 5000$$
$$\therefore \textit{Marginal cost of sales} = \underline{\underline{£20{,}000}}$$

Despite the simplicity of the formulae used, students are strongly advised to practise using logical argument to solve problems.

NOTE: Using logical argument, one can often use the fact that *the contribution at break-even exactly equals the fixed cost.*

EXAMPLE 3.

Reworking Examples 1 and 2 using logical argument:

1. Now contribution at break-even = fixed cost (*i.e.* contribution exactly covers fixed cost), and since break-even is 1000 units and fixed costs £2000, then £2000 is the contribution from 1000 units.

$$\therefore \text{Contribution per unit} = \frac{2000}{1000} = £2$$

∴ Since selling price is £6, marginal cost must be $6 - 2 =$ £4 per unit.

And also the total contribution from 1500 units at £2 unit is £3000.

Out of this, £2000 fixed costs must be paid leaving profit of £1000.

2. Since the total contribution is made up of fixed cost and profit, then a total contribution of $4000 + 1000 =$ £5000 is obtained here from the level of sales attained.

Now since contribution at break-even equals the fixed cost, then at break-even a contribution of £4000 is obtained from the given break-even sales of £20,000.

Also sales and contributions are in proportion to each other, and so to have lifted the contribution from £4000 to £5000 (*i.e.* a quarter) we must have raised sales by a quarter, that is, from £20,000 to £25,000.

(Alternatively, contribution of £4000 from £20,000 sales gives a P/V ratio of $\frac{4000}{20,000} = \frac{1}{5}$. Therefore sales required to give contribution of 5000 is $5000 \times 5 =$ £25,000.)

And finally, since £5000 of this £25,000 sales is contribution, then the remainder, £20,000, must be the marginal cost of sales.

At this point the student is recommended to attempt questions 1 and 2 in Progress Test 15 (p. 176).

MARGINAL COST STATEMENTS AND ACCOUNTS

7. Cost bases: time and production. So far it has only been stated that variable costs vary in proportion to activity whereas fixed costs remain unchanged. It is important also to appreciate why this is so. Basically it is that individual costs (or parts of costs) are either *time based* or *production based*, *i.e.* they depend for their value on either time or production. For instance, the amount of rent or debenture interest one pays depends upon *how long* one has the use of the premises or the capital. Such costs are independent of production and so, not changing with activity, are the fixed costs. On the other hand, the amount one pays for material depends upon *how much* one uses and time does not come into it. Material costs, therefore, vary with production and so are among the variable (marginal) costs.

It is because nearly all costs (or parts of costs) are either time or production based that they are either fixed or variable.

NOTE: With costs such as debenture interest, when the time-span extends we can ask "how much?" as well as "how long?" since long time spans allow changes in debenture size. Thus debenture interest becomes partly variable. This is why all costs tend to be variable in the long run.

8. Fixed costs and multi-products. It follows, then, that when a factory makes more than one product the fixed costs are found to remain unchanged, not only as regards changes in activity but also as regards changes in the product proportions, since they are affected only by time, not by production. If, for example, a factory made tables and chairs, the fixed cost would remain the same no matter which were made in a specific period, although sales, marginal costs and contributions might vary considerably, depending upon which product was dominant. Under these circumstances, then, it may well be argued that if fixed costs are quite unconnected with production and their amounts quite independent of production there is *no point in apportioning them to products.* Instead products should be identified with the sales, marginal costs and contributions they give rise to, and fixed costs treated as an indivisible over-all charge against the business as a whole.

This viewpoint is the basis of the marginal cost technique.

9. Basic pattern of marginal cost statements. Following this approach through, marginal cost statements adopt a basic pattern that aims at detailing sales, marginal costs and contributions for individual products or cost units, and deducting fixed costs *en bloc* from the over-all contribution to arrive at the profit. This pattern can be shown so:

Marginal cost statement

For each product or cost unit:	Sales (or selling price)	√
	Less Marginal costs	√
	Contribution	√
For the enterprise as a whole:	Total of all contributions	√
	Less Fixed costs	√
	Profit	√

10. Marginal cost statements illustrated. Two uses of marginal cost statements are now illustrated.

(*a*) *The effect of changes in levels of activity.* This is a very simple statement indicating the relationship between profit and activity, a relationship already examined graphically in the form of the break-even chart.

(Selling price £10 unit; marginal cost £6 unit; fixed cost £8,000.)

	Activity			
	1,000 units	*2,000 units*	*3,000 units*	*4,000 units*
Sales	£10,000	£20,000	£30,000	£40,000
Less Marginal costs	6,000	12,000	18,000	24,000
Contribution	£4,000	£8,000	£12,000	£16,000
Less Fixed costs	8,000	8,000	8,000	8,000
Profit	£4,000 Loss	Nil (B/E)	4,000	8,000

(*b*) *Trading results in a three-product factory.*

	Product A (£)		*Product B* (£)		*Product C* (£)		*Total* (£)	
Sales		45,000		40,000		20,000		105,000
Marginal cost:								
Materials	£9,000		£4,000		£2,000		£15,000	
Labour	£10,000		£15,000		£5,000		£30,000	
Variable overheads	£8,000	27,000	£1,000	20,000	£1,000	8,000	£10,000	55,000
Contribution		£18,000		£20,000		£12,000		£50,000
							Fixed costs	30,000
							Profit	£20,000

Note the double columns of figures for each product. This is often a useful device, since the detail can be put in the left-hand column and the right-hand one reserved for the main figures.

Notice that the effect on profit of dropping any one product is simply the reduction of profit by the amount of the contribution lost (assuming neither remaining product is expanded to replace the dropped product). Also the effect of, say, doubling the sales of a product can be seen to result in the doubling of the product contribution, and so the profit increases by exactly this contribution increase.

Thus *a marginal cost statement shows the profitability of different products.* On a total absorption cost statement this factor would not be revealed with such clarity; indeed, such

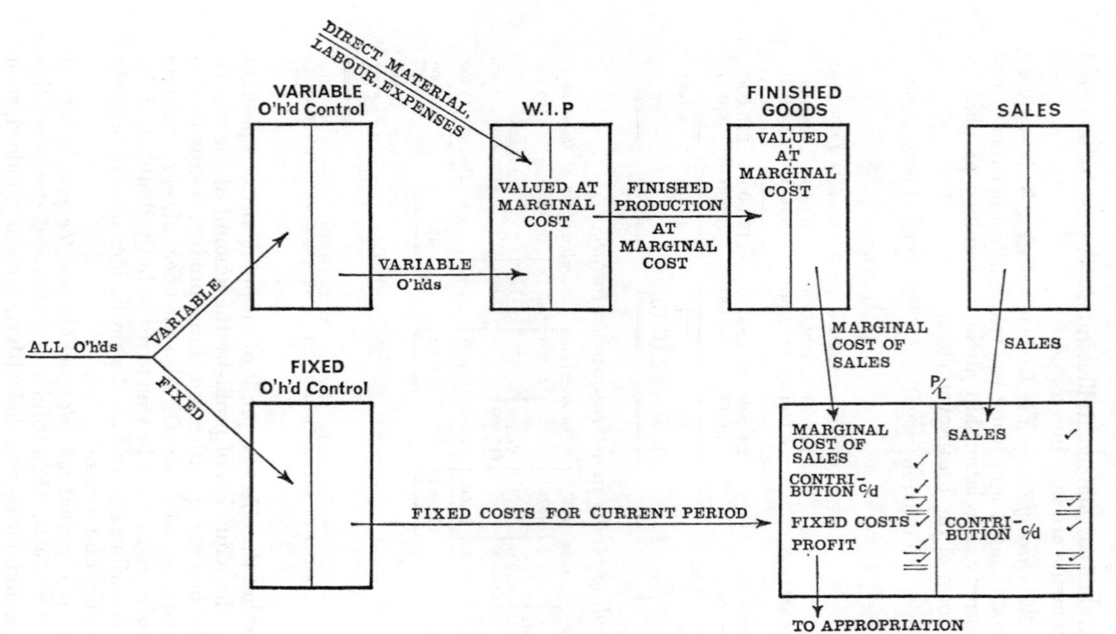

FIG. 23.—*Chart of marginal cost accounting*

This chart indicates how the Overhead, Work-in-Progress, Finished Goods, and Profit and Loss Accounts under marginal cost accounting differ from the same accounts under normal integral accounting (*see* Fig. 11).

a statement could easily reverse the true picture and so totally mislead management. For example, if the fixed costs above were absorbed into products using the percentage direct wages method (*i.e.* 100% direct wages) the "profit" on A and B would be £8000 and £5000 respectively, implying that A was the more profitable product.

11. Marginal cost accounting. Marginal cost accounting differs from the accounting discussed in Chapter XI only as regards the fixed costs. In marginal costing it is argued that since fixed costs are time and not production based, they should be charged against time, *i.e.* written off to Profit and Loss in the period in which they are incurred. They should not under any circumstances be charged to production.

In the accounts this has two effects:

(*a*) Fixed costs are charged to a Fixed Overhead Control Account, and then written off direct to Profit and Loss.
(*b*) Since fixed costs are in no way charged to production, they cannot become part of the production cost, and therefore *stocks are valued at marginal cost only.*

The essential part of a chart of marginal cost accounts is shown diagrammatically in Fig. 23.

MARGINAL COSTING AND DECISION-MAKING

12. Role of marginal costing in decision-making. Decision-making involves essentially a choice between alternatives. Clearly, when evaluating alternatives there is little to be gained by including any factor which is common to all. Indeed, common factors are better excluded altogether, leaving only the *differences* between alternatives to be examined. In this way they can be more effectively compared.

Now in many decisions the fixed costs are the same for all alternatives; only the sales and marginal costs differ. Consequently, a marginal cost statement that excludes the final part detailing the fixed costs is very suitable for many decision-making situations.

13. Acceptance of a special contract. One type of decision often to be made is the acceptance or otherwise of a special contract under which units are sold below normal selling prices. In such circumstances the contribution is the relevant figure, since the whole of any contribution must be extra profit if the enterprise is over the break-even point, or a reduction of the loss if below this point. Either way the enterprise is better off by the amount of the contribution. From this we see that *it is always better to take a special contract if there is some contribution, no matter how small, than to reject the contract and have no contribution.* Note, however, two qualifications to this:

(*a*) It is assumed that the fulfilment of the contract *will not affect normal sales.* Nothing is gained by selling units at £4 which otherwise would have been sold at £5.

(*b*) It is also assumed that *nothing better is likely to come along.* A business that fills its workshops with many low-contribution contracts and then has to turn away high-contribution work is not making the best decisions. Whether or not anything better is likely to come along is a judgment that must be made by management itself.

14. Key factors. There is always something that limits an enterprise from achieving an unlimited profit. Usually this is sales, *i.e.* the enterprise cannot sell as much as it would like. Sometimes, however, an enterprise can sell all that it can produce, but output is limited by the scarcity of some economic "factor of production," *e.g.* materials, labour, machine capacity or cash. Such a factor is called a *key factor*; (alternatively, *limiting factor of production*).

15. Contribution per unit of key factor. If a key factor is operating, then it is important that the enterprise makes as much profit as it can each time it uses up one of its scarce units of key factor. Since fixed costs do not alter, this means *maximising the contribution per unit of key factor.*

EXAMPLE

Data: Materials are limited to 1000 tons. A choice must be made between two jobs requiring such materials, A and B. Job details are as follows:

	Job A	*Job B*
Selling price	£300	£200
Marginal cost	£100	£120
Contribution	£200	£80
Tons required	4	1

Method: On the face of it A is in all respects the more profitable; it has higher selling price, lower marginal cost and a contribution over twice that of B. But in using 4 tons of materials it earns a contribution of only £50 a ton, *i.e.* if all jobs were of this type our 1000 tons would allow us to earn only £50,000 contribution. B, on the other hand, earns a contribution of £80 a ton, so jobs of this type would allow us to earn £80,000 contribution. Type B jobs are therefore more profitable in these circumstances, and so should be selected in preference to type A jobs.

Where a key factor is involved, therefore, the work that gives *the highest contribution per unit of key factor used should be chosen.*

16. Make-or-buy decisions. Another type of decision, called a *make-or-buy decision,* arises when the product being manufactured has a component part that can either be made within the factory or bought from an outside supplier. On the face of it, since the only extra cost to make the part is the marginal cost, then the amount by which this falls below the supplier's price is the saving that arises on making. However, this is a deception, as it is also important to consider what work would have been carried out using the relevant facilities if the part had not been made. This is necessary, since if making the part involves putting aside other work, then the business will *lose the contribution this work would otherwise have earned.* Such a loss of contribution must be added to the marginal cost of the part.

NOTE: In economics such a cost is called an *opportunity cost.* An opportunity cost is one that is represented not by money paid out but by the loss of income that would otherwise be obtained (*see* I, 5).

To summarise, in a make-or-buy decision compare:

(*a*) the supplier's price; with
(*b*) the marginal cost of making, plus the loss of contribution of displaced work.

This loss of contribution is usually best found by use of the contribution per unit of key factor (*see* **15**).

EXAMPLE

Data: An X takes 20 hours to process on machine 99. It has a selling price of £100 and a marginal cost of £60. A Y (a component part used in production) could be made on machine 99 in 3 hours for a marginal cost of £5. The supplier's price is £10. Should one make or buy Ys?

Method: Now contribution per X = 100 − 60 = £40.

∴ Contribution earned per hour on machine 99 is $\frac{40}{20}$ = £2. If then a Y is made in 3 hours, £6 contribution is lost.

∴ Full cost to make Y = £5 + £6 = £11.

This is more than the supplier's price of £10, and so it is better to buy than make.

This decision assumes that machine 99 is working to full capacity and machine time then, is the key factor.

17. Differential costs. Decisions sometimes arise in which the fixed costs *do* alter between alternatives. For example, a decision may need to be made as to whether or not a department should be closed. Marginal costing shows a departmental contribution of £4000, so on the face of it profits would drop by this amount if the department was closed. However, certain fixed costs could well be saved by such a closure, *e.g.* departmental supervision, clerical staff and plant depreciation. If this amounts to over £4000, then clearly the fixed-cost savings exceed the departmental contribution, and the department should therefore be closed.

The fixed costs brought into the calculations must, of course, only be those which are incurred wholly on account of the existence of the department, *i.e.* "direct" fixed costs, and which would no longer be incurred if the department closed. These clearly will not include any apportioned overheads such as rent, general administration salaries, etc. These former costs are sometimes called *identifiable fixed costs* and in cost statements should be shown as a deduction from the contribution of the department concerned so that only the net contribution is shown as the amount the department contributes to the enterprise as a whole.

This costing technique can be applied to other types of decisions, changing machines, for example. It is sometimes referred to as *differential costing* and can be defined generally as a cost technique in which the differences between alternatives is examined. It differs from marginal costing in that it takes into consideration identifiable fixed costs.

18. Profit planning. Very often an enterprise plans its sales, costs and activity, and then computes what profit will emerge.

In profit planning this is reversed; the enterprise decides what profit it wants (which is usually based on a reasonable return on capital employed) and then works *backwards* to see what sales, costs and activity are needed to produce that profit.

In practice, certain factors are usually fixed before planning begins (*e.g.* capacity may be limited, or selling prices determined by competitors' activities) and then profit planning indicates the value that the remaining factors must take to achieve the profit target.

EXAMPLE

Data: A company manufacture a single product having a marginal cost of £0·75 a unit. Fixed costs are £12,000. The market is such that up to 40,000 units can be sold at £1·50 a unit, but any additional sales must be made at £1·00 a unit. There is a planned profit of £20,000. How many units must be made and sold?

Method:

Planned profit (£20,000) + Fixed costs (£12,000) = Planned contribution.

∴ Planned contribution = £32,000.

Now the first 40,000 units give a contribution of 40,000 × £(1·50 − 0·75) = £30,000.

This is £2,000 contribution short of plan.

Since the contribution per unit on sales over 40,000 units is £(1·00 − 0·75) = £0·25, then the number of additional units needed to give a contribution of £2,000 = $\frac{£2,000}{£0{\cdot}25}$ = 8,000.

∴ Total number of units to be made and sold = 40,000 + 8000 = 48,000 units.

19. A fundamental decision-making principle. A number of variations of the marginal cost technique have now been examined, and the student may feel a little bewildered and be in need of some way of determining which one he should use in any given situation. There is, of course, no simple answer, but if he bears in mind that *when comparing alternatives it is necessary to introduce every factor that has an effect on the enterprise's over-all profit* (*e.g.* extra contribution; use of units of a factor in short supply; contribution loss from work displaced; changes in fixed costs), then his own common sense should enable him to pick his way successfully. There are no rules, and the only guide is a sound appreciation of just what is required.

MARGINAL COSTING VERSUS TOTAL ABSORPTION COSTING

For many years the more progressive cost accountants have argued that marginal costing is the correct technique and that total absorption costing is obsolete. In this section the two techniques are contrasted.

20. Advantages of marginal costing. The following advantages are claimed for marginal costing over total absorption costing:

(*a*) No attempt is made to relate fixed costs, which are incurred on a time basis, with products, since such costs are independent of production. This avoids complicated and misleading statements.

(*b*) Under- or over-absorption of overheads cannot arise.

(*c*) Fictitious profits cannot arise due to fixed costs being absorbed and capitalised in unsellable stock (*e.g.* assume 100 units are produced for a cost, all fixed, of £1000, *i.e.* £10 a unit. 20 only are sellable and are sold for £15 each. If the remainder are valued in stock at £10 each the Profit and Loss Account will show a profit of £100, when a loss of £700 would be a truer figure.)

(*d*) Marginal costing avoids the false sense of security that total absorption costing can give when all products show a satisfactory profit, but owing to the activity level being lower than that planned, such profits are unknowingly being more than offset by under-absorbed overheads.

(*e*) Contribution is a more correct measure of the effect of *making and selling a product* than the product profit figure obtained from total absorption costing, which is not only incorrect when the activity level is different from that planned but may even indicate quite the reverse of the true situation.

(*f*) Marginal costing is simpler and less ambiguous than total absorption costing, and avoids the complexities of apportionments which are really only arbitrary divisions of indivisible fixed costs.

(*g*) If a variety of products is offered to customers, marginal costing enables the planned profit to be made (assuming the activity is as planned) regardless of sales mix (*e.g.* if a contribution of £1 per hour is obtained in respect of all products, then if the planned activity is reached, the contribution and hence the profit obtained will be that planned).

(*h*) Pricing can be done more intelligently since the contribution to be added onto any cost unit will:

(*i*) be based on the total contribution required from all production (*i.e.* planned profit and fixed costs);

(*ii*) take account of the use made by the unit of any relevant key factor.

21. Advantages of total absorption costing. The following advantages are claimed for total absorption costing over marginal costing:

(*a*) Since production cannot be achieved without incurring fixed costs, such costs *are* related to production, and total absorption costing attempts to make an allowance for this relationship. This avoids the danger inherent in marginal costing of creating the illusion that fixed costs have nothing to do with production.

(*b*) Fictitious losses cannot arise as they can in marginal costing owing to fixed costs being written off in a period when good, merchantable goods are produced and stocked for sale in a later season (*e.g.* fireworks).

(*c*) Use of total absorption costing avoids the stock valuation anomalies associated with marginal costing. For example, a manufacturer may pay a fixed monthly rental for a machine. Under marginal costing such a charge would not be included in the stock value. If, though, he renegotiates to pay a rental based on his *production*, then this charge will be included in the stock value. Thus, although an article remains exactly the same, and is made in exactly the same way, nevertheless under marginal costing its stock value increases.

(*d*) When pricing, finding the marginal cost alone is not sufficient, since it is essential that the added contribution should relate to fixed costs; otherwise an enterprise with a high fixed cost could set prices that gave too small a contribution and so resulted in an inadvertent loss. In total absorption costing an addition is automatically made based on the utilisation of the fixed cost facilities by the different products.

NOTE: This claim is valid only if the cost accountant is not setting prices as outlined in **20**(*h*) but is simply adding an arbitrary contribution to the marginal cost.

(*e*) Use of marginal costing in pricing tends to lead to low prices being quoted at a time of slack demand. Customers may then expect the business to maintain such prices on future occasions.

(*f*) If a wide range of goods involving differing fixed cost requirements are offered to customers and no pre-knowledge of likely demand is available, then total absorption costing enables a more consistent profit to be earned.

NOTE: This situation differs from that referred to in **20**(*g*) in that here fixed costs are expected to change with different product mixes.

22. Choice of technique. The paragraphs above (**20, 21**) indicate that the choice of technique is not easy to make. Unfortunately, no rules can be given; all that can be said is that the technique which is most appropriate to the circumstances should be chosen.

At the heart of the controversy lies the implication that since fixed costs are incurred on a time basis and are irrespective of the volume of production, they cannot form part of the individual costs of units produced. This is not so. Without the fixed costs the units could not be produced at all. The relationship between fixed costs and cost units may be tenuous and changing, but the problem cannot be solved by denying the relationship entirely.

In the ultimate analysis the two techniques are not really contradictory; they simply represent the extremes of this elusive relationship, and cost accountants serve management best by ensuring that their statements reflect the appropriate relationship existing in any given circumstances.

PROGRESS TEST 15

Practice

1. Find the break-even point and the profit from sales of £40,000 when: Selling price is £5; marginal cost £3; fixed cost £10,000.

2. Find the profit when: Sales figure is £80,000; marginal cost of sales £60,000; break-even point £60,000 sales.

3. In the materials handling department of a company a task is done manually by operators who can move 1500 pallets per week

each and whose wages are £13 per week each. The cost of expendable supplies in this task is £2 per 1000 pallets.

As a result of a work-study investigation it is found that the task can be undertaken by a piece of equipment costing £1000, with a capacity of up to 6000 pallets per week. This equipment involves the following costs:

Operator's pay	£16 per week
Maintenance	£3 ,, ,,
Operating costs	£1 per 1000 pallets
Expendable supplies	£2 ,, ,, ,,

Company policy will be to depreciate this equipment on a 5-year straight-line basis of 50 weeks per annum.

You are required to calculate in pallets the weekly level of activity beyond which there is a cost saving to the company by having the task done by use of the equipment instead of manually. Show your workings. (*I.C.W.A.*)

4. The following information is available for XY Ltd which manufactures a standard product:

Quarterly budget for each of quarters 3 and 4 of 1963:

		Total		Per unit
		£		£
Sales (30,000 units)		30,000		1·00
Production cost of sales:				
Variable	£19,500		£0·65	
Fixed overhead	£6,000	25,500	£0·20	0·85
		4,500		0·15
Selling and administration cost (fixed)		2,100		0·07
Profit		£2,400		£0·08

Actual production, sales and stocks in units for quarters 3 and 4 of 1963:

	Quarter 3	Quarter 4
Opening stock	—	6,000
Production	34,000	28,000
Sales	28,000	32,000
Closing stock	6,000	2,000

You are required to show in tabular form trading and profit and loss accounts for each of the quarters:

(*a*) when fixed production overhead is absorbed into the cost of the product at the normal level shown in the quarterly budget;

(*b*) when fixed production overhead is not absorbed into the cost of the product, but is treated as a cost of the period and charged against sales.

(*N.B.*—The bases of calculations should be shown.) (*I.C.W.A.*)

5. The Mix Chemical Company Ltd. produces joint products A, B and C from input material X. From 150 lb of X which costs 33½p per lb, 50 lb of A, 45 lb of B and 45 lb of C can be produced, The 10 lb of process scrap is sold at 10p per lb, as can be any of the finished products which cannot be disposed of on the open market. The standard costs and revenues of A, B and C are as follows:

Joint Products A, B and C—Standard Cost and Revenue Table

	A		*B*		*C*	
Quantity		50 lb		45 lb		45 lb
		£		£		£
Standard Revenue		50·0		55·0		35·0
Less Joint Costs:						
Material	17·5		19·25		12·25	
Labour	12·5	30·0	11·25	30·5	11·25	23·5
		20·0		24·5		11·5
Less Direct Costs:						
Finishing	5·0		5·0		1·0	
Packing	5·0		4·5		4·5	
Distributing	5·0	15·0	4·5	14·0	4·5	10·0
Standard Direct Profit		5·0		10·5		1·5
Standard Cost per lb		0·90		0·99		0·74

Note: Joint Cost basis of allocation—Materials allocated on standard revenue; Labour allocated on standard weight.

The company has received, from its biggest customer, an additional order of 10,000 lb per annum of product A at a price of 95p per lb. You have been asked to advise as to whether this order should be accepted, and if so what will be the additional profit, and what is the minimum price the company could accept so that a loss would not be made? The answers to these questions have to be made under each of the following assumptions:

(*a*) At present because of the demand for B and C, 12,000 lb per annum of product A has to be sold as scrap because it cannot be sold on the open market.

(*b*) The present demand for product A is such that all of production of B and C cannot be sold on the open market and has to be scrapped.

(*c*) The whole of the present production is being sold on the open market, and there is an unlimited demand, at standard selling price, for product C, but it is estimated that only an additional 6750 lb of B can be sold annually on the open market.

Interest charges can be ignored.

(*A.C.C.A.* Adapted)

6. The Chairman of a company faces a difficult board meeting. Last period the company lost £2000 and the Chairman's four colleagues on the Board are far from happy. Each has a pet proposal, he would like to see adopted, at the expense if need be, of his colleagues. The only thing they are all agreed on is that they should have a profit target of £4000 per period.

To assist in evaluating each director's proposal the Chairman has invited you to the meeting, so as to be able to give figures implied by the different proposals. You know that the Company has a fixed cost of £20,000 per period, and a variable cost per unit of £5 up to 12,000 units, and £6 for units in excess of 12,000. Last period 9000 units were sold.

Director	*Proposal*	*Chairman requests:*
A	Improve package of product at a cost of £0·50 a unit and so increase sales.	Percentage increase in sales required.
B	Spend £2000 on advertising.	Percentage increase in sales required.
C	Drop the selling price by £0·50 a unit.	Percentage increase in sales required.
D	Buy more efficient machinery. This will cut the variable cost per unit by £1 at all levels. Sales to remain as before.	Maximum increase in fixed machine cost per period to justify the proposal.

PART FIVE

COST PLANNING AND CONTROL

CHAPTER XVI

INTRODUCTION TO COST CONTROL

THEORY OF COST CONTROL

1. Cost control. *Control is compelling events to conform to plan.* Cost control may, then, be defined as compelling actual costs to conform to planned costs. This clearly involves:

(*a*) *Planning* costs.
(*b*) *Comparing* actual costs with planned costs.
(*c*) Taking *action* to correct divergencies between planned and actual costs.

Cost control is essentially a *function of management*. It is the cost accountant's task to *assist*, not to carry it out himself.

2. Cost plans. Cost plans can be prepared on two different bases:

(*a*) The costs relating to a *period of time* can be planned.
(*b*) The costs relating to a *cost unit* can be planned.

The former plan is known as a *budget*, and the latter a *standard cost*.

A moment's thought regarding these two bases will show that a budget is the logical plan for control of costs that use time-based, *i.e.* fixed, costs, and that a standard cost is the logical plan for control of costs that are production-based, *i.e.* variable costs. As will be seen in later chapters, current practice tends to allow budgets and standard costs to overlap so that variable costs enter into budgetary control and fixed costs enter into standard cost control. In Chapter XXII (**7–9**) the more modern approach of standard marginal costing is briefly examined, and the student will be able to note that this technique gives a more appropriate division of control work between the two cost bases.

3. Preparing a cost plan. It cannot be emphasised enough that *cost control is a managerial function*, the cost accountant being essentially an assistant. Consequently, when preparing a cost plan it is management's task to determine all the technical figures upon which the plan is based. It is for management to decide material quantities, specifications and prices; labour grades, times and rates; sales products, levels and prices; production lines, levels and schedules; service provisions, equipment requirements and staffing ratios; all this information management provides and the cost accountant simply collates and processes the data so that a cost plan is built up.

The managerial aspect is again emphasised when it is observed that an accepted cost plan is *an executive order*. In cost control, a planned cost of £x is a definite order to the person responsible not to incur a cost in excess of £x. That it is expressed in the form of a budget or standard cost rather than a management memorandom does not alter the fact that an instruction has been given by management.

All this, however, is not to be construed as a suggestion that the cost accountant should wait passively for management to feed him with the necessary information. He more than anyone is probably aware of the precise data required, and he should exert himself in directing management's efforts to obtaining this, and gently extracting such data from managers who tend to be reluctant to commit themselves to anything definite. What must be appreciated, however, is that the cost accountant has no authority to insert any such figures in a cost plan himself.

4. Comparison of actual cost with planned cost. It is in this aspect of cost control that the cost accountant brings to bear his own important skills. It is his responsibility:

(*a*) *To collect actual costs*. This requires a knowledge of the methods outlined earlier in this book.

(*b*) *To find the divergencies between actual costs and planned costs*. These divergencies are termed variances, and finding them is essentially a mathematical technique called variance analysis and is explained in later chapters.

(*c*) *To ascertain the reason for the variances*. This is partially achieved by variance analysis, but very often there is more valuable information that only emerges as a result of detailed up-to-date knowledge of factory activities coupled with good relationships with managers at all levels, particularly foremen.

NOTE: Students should appreciate that it is this latter aspect of the cost accountant's work that determines his value to the organisation, not his computational ability, which management should be able to take for granted.

5. Action. Once the variances have been fully and intelligently reported to management, the responsibility passes back again to management. They will issue instructions on a basis of the cost accountant's report which will aim to rectify adverse variances and so ultimately enable the cost plan to be achieved. Although at this stage of control the cost accountant may advise management, it is important to appreciate that the cost accountant has no right whatsoever to issue instructions to line management himself.

VARIANCES

6. Definition. A *variance* is the divergence between any planned result and the actual result measured in money. For example, if the planned cost is £60 and the actual cost £70, then the variance is £10.

7. Variance analysis. The overall variance between a planned cost and an actual cost is usually due to a number of factors. Ascertaining the contribution of each factor to the over-all variance is termed *variance analysis*. For most variances this is ascertained by computing the effect on profit of each divergence, on the basis of the assumption that *all factors other than the one under consideration were as planned*. For example, if a usage of 100 tons at £5 ton was planned and 103 tons was actually used, then the 3 tons *excess usage* would be valued at the planned price of £5 ton, no matter what the actual price paid for the material had happened to be.

8. Direction of variance. Any variance must be either:

(*a*) *a favourable variance* (F) which on its own would result in the ultimate profit being *better* than that planned; or
(*b*) an *adverse variance* (A), which on its own would result in the ultimate profit being *worse* than that planned.

All variances *must* state the direction of the variance as well as the amount, thus the variance of £10 mentioned above (in 6) must be given as £10 *adverse*.

9. Controllable and uncontrollable variances. Cost control ultimately depends on action which is based on variances.

However, action can be taken only by people who have the appropriate authority. There is little to be gained, therefore, by presenting variances to a person if they relate to matters outside his authority. Such variances are termed *uncontrollable*, and those relating to matters within his authority are termed *controllable*. A *controllable variance*, therefore, can be defined as a variance that relates to factors within the authority of the person to whom it is presented.

PROGRESS TEST 16

Principles

1. What is cost control? (1)
2. Explain fully the difference between a budget and a standard cost. (2)
3. Who is responsible for cost control? (3)
4. Define:
   (*a*) Variance. (6)
   (*b*) Favourable variance. (8)
   (*c*) Controllable variance. (9)

CHAPTER XVII

BUDGETS

INTRODUCTION

1. Definition. A *budget* is a cost plan relating to a period of time. Time is a fundamental factor in any budget. This definition is easily remembered, but it is important to appreciate the implications of the word "cost." As we saw in I, **5**, a cost is the value of economic resources used. Thus a *cost plan* is essentially a resources plan in terms of value (*see* **7**).

2. Forecasts and budgets. It is important to note carefully the distinction between a forecast and a budget:

(*a*) A *forecast* is a prediction of what will happen as a result of a given set of circumstances.
(*b*) A *budget* is a planned result that an enterprise aims to attain.

From this it follows that a *forecast* is a judgment that can be made by anybody (provided they are competent to make judgments), whereas a *budget* is an enterprise objective that may be set only by the authorised management. (Moreover, the announcement of a plan is an implicit instruction to employees to work to achieve that objective.)

3. Main steps in preparing a budget.

(*a*) Prepare forecast.
(*b*) Determine enterprise policy (*e.g.* product range; normal hours of work per week; channels of distribution; stocks; research and development appropriation; investments).
(*c*) Compute requirements in terms of quantities required to comply with forecasts and policies (*e.g.* men; machines; tons of material) and convert to money values. This results in the initial budget.
(*d*) Review the forecast, policies and initial budget. Amend the policies or budget or both, until an acceptable budget emerges.
(*e*) Formally accept the budget. It then becomes the "master budget," and as such an executive order.

4. Budget period. A *budget period* is the period of time for which a budget is prepared and employed.

Budget periods will depend very much on the type of budget involved and also on circumstances. The following gives a general indication of the extent of budget periods used with the main types of budget:

(*a*) *Trading budgets*—one year.
(*b*) *Capital expenditure budgets*—many years.
(*c*) *Research and development budgets*—some years.

5. Types of budget. Although budgets frequently overlap each other, they do tend to be one of the following two types:

(*a*) *Operating budgets.* Budgets of this type relate to the operating of the enterprise. They involve:

(*i*) Budgeted income and expenditure figures.
(*ii*) Budgeted profit and loss statements.
(*iii*) Cash budgets (monthly).
(*iv*) The budgeted concluding balance sheet is usually included also, for the sake of completeness.

Operating budgets usually run for one year.

(*b*) *Capital budgets.* Budgets of this type relate to the capital structure and liquidity of the enterprise. They involve:

(*i*) Budgeted working capital.
(*ii*) Budgeted fixed assets.
(*iii*) Budgeted equity and loan capital.
(*iv*) Cash budgets (long term).

Capital budgets usually (not always) relate to periods of time in excess of one year. These budgets do involve consideration of operating figures, of course, but such figures are generally based on simple assumptions and are the less important aspect of the budgets.

NOTE: Although the fields of management accounting and cost accounting merge when considering budgets, it seems to be accepted by most authorities that capital budgets lie essentially in the domain of the management accountant, and therefore they will not be discussed further in this book.

6. Essentials of budget preparation. Budget preparation involves two essentials, clear thinking and common sense. Unfortunately no book can help students with these, and so budgeting is the easiest technique to learn and the hardest to apply. In this chapter a few useful words are defined and a logical approach suggested. In the majority of budget problems, however, the student must use his own initiative.

7. The importance of quantities. In practice, it is important never to lose sight of the fact that it is the *quantities* (such as those discussed in XVI, 3) which are budgeted, not money figures. The money figures are merely a way of expressing quantities in the form of a common measure (*see* I, 3(*b*)).

8. Fixed and flexible budgets. Students must appreciate that budgeting can be used *quite separately* as a planning technique and as a control technique.

(*a*) *Planning technique.* In this technique the budget is used to give a preview of the expected position at a future moment in time. If this position is unsatisfactory the budget is amended until an acceptable position is shown. Such a budget is termed a *fixed budget*, since the figures are not subsequently adjusted to allow for the actual levels of activity achieved.

(*b*) *Control technique.* If a budget is to be used for control, then a fixed budget is useless, since the actual level of activity is virtually certain to be different from the planned level, and this will affect actual costs. Since the level of activity will be uncontrollable by many managers (as this often depends on customer demands), it is important that new budgets are drawn up that make allowances for the changed activity. A budget initially prepared for such amendment is termed a *flexible budget.*

Contrasting these two types of budget, it should be observed that a fixed budget is primarily concerned with a *future period*, whereas a flexible budget paradoxically is concerned with a *period just concluded.* In other words, a flexible budget is used to ascertain what costs *should have been* incurred in view of actual activity. A comparison of these with actual costs can then be made, and this, of course, enables the cost performance of individual managers to be controlled.

FIXED BUDGETS

9. Definition. A *fixed budget* is a budget which is designed to remain unchanged irrespective of the level of activity actually attained. Its usual purpose is to lay down the major objectives of the enterprise and to co-ordinate and define the minor objectives that must be achieved by the sectional parts of the enterprise to attain these ends.

10. Principal budget factor. There is always some factor that prevents an enterprise from immediately expanding to infinity. This factor is usually sales, the enterprise being unable to sell all it can produce. However, there are other possible factors which may limit enterprise activity, such as shortage of machinery, cash, labour, space, materials and managerial ability.

Such a factor is termed the *principal budget factor*, for, clearly, it must be determined and its value assessed before any other factors can be budgeted. Indeed, part of the art of management is to make plans so that use of the principal budget factor is maximised. We have already discussed this aspect of maximising return from the use of a limiting factor (*see* XV, **14**, **15**).

The principal budget factor does not remain constant. If the limitations imposed by one factor are removed, then another takes its place and becomes the principal budget factor. In practice, it is important that one is aware when this type of switch-over is imminent.

11. Functional budgets. When budgeting, each function within the enterprise prepares its own *functional budget* on a basis of the enterprise objectives. Obviously these budgets are interrelated, data from one being required in the preparation of another (*see* Fig. 24).

On the assumption that sales is the principal budget factor, the basic information required for each functional budget is given by the answers to the following questions:

(*a*) *Sales.* In view of this being the principal budget factor, what quantities can be sold and at what prices?
(*b*) *Finished goods stock.* What finished goods stock will be required to support the budgeted sales?
(*c*) *Production.* What production must be achieved to meet budgeted sales and secure the budgeted finished goods stock?
(*d*) *Materials.* What materials will be required to meet the budgeted production?
(*e*) *Raw material stores.* What raw material stocks will be required in view of the materials budget?

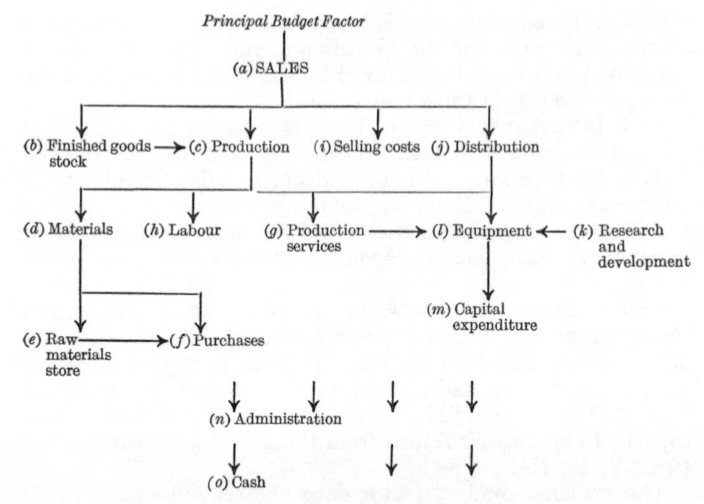

FIG. 24.—*Inter-relationship of functional budgets*

It is assumed here that the principal budget factor is sales. The letters in brackets refer to the sections of paragraph **11**.

(*f*) *Purchases.* What purchases must be made to secure the budgeted materials and raw material stocks, and at what prices?

(*g*) *Production services.* What production services will be required to support the budgeted production, and at what cost?

(*h*) *Labour.* What labour must be employed to achieve the budgeted production and man the budgeted services, and at what rates?

(*i*) *Selling costs.* What selling services will be required to achieve the budgeted sales, and at what cost?

(*j*) *Distribution.* What distribution services will be required to distribute the budgeted sales, and at what cost?

NOTE: Students often make the error of basing these last two budgets on production instead of *sales.*

(*k*) *Research and Development.* What research and development will be needed and at what cost?

NOTE: This budget in practice is often set independently of the others.

(l) *Equipment.* What equipment will be needed to enable budgeted production, research and development to be achieved, and budgeted services to be set up?
(m) *Capital expenditure.* What capital expenditure will be needed in the budget period to supply the budgeted equipment?
(n) *Administration.* What administration will be required, and at what cost, to administer effectively an enterprise engaged in achieving all the foregoing budgets?
(o) *Cash.* What cash will be involved, and need to be raised, to finance all the foregoing budgets?

12. Cash budget. Cash fluctuations can be very rapid and involve large sums, and for this reason the cash budget should be prepared on a *monthly* basis.

The preparation is essentially this:

(a) Begin with the cash balance at the start of the month.
(b) Add receipts and deduct payments for the month.
(c) Finish with the cash balance at the end of the month.

The *cash pattern may differ considerably from the income and expenditure pattern,* particularly as regards timing. It is necessary to watch out carefully for such factors as credit trading (this will "shift" the cash flow into a later period than the date of the sales or purchases), capital payments and receipts, tax and dividend payments, non-trading income and expenditure.

13. Summary budget. A *summary budget* is a budget that is prepared from, and summarises, all the functional budgets. The end products of the summary budget are:

(a) *The budgeted Profit and Loss Account.* By abstracting the budgeted income found in the sales budget, and the budgeted costs found in the other budgets, a budgeted Profit and Loss Account can be built up.
(b) *The budgeted balance sheet.* This is built up by:

(i) Taking the final cash balance in the cash budget.
(ii) Bringing in the budgeted values of the other assets and liabilities at the end of the budget period.
(iii) Adding the budgeted profit retained to the opening net worth.

14. Master budget. The budgeted Profit and Loss Account and Balance Sheet will indicate the enterprise results to be expected by the end of the period. If the results are judged to be unsatisfactory the functions are rebudgeted. This process continues until an overall satisfactory budget is drafted. The budget is then accepted by top management (or, often, the Board of Directors), and upon acceptance the budget is termed the *master budget*. From that moment on it ceases to be merely a plan; it is also an executive order.

FLEXIBLE BUDGETS

15. Definition. A *flexible budget* is a budget which is designed to change in accordance with the level of activity actually attained.

The object of a flexible budget is to assess what any individual cost should have been in view of the *actual* level of activity attained.

Flexible budgets are necessary for *control*; a manager's actual achievement can only be compared with what he should have achieved in the actual circumstances prevailing, not with what he should have achieved under quite different circumstances.

16. Limitation of the fixed budget. Assume we have budgeted for 1000 units at a cost of £1000. At the end of the period the actual output is found to be 800 units and actual expenditure £900. Has the manager concerned done well or badly in respect of costs?

From one point of view we could say that costs dropped by 10%, but then production dropped by 20%. If costs are all variable, then only £800 should have been spent, and therefore the manager has over-spent his budget by £100. Conversely, if costs are all fixed, then they would not be affected by the fall in production and the £100 difference can only be due to careful economy on the part of the manager.

A fixed budget, by its failure to distinguish between fixed and variable costs, does not enable us to assess the performance of managers and is therefore of little use for cost control.

17. Budget allowances. If we are to control effectively we must know exactly how much a manager should have spent in view of the level of activity attained. This amount is known as the *budget cost allowance* and may be defined as the cost which should have been incurred in view of the *actual activity level*.

If the costs relate only to overheads it is termed the *budget overhead allowance.*

Students should fully understand these phrases. They are of the greatest importance, for all cost control hinges on the comparison of actual figures with *allowed* figures, not the original planned figures.

18. Preparation of a flexible budget: formula method. Flexible budgets are based upon a clear distinction between fixed and variable costs. One method of preparing such a budget, then, is as follows:

(*a*) *Before* the period begins:

(*i*) Budget for a normal level of activity.
(*ii*) Segregate fixed and variable costs.
(*iii*) Compute the variable cost per unit of activity.

(*b*) At the *end* of the period:

(*i*) Ascertain the actual activity.
(*ii*) Compute the variable costs allowed for this level and add the fixed costs to give the budget cost allowance.

This is expressed in the formula:

$$\textit{Allowed cost} = \textit{Fixed cost} + \left(\textit{Actual units of activity for period} \times \textit{Variable cost per unit of activity}\right)$$

EXAMPLE: overheads only (£).

Preparation of flexible budget before period begins: Budgeted activity: 80% capacity					*Application of flexible budget at end of period:* Actual activity attained: 90% capacity			
Overhead	*Budget* *	*Fixed o'h'ds* *	*Var. o'h'ds* *	*Var. o'h'd per 1% activity*	*Var. o'h'ds allowed*	*Total budget o'h'd allowance*	*Actual o'h'ds*† (*see* **22**)	*O'h'd variance* (*see* **22**)
Power	400	—	400	5	450	450	480	30 (A)
Rent	600	600	—	—	—	600	600	—
Indirect Labour	2300	700	1600	20	1800	2500	2600	100 (A)
Maintenance	900	100	800	10	900	1000	860	140 (F)
Heat and light	200	40	160	2	180	220	220	—
Supervision	1000	760	240	3	270	1030	1020	10 (F)
Total	£ 5400	2200	3200	40	3600	5800	5780	20 (F)

* The figures in these columns are assumed in this example. In practice, they would be found by first preparing a fixed budget and then segregating the fixed and variable overheads by the analysis detailed in Chapter XIV (*see* **6, 7**).

† These figures are also assumed. In practice, they would be obtained from records of actual costs.

19. Preparation of a flexible budget: multi-activity method. An alternative method of preparing a flexible budget involves preparing a budget for every major level of activity. When the actual level of activity is known the allowed cost is found by "interpolating" between the budgets of the activity levels on either side.

EXAMPLE: overheads only (£).

	Activity level: % capacity					
Overhead	50%	60%	70%	80%	90%	100%
Rent	500	500	500	500	500	500
Depreciation	400	400	400	450	500	500
Indirect labour	2,000	2,400	2,800	3,200	3,600	4,000
Indirect materials	100	100	120	140	150	160
Power	100	120	140	160	180	200
Supervision	1,000	1,000	1,000	1,100	1,400	1,500
Maintenance	300	300	350	450	600	900
Storekeeping	200	200	250	250	300	300
Administration	1,300	1,400	1,500	1,700	2,000	2,000
Total	£ 5,900	6,420	7,060	7,950	9,230	10,060

If the actual activity level was 72%, then the allowed overheads would be computed by interpolating between the 70% and 80% budget levels (*i.e.* adding two-tenths of the difference to the 70% figures) as follows:

	£
Rent	500
Depreciation	410
Indirect labour	2880
Indirect materials	124
Power	144
Supervision	1020
Maintenance	370
Storekeeping	250
Administration	1540
Total	£7238

These allowances would then be compared with the actual costs incurred and the variances computed as in the last three columns of the example shown in **18** above.

20. Choice of method of preparation. The choice of method depends upon how "fixed" the fixed costs are. If they are likely to change significantly over the expected range of activity (due to major "stepping," *see* XIV, **13**(*b*)), then the second method should be employed. If, on the other hand, fixed costs remain relatively unchanged over this range, then the first method is perfectly satisfactory and requires less work in preparation.

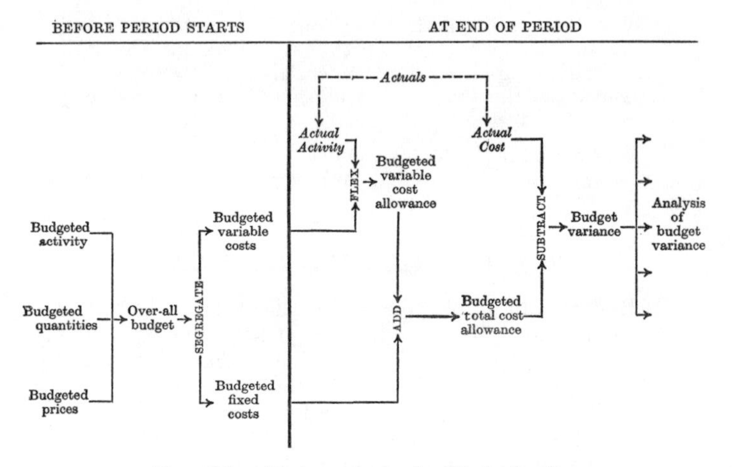

FIG. 25.—*Main steps in flexible budgeting*

Before the period begins budgeted fixed and variable costs must be segregated. At the end of the period the actual figures are compared with the budget allowances (*not* with the original budgeted figures). Determining the variable cost allowances is called "flexing the budget."

21. Measuring activity. In the chapter on break-even charts we discussed the problem of measuring activity (*see* XIV, **8**). This problem again arises with flexible budgets.

It should be noted that whereas production is often an excellent measure when dealing with the usual direct costs, this is not necessarily so in the case of overheads. Most overheads that vary at all vary more with *hours worked*. For instance, power, light, heat, shop-floor administration costs (including supervision) and many indirect labour costs, such as the canteen, all tend to vary far more in relation to actual working hours than to actual production. For this reason hours worked are usually employed as the measure of activity when dealing with variable overheads.

22. Budgetary control. Control is attained by comparing

budget figures with actual figures and taking action to correct divergencies. Note the following points in this connection:

(*a*) The difference between a budget figure and an actual figure is called a *budget variance*.

(*b*) When computing budget variances it is always the *budget allowance* that is compared with the actual figure. The original budgeted figure has no relevance. (Note, however, that for fixed costs the budget cost allowance is the same as the original budgeted cost.)

23. Flexible budget chart. A chart depicting the main steps taken when using the flexible budget technique is shown in Fig. 25.

BUDGET ADMINISTRATION

24. Budget committee. We said earlier that budgeting is a management technique, and consequently management is responsible for the compilation of budgets. Since these usually involve managers throughout the whole enterprise, a committee with representatives from all sections of the business should be appointed to plan and co-ordinate the budgets.

25. Budget officer. In addition to the committee, a budget officer should also be appointed. His work is essentially that of secretary to the committee, and entails:

(*a*) Ensuring that the committee secretarial work is carried out (*e.g.* agendas, minutes, notice of meetings).

(*b*) Ensuring that committee instructions are passed to the appropriate people.

(*c*) Collecting data and opinions for consideration by the committee.

(*d*) Keeping managers to the budget time-table (*see* **26** below).

(*e*) Co-ordinating and briefing the members of the committee.

Since the cost accountant, in the course of his own budget work, has close contact with all the managers, he is well suited for, and often appointed to, this post.

26. Budget time-table. When preparing major budgets it is first necessary to prepare many of the smaller, but key, budgets. If these smaller budgets are not completed quickly, then the preparation of the major budgets will be held up, which in turn will hold up the summary budget and ultimately the master budget. Delay in issuing the master budget is clearly serious, for a budget issued after the start of a period has very much reduced value, and many even result in the delay of vital projects. In order, then, that the master budget can be issued before the period begins, it is necessary to prepare a carefully thought-out time-table for all budget activities. Such a time-table must be rigidly adhered to, since delays in this type of work tend to snowball and quickly assume serious proportions.

27. Budget manual. To assist everyone engaged in budgeting and budget administration, a budget manual should be issued. A *budget manual* is a manual that sets out such matters as the responsibilities of the people engaged in, the routine of, and the forms and records required for, budgeting and budgetary control.

More generally, this manual will set out all information needed by all persons involved in budgeting and budgetary control to enable them to maximise both:

(*a*) their contribution to the budget compilation; and
(*b*) their benefit from the control data ultimately reported back to them.

28. Budget centres. Control can only be attained through people, and therefore budget cost allowances and actual costs must be assigned to individuals who can be held responsible for these costs. To do this the organisation is broken down into budget centres. Budget centres are very similar to cost centres, except that they must relate to the areas of authority and responsibility of individuals. A *budget centre*, then, is a location to which costs may be charged, the responsibility of these costs being wholly and exclusively borne by a single member of the organisation. For example, a whole department, if under the control of a single foreman, would be a budget centre, and so would an office under a specified office manager.

In connection with budget centres note that:

(*a*) Centres group to form bigger centres. Thus all the factory centres will form a single factory budget centre under the control of the factory manager.

(*b*) Occasionally costs charged to a cost centre may be charged to a budget centre that does *not* take in that cost centre. For example, paid leave specifically granted by the personnel manager to a shop-floor employee may be charged in the *accounts* to the shop-floor as an overhead, but it would be charged for *control* to the personnel officer budget centre, since the personnel manager was responsible for sanctioning the cost.

PROGRESS TEST 17

Principles

1. What is the difference between a forecast and a budget? (2)
2. What, and how long, is a budget period? (4)
3. Distinguish between an operating budget and a capital budget. (5)
4. Distinguish between fixed budgets and flexible budgets. (8)
5. What is the principal budget factor? (10)
6. What is a master budget and what is specially significant about it? (14)
7. What is the major disadvantage of a fixed budget? (16)
8. What is a budget allowance and why is it important? (17)
9. Explain the main points in budget administration. (24–28)
10. What is a budget centre? (28)

Practice

11. You are given the following data regarding the operation of a company for a 4-week period at two forecasted levels of activity:

	Forecast A	*Forecast B*
Sales (at £5 per unit)	50,000 units	100,000 units
Variable and semi-variable overheads:		
Indirect labour	80 men	140 men
Power	£5,000	£10,000
Maintenance	£15,000	£25,000
Distribution	£10,400	£14,800

In addition, the following information applies to both forecasts:

Direct materials	50% sales value
Direct labour	1 man produces 50 units a week
Depreciation	£5,000
Other fixed costs	£15,000
Selling costs	$2\frac{1}{2}$% sales
Labour costs	£25 per man per week

(*a*) Prepare comparative forecasted profit statements.
(*b*) As it happened the actual activity was:

Production 60,000 units.
Sales (cash) 40,000 units.

(*i*) Compute all the allowed costs.
(*ii*) If the opening bank balance was £31,850 and 10% of the direct materials used are as yet unpaid for, what should the closing bank balance be?

12. A chemical manufacturing company produces two products, C 100 and C 300. From the information given below you are required to produce the following statements relating to the ensuing year:

(*a*) A standard cost statement for 1000 grams of each product.
(*b*) A profit forecast for the year in an appropriate form.
(*c*) A cash forecast for the year.
(*d*) The estimated closing balance sheet at the end of the year (estimated to the nearest £).

Supporting schedules showing clearly how these statements have been built up are to be supplied where appropriate.

Taxation may be ignored.

The direct cost method is to be used: that is to say, overhead expenses are not to be allocated to products and stocks are to be valued at prime cost.

The information is as follows:

Production specifications:

	Batches of 1000 grams	
	C 100	C 300
Direct materials:		
XY	110 grams	60 grams
DR	900 grams	1000 grams
Cost of energy used	£4	£5
Direct labour time:		
Process 1	1 hour	1 hour 20 minutes
Process 2	30 minutes	30 minutes
Standard material prices are:		
XY	10p per 10 grams	
DR	15p per 10 grams	
Standard labour rates are:		
Process 1	30p per hour	
Process 2	40p per hour	

Budgeted manufacturing overheads for the ensuing year are £4500, of which £600 is depreciation.

Budgeted sales for the year are:

	C 100	C 300
Batches of 1000 grams	1800	1000
Price per 1000 grams	£24	£26

Purchases of materials, and sales, are expected to be constant from month to month.

Planned stocks at year-end are:

C 100	260 batches of 1000 grams
C 300	135 batches of 1000 grams
XY	12,000 grams
DR	125,000 grams

General administrative overheads are budgeted at £3800, of which £100 is depreciation.

Debtors and creditors at the end of the year are planned to represent one month's sales and purchases respectively. It may be assumed all other costs except depreciation are cash outlays.

The capital expenditure budget includes £2200 for new equipment, to be spent in cash during the year.

The balance sheet at the beginning of the year is expected to be as follows:

	£		£	£
Share capital	50,000	Equipment:		
Profit and loss	13,863	Cost	62,000	
Creditors	2,920	Depreciation	8,000	
				54,000
		Stock*	4,283	
		Debtors	6,200	
		Cash	2,300	
				12,783
	£66,783			£66,783

* Details of the stock are as follows:

		£
C 100	60 batches of 1000 grams at £19·1	1146
C 300	35 batches of 1000 grams at £21·2	742
XY	22,000 grams at 10p per 10 grams	220
DR	145,000 grams at 15p per 10 grams	2175
		£4283

There will be no opening or closing work-in-progress.

(*A.C.C.A.* Adapted)

CHAPTER XVIII

SETTING STANDARDS

DEFINITIONS

1. The meaning of standard. The word *standard* means a criterion or bench-mark. Consequently, a standard figure is one against which we can measure an actual figure to see by how much the actual differs from the standard. The two main features of any standard are:

(*a*) It is *accepted* (by the people who must use it: XII, 2).
(*b*) It is relatively *permanent*.

2. Standard cost. A *standard cost* is a cost plan relating to a single cost unit. The term also refers to the total planned cost of any given number of units, found by multiplying the number of units by the unit standard cost.

Since both standard costs and budgets are cost plans, there is considerable similarity in their preparation and much that is relevant to preparing a budget is relevant to setting a standard cost. However, setting a standard cost involves much more consideration of the direct costs, overheads being regarded very much as a secondary factor.

3. Cost standards. As was explained in Chapter I (**6**), every cost is made up of a usage component and a price component. Consequently, when planning a cost one must first plan the usage and the price. Often it is also necessary to plan other factors, such as the specification of material, or grade of labour, or loss in process. All these must be planned first before we can compute our standard cost, and since they, too, form criteria, they are also standards and, since they are used for costing, they can be called cost standards. A *cost standard*, then, is a usage, price or other standard upon which a standard cost is based.

Clearly, the first step in setting a standard cost is to determine the cost standards.

4. Ideal and expected standards. Before management begin to determine the cost standards they must decide which of two types of standards they wish to use. These are:

(*a*) *Ideal standards* which are based on perfect performance. It is assumed there is no wastage, no inefficiencies, no idle time, breakdowns or other imperfections in the manufacturing process. The standards reflect only what would be necessary if everything went perfectly.

(*b*) *Expected standards* which are based on expected performance (albeit that the expected performance is assumed to be at high efficiency). Thus unavoidable wastage is allowed for, and a reasonable allowance made for breakdowns and other inevitable lapses from perfect efficiency.

Ideal standards are used to measure the loss resulting from imperfection and indicate the points where a close investigation may result in large savings. However, since such standards can never be achieved in practice, they tend to dishearten managers. This is not true, however, of expected standards. Managers can hope to achieve and even better expected standards and, indeed, they pose a definite challenge. Because of this valuable psychological incentive that expected standards possess, virtually all standards today are of this type.

It should be noted, however, that such standards now fulfil two functions, that of a *criterion* and that of a *target*. These functions are occasionally opposed to each other, and so sometimes lead to awkward dilemmas (*see* **15** below).

SETTING STANDARDS

5. Summary of steps. Setting a total standard cost for a product follows much the same procedure as preparing a job cost except that planned figures are used in lieu of actuals. For any given unit or product the following standards must be determined:

(*a*) Standard materials costs.
(*b*) Standard wages costs.
(*c*) Standard direct expenses.
(*d*) Standard variable overhead costs.
(*e*) Standard fixed overhead costs.
(*f*) Standard selling and distribution costs.
(*g*) Standard selling price and profit.

6. Standard materials costs. Determining the standard materials costs involves deciding upon:

(*a*) *Standard materials specifications.* This requires consideration of design (appearance and strength requirements), quality policy, range of materials available and even decisions regarding which components are to be bought and which made. The design department is clearly involved in setting these standards.

(*b*) *Standard materials usage.* Here consideration must be given to finished sizes (or volumes) and the inevitable losses (due to machining, off-cuts, evaporation) that arise when processing materials. Any expected breakage or similar losses must also be allowed for. Assistance in determining these standards will come from both the design department and the workshops.

(*c*) *Standard materials prices.* Essentially this is a forecast of the average prices of materials during the future periods. Bulk and other discounts and also freight and handling charges should be allowed for. The department that will aid here is, of course, the buying department.

The standard materials costs can now be computed.

7. Standard wages costs. Determining the standard wages costs involves deciding upon:

(*a*) *Standard labour grades.* This requires consideration of the operations involved, skills required and the anticipated volume of work, this latter factor being needed to estimate how far division of labour can be carried out and relatively unskilled personnel be highly trained for skilled but very limited operations. The availability of labour must also be taken into account, since there is no point in planning for a grade which is not available. The work study and personnel departments will assist with this standard.

(*b*) *Standard labour times* (standard hours). The usage of labour is measured in hours. The hours required of each grade in each cost centre to manufacture the cost unit will be determined. This is a major task involving many work study techniques, and indeed the work study department will be almost wholly responsible for these standards. Note that the planned hours are termed *standard hours*, and, as will be seen, form a major concept in standard costing.

(*c*) *Standard wages rates.* Knowing the labour grades, this simply involves a forecast of the relevant rates over the future period. The personnel department will undertake the determination of these standards.

The standard wages costs can now be computed.

8. Standard direct expenses. If there are any direct expenses relating to the cost unit, standards for these, too, must be set. Setting these is usually quite simple and is essentially no more than a matter of common sense.

9. Standard variable overhead costs. In modern standard costing, overheads are nearly always segregated into fixed and variable overheads and usually absorbed on a basis of direct labour hours. Determining the standard variable overhead costs, then, involves ascertaining:

(*a*) *Standard variable overhead absorption rates.* These are computed for each cost centre in the same way that normal pre-determined overhead rates are computed (*see* IX, **19**).

$$Standard\ V.OAR = \frac{Budgeted\ cost\ centre\ variable\ overheads}{Budgeted\ cost\ centre\ direct\ labour\ hours}$$

This formula requires a decision regarding the levels of activity to be adopted. In standard costing this is usually regarded as *the level of activity at which the cost centre would operate in normal economic circumstances.* For reporting purposes these levels are often classed as 100% capacity.

(*b*) *Standard overhead usage* (standard hours). Since overheads are absorbed on the basis of direct labour hours, all that is necessary in this instance is to use the standard labour times previously decided upon (*see* **7**(*b*)).

The standard variable overhead costs can now be computed by multiplying for all cost centres the standard hours for the cost unit by the standard variable overhead rates.

10. Standard fixed overhead costs. The standard fixed overhead costs are found in exactly the same way as the standard variable overhead costs, except that budgeted fixed costs are used in lieu of budgeted variable costs when computing what will now be the fixed overhead absorption rates.

Note that setting standard overhead costs entails the preparation of full overhead budgets.

11. Standard selling and distribution costs. The standard selling and distribution costs are found by making a careful study of the costs involved in selling and distributing a cost unit. Packages, packing time, freight, sales commission and a share of the advertising and sales administration costs are all considered in fixing this charge. The sales and distribution departments will obviously be able to assist in setting these standards.

12. Standard selling price. The *standard selling price* is the price at which it is planned to sell the cost unit. It is, of course, an alternative term for budgeted selling price. It is usually set by the sales manager in consultation with the managing director.

13. Standard sales margin. The *standard sales margin* is the difference between the total standard cost of a product and its standard selling price. Traditionally the product total standard cost is set to include all costs, and so the product standard sales margin is the same as the product standard profit. This approach has been adopted in this book. Students, however, are warned that this need not always be the case (*e.g.* the standard cost may only relate to marginal cost, *see* XXII, **7–9**), and future developments will almost certainly move away from the traditional approach.

14. Standard cost card. All the above standards should be recorded on a *standard cost card*. Such a card, which is very similar to a job card, is made out for each cost unit manufactured and forms a complete record of all the cost standards and standard costs relating to that unit. In practice, it should be laid out in such a way that the standard cost of the unit when only partly completed can be quickly found. This is important for valuing work in progress.

The data which would appear on a simple standard cost card are shown in the chapter on cost variances (*see* XIX, **4**(*a*)).

NOTE: When solving standard cost problems the standard cost card is an invaluable source of data. If a question does not give a standard cost card, the student is strongly advised to prepare his own before attempting to calculate variances.

15. Revision of standards. If some economic factor alters permanently (*e.g.* if the unions negotiate an increased wages rate), then the question arises as to whether or not the standard cost should be amended. This problem can be considered both theoretically and practically:

(*a*) In theory, this is one of the difficulties that arise from using a standard as both a criterion and a target, for:

(*i*) As a *criterion*, standards should rarely be altered. A standard that was always changing would be like a tape-measure made of elastic. A relatively unchanging standard enables comparisons to be made between different periods. Revise it too frequently and this advantage is lost.

(*ii*) As a *target*, standards must be revised. Out-of-date standards provide no incentive. There is no challenge in attempting to keep wages rates down to impossible levels.

(*b*) In practice, revising a standard cost involves considerable work and sometimes leads to serious confusion. For instance, the revision of one single minor raw material cost standard means a careful revision of:

(*i*) All standard cost cards of products using the material.

(*ii*) All price lists detailing standard prices of the material *and* products.

(*iii*) All valuations of stores, work in progress and finished goods stocks.

For all these reasons standard cost revisions are usually made only at year-ends. Where factors alter during the year, then in order to maintain the "target" appeal of standards, the *effect* of the revision is allowed for in management statements, although the revision is not taken into the standard costs (*see* XIX, **36**).

PROGRESS TEST 18

Principles

1. Define:

(*a*) standard cost; (**2**)

(*b*) cost standard. (**3**)

2. What is the difference between ideal standards and expected standards? (**4**)

3. What is the main disadvantage of ideal standards? (**4**)

4. What are the steps taken when setting a full standard cost for a product? (**5**)

5. What factors should be taken into account when setting:

   (*a*) a standard materials cost; **(6)**
   (*b*) a standard wages cost? **(7)**

6. What are standard hours? **(7(*b*))**
7. How are standard overhead rates computed? **(9, 10)**
8. What is a standard sales margin? **(13)**
9. What is the value of a standard cost card? **(14)**
10. Should standards be revised? **(15)**
11. Which departments assist in setting which standards? **(6–12)**

CHAPTER XIX

VARIANCE ANALYSIS: COST VARIANCES *

INTRODUCTION TO VARIANCE ANALYSIS

1. Profit variance. At the beginning of a period an enterprise will aim to earn a planned (budgeted) profit. At the end of the period an actual profit will have been made. The difference between actual profit and budgeted profit is the *profit variance.*

2. Variance analysis. Clearly management will wish to have the profit variance explained in terms of all the factors that varied from plan over the period. To give management this information the profit variance is analysed into sub-variances, and this analysis is called a *variance analysis.*

3. Chart of variances. Fig. 26 is a chart showing all the sub-variances into which the profit variance can be analysed.

The chart is mathematically consistent, *i.e.* where a variance subdivides into two other variances the sum of these latter variances equals the original variance (*see* **16**).

From the chart it can be seen that the profit variance analyses initially into the *total cost variance* and the *sales margin variance.* In this chapter the analysis of the total cost variance is detailed and the analysis of the sales margin variance is covered in the next chapter (XX).

All the formulae for computing variances are listed in **5** below, together with examples which are based on the standards and actuals given in **4**.

4. Illustrative figures: standards and actuals. These figures are used to illustrate the formulae for computing the variances listed in **5**.

(*a*) *Standard cost card:*

	£
75 cwt of X at £2 cwt	150
50 cwt of Y at £5 cwt	250
125	400
−25 cwt, standard loss (20%)	—
100 cwt of Z, standard yield (80%)	400

* See **3** in Preface.

	£
Standard materials cost of 1 cwt Z	4·00
Labour: 2 hrs at £0·50 hr	1·00
Variable overheads: 2 hrs at £0·25 hr	0·50
Fixed overheads: 2 hrs at £1 hr	2·00
Production royalty: £0·10* cwt	0·10
Standard production cost, 1 cwt	7·60
Selling and distribution costs: £1·40 cwt	1·40
Total standard cost per cwt	9·00
Standard sales margin (profit)	1·00
Standard selling price per cwt Z	£10·00

* To be revised at £0·125 cwt.

NOTE: Since 2 labour hours are planned for 1 cwt then 1 cwt production = 2 standard hours.

(*b*) *Budget for period:* Production and sales, 10,000 cwt Z

NOTE

(*i*) If 10,000 cwt are budgeted, then at 2 hrs a cwt 20,000 *working hours* are budgeted. Also *budgeted fixed overheads* must be 20,000 × £1 = £20,000.

(*ii*) From these figures the *budgeted profit* can be computed as £10,000 (*i.e.* 10,000 cwt at £1 profit per cwt).

(*c*) *Actuals for period:*

Sales (cash): 7000 cwt Z at £10·10 per cwt
Production 8000 cwt Z
Costs: Material purchases (credit) and issues

	X 6000 cwt at £2·05 cwt
	Y 4400 cwt at £4·75 cwt
Direct labour	18,000 hrs at £0·55 hr
Variable overheads	£4,100
Fixed overheads	£19,000
Royalties	£1,000
Selling and distribution	£9,200

NOTE

(*i*) 8000 cwt production = 8000 × 2 = 16,000 standard hours of production.

(*ii*) From these figures the actual profit can be computed as £1900 (*see* XXII, 4).

5. Computation of variances. The different variances are listed together here for purposes of comparison and summary.

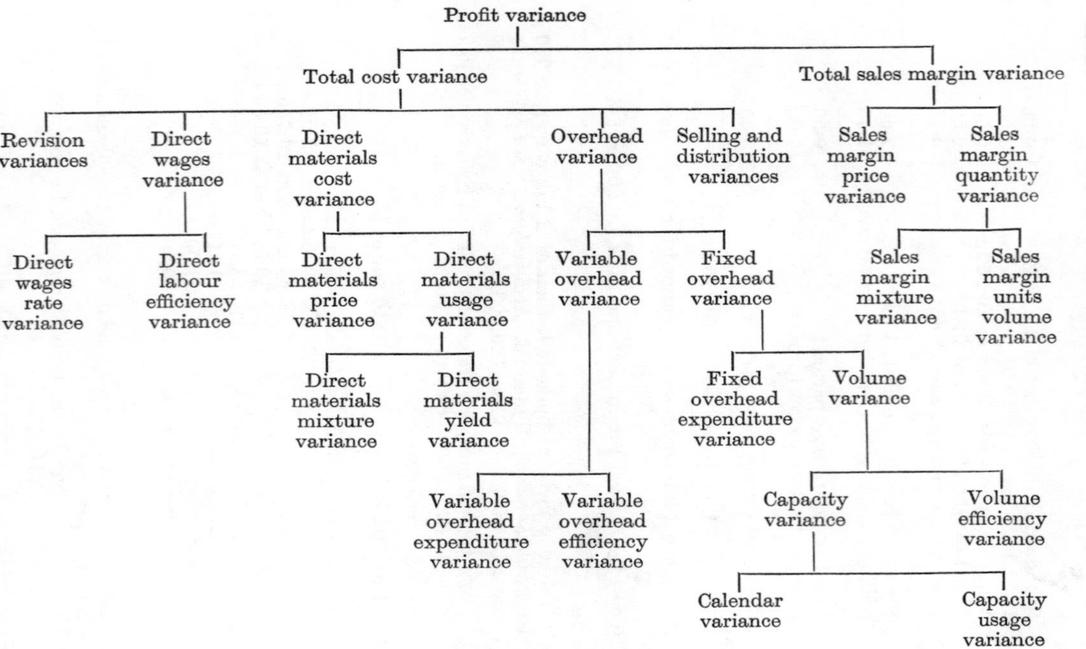

FIG. 26.—*Chart of cost variances*

This chart shows the profit variance and all its sub-variances, as they are dealt with in Chapters XIX and XX.

The formula for each variance is set out and illustrated in a brief worked example using the standards and actuals given in **4** above. Variances are discussed in detail in the rest of this and the next chapter.

The following points should be noted:

(*a*) In this book three abbreviations are used in variance analysis, which the student should learn at this point. They are:

SHP = *Standard hours (of) production.*
F.OAR = *Fixed overhead absorption rate.*
V.OAR = *Variable overhead absorption rate.*

(*b*) The numbers given after the name of each variance refer to the paragraphs dealing with that variance.

(*c*) Those variances which are *not* further subdivided (*see* Fig. 26) are italicised.

Variance	*Formula*	*Example* (data as in **4**)
Profit (**1**)	Actual profit − Budgeted profit	£1,900 − £10,000 = £8,100 (A)
Total cost (**7**)	Total actual cost incurred − (Standard cost of production + standard selling and distribution costs of sales)	Actual cost* = £67,200 + £9,200 = £76,400 Standard cost = £(8,000 × 7·60) + £(7,000 × 1·40) = £70,600 ∴ Variance = £5,800 (A)
Direct wages (**13**)	Actual direct wages cost − Standard direct wages cost	(18,000 × £0·55) − (8,000 × £1) = £1,900 (A)
Direct wages rate (**14**)	(Actual wages rate − Standard wages rate) × Actual hours	(£0·55 − £0·50) × 18,000 = £900 (A)
Direct labour efficiency (**15**)	(Actual hours worked − SHP) × Standard wages rate	(18,000 − 16,000) × £0·50 = £1,000 (A)
Direct materials cost (**17**)	Actual direct materials cost − Standard direct materials cost	(6,000 at £2·05 + 4,400 at £4·75) − (8,000 × £4) = £1,200 (A)
Direct materials price (**10, 11, 18**)	(Actual price† − Standard price) × Actual usage (*or* Actual purchases, *see* **18**)	X: £(2·05 − £2·00) × 6,000 = £300 (A) Y: £(4·75 − £5·00) × 4,400 = £1,100 (F) Total = £800 (F)
Direct materials usage (**9, 18**)	(Actual usage − Standard usage for actual production) × Standard price	As there are both mixture and yield variances involved here, these two variances are added (*see* **18**(*b*)). Mixture £720 (A) Yield £1,280 (A) Usage = £2,000 (A)

* *See* the profit and loss statement given in XXII, **4** (Example 1).

† If the actual price is not known, an alternative formula is: (Standard price × Actual usage) − Actual cost.

Variance	*Formula*	*Example* (data as in **4**)
Direct materials mixture (**19**)	*See* layout given in **19**	X: 6,000 at £2 = £12,000 Y: 4,400 at £5 = £22,000 10,400 £34,000 X($\frac{3}{5}$): 6,240 at £2 = £12,480 Y($\frac{2}{5}$): 4,160 at £5 = £20,800 10,400 £33,280 ∴ Mixture variance = £34,000 − £33,280 = £720 (A)
Direct materials yield (**20**)	(Actual yield − Standard yield for actual input) × Standard cost per unit of output	(8,000 − 80% of 10,400) × £4 = £1,280 (A)
Overhead (**24**)	Actual overheads − (SHP × (F.OAR + V.OAR))	£(4,100 + 19,000) − (16,000 × £(1·00 + £0·25) = £3,100 (A)
Variable overhead (**25** (*b*))	Actual variable overheads − (SHP × V.OAR)	£4,100 − (16,000 × £0·25) = £100 (A)
Variable overhead expenditure (**26**)	Actual variable overheads − (Hours worked × V.OAR)	£4,100 − (18,000 × £0·25) = £400 (F)
Variable overhead efficiency (**27**)	(Hours worked − SHP) × V.OAR	(18,000 − 16,000) × £0·25 = £500 (A)
Fixed overhead (**25** (*a*))	Actual fixed overheads − (SHP × F.OAR)	£19,000 − (16,000 × £1) = £3,000 (A)
Fixed overhead expenditure (**28**)	Actual fixed overheads − Budgeted fixed overheads	£19,000 − £20,000 = £1,000 (F)
Volume (**29**)	(SHP − Budgeted hours) × F.OAR	(16,000 − 20,000) × £1 = £4,000 (A)
Volume efficiency (**30**)	(Hours worked − SHP) × F.OAR	(18,000 − 16,000) × £1 = £2,000 (A)
Capacity (**32**)	(Hours worked − Budgeted hours) × F.OAR	(18,000 − 20,000) × £1 = £2,000 (A)
Calendar (**33**) (sub-variance of capacity)	(Working days in actual month − Working days in year ÷ 12) × Total no. of working hours per day × F.OAR	No figures in this example. *See* **33** for worked example.
Capacity usage (**34**) (only arises if capacity variance includes a calendar variance)	(Actual hours worked − Hours planned for actual month) × F.OAR	No figures in this example. *See* **34** for worked example.
Revision (**36**)	(Existing cost standard − Revised cost standard) × Appropriate factor*	Royalty revision: (£0·10 − £0·125) × 8,000 = £200 (A)
Selling and distribution (**37**)	Actual selling and distribution costs − (No. of units sold × Standard selling and distribution cost per unit)	£9,200 − (7,000 × £1·40) = £600 (F)

* Factor depends on which cost standard is revised. A revision variance can occur at any point in the analysis.

Variance	*Formula*	*Example* (data as in **4**)
Total sales margin (XX, 4(*a*))	(Actual sales − Standard cost of sales) − Budgeted margin	(7,000 × £10·10 − 7,000 × £9) −(10,000 × £1) = £2,300 (A)
Sales margin price (XX, 4(*b*), 5)	(Actual margin per unit* − Standard margin) × Units sold *Or:* Actual sales − (Actual units sold × Standard selling price)	£(1·10 − 1·00) × 7,000 = £700 (F) *Or:* (7,000 × £10·10) − (7,000 × £10) = £700 (F)
Sales margin quantity (XX, 4(*c*), 5)	(Actual units sold − Budgeted units) × Standard margin per unit	(7,000 − 10,000) × £1 = £3,000 (A)
Sales margin mixture and units volume (XX, 4(*d*), 5)	*See* worked example in XX, **5**	*See* worked example in XX, **5**

* Actual margin per unit here = Actual selling price − Total unit standard cost.

6. General definition applicable to most variances. There are a large number of variances, and this means that there are a large number of definitions to be learnt. However, most of them are very similar, and so it is possible to devise a single definition that can be applied to almost any variance. This definition runs:

An X variance is the variance arising due to the actual X differing from the planned X, where "X" stands for the title of the variance defined. (For example, a "capacity variance" can be defined as "the variance arising due to the actual capacity differing from the planned capacity.")

7. Total cost variance. The *total cost variance* is the difference between the total actual cost incurred and the total standard cost of the actual production. (If sales and production do not match, then the selling and distribution part of the total standard cost is based on actual sales, not on production.) The chart in Fig. 26 shows how this variance can be analysed.

8. Price and usage variances. Since all costs are primarily composed of price factors and usage factors, variances due to each of these factors occur frequently in variance analysis. Students should therefore be fully conversant with these types of variances and be able to recognise them instantly. They are dealt with in turn below.

9. Usage variances. A *usage variance* is the variance arising due to the actual usage differing from the planned usage. To compute this variance then, find the difference in usage and multiply by the *standard price*, since in variance analysis, other than in exceptional cases, all other factors are deemed to be at standard.

The formula, therefore is:

Usage Variance =
(*Actual usage* — *Standard usage for actual prod.*) ×
Standard price

For example: Standard, 6 ft at £0·50 ft
Actual, 8 ft at £0·60 ft

Usage variance = (8 — 6) × £0·50 = £1·00 (*A*) (adverse because it affects the profit adversely).

10. Price variance. A *price variance* is the variance arising due to the actual price differing from the planned price.

To compute this variance one would expect the difference between prices to be multiplied by the standard usage, but this is one of the exceptions. If it were calculated in this way the price and usage variances would not add to give the material cost variance. One of these two variances must be multiplied by an *actual* figure and an arbitrary choice is made. By convention we subject the price variance to this special treatment and so the formula becomes:

Price variance = (*Actual price* — *Standard price*) × *Actual usage*

For example: Standard, 6 ft at £0·50 ft
Actual, 8 ft at £0·60 ft

Price variance = (£0·60 — £0·50) × 8 = £0·80 (*A*)

11. Price variance; an alternative method of computation. Very often the actual price is not given, only the total actual cost. The actual price can be computed, of course, simply by dividing the actual usage into this actual cost, but an alternative formula exists which gives exactly the *same result* but saves this awkward step. This formula is:

Price variance = (*Standard price* × *Actual usage*) — *Actual cost*

For example (as in **10**):
Price variance = (£0·50 × 8) — (8 × £0·60) = £0·80 (A)

In view of the fact that it is often the more suitable formula, it is worth expressing it in a verbal form; *i.e.* the price variance is the difference between what it actually cost and what it *would* have cost if the actual usage had been paid for at standard price.

Note that *actual prices are never used in variance analysis except to compute price variances*. Remembering this will enable the student to avoid puzzling over whether to use the standard or the actual price.

12. Determining the direction of variances. It is possible by correct layout of formulae to be able to tell if the direction of a variance (XVI, **8**) is adverse or favourable by noting whether the answer is plus or minus. However, this method does make strict demands on the student's memory, and so he is strongly advised to determine the direction by inspection, *i.e.* by looking at the figures involved and deciding the direction by common sense. Experience shows this method to be the freer of errors.

NOTE: At this point the student is recommended to attempt Question 1 in Progress Test 19 (p. 228).

WAGES VARIANCES

Wages variances include the direct wages variance, the direct labour efficiency variance and the direct wages rate variance. These are sometimes called "labour variances."

13. Direct wages variance. The *direct wages variance* is the variance arising due to the actual direct wages differing from the standard direct wages. The formula is:

Direct wages variance =
Actual direct wages cost − Standard direct wages cost

For example: Standard, 16 hours at £0·50 hour
Actual, 20 hours at £0·45 hour

∴ Actual direct wages cost = 20 × £0·45 = £9·00
Standard direct wages cost = 16 × £0·50 = £8·00

∴ *Direct wages variance* £1·00 (*A*)

14. Direct wages rate variance. The *direct wages rate variance* is the variance arising due to the actual direct wages rate differing from the standard direct wages rate.

This is obviously a price variance, a wages rate being the "price" at which one buys labour. The formula is:

Direct wages rate variance =
(Actual wages rate − Standard rate) × Actual hours

For example (as in **13** above):

Direct wages rate variance = (£0·45 − £0·50) × 20 = £1·00 (*F*)

15. Direct labour efficiency variance. The *direct labour efficiency variance* is the variance arising due to the actual direct labour efficiency differing from the standard direct labour efficiency.

This is simply a usage variance. It is termed labour *efficiency* variance because labour usage is measured in hours, and any saving or loss of hours is directly attributable to efficiency.

The formula is:

Direct labour efficiency variance =
(*Actual direct hours worked* − SHP) × *Standard wages rate*

For example (as in **13**):

Direct labour efficiency variance = (20 − 16) × £0·50 = £2·00 (*A*)

16. Variances cross-check. Note that the sum of the direct labour efficiency and wages rate variances is £2 Adverse + £1 Favourable = £1 Adverse, which agrees with the direct wages variance computed in **13** above. Students should use this technique of comparing the sum of the two sub-variances with the higher variance as a cross-check to prove their arithmetic.

NOTE: Sometimes students compute only two variances and extract the third one from these. This is not recommended, since if one of the first two variances is wrong, the third will be wrong also and there will be nothing to indicate to the student that any error exists at all.

At this point the student is recommended to attempt Question 2 in Progress Test 19 (p. 228).

MATERIALS VARIANCES

17. Direct materials cost variance. The *direct materials cost variance* is the variance arising due to the actual direct materials cost differing from the standard direct materials cost. The formula is:

Direct materials cost variance =
Actual direct materials cost − *Standard direct materials cost*

For example: Standard, 6 ft at £0·50 ft
Actual, 8 ft at £0·60 ft

Direct materials cost variance = (8 × £0·60) − (6 × £0·50)
= £1·80 (*A*)

18. Direct materials price and usage variances. These were examined earlier in the chapter (*see* **8–11**).

(*a*) Note that, in connection with price variances, in practice the variance is computed for the *purchases* in the period, *i.e.* instead of multiplying by the actual quantity used at the time of using, we multiply by the actual quantity purchased. It is clearly more logical to control purchase prices at the time of purchase rather than later at the time of usage.

It should be appreciated that price variances can be computed in the normal way regardless of whether or not there are mixture or yield variances. Calculating the price variances is, in fact, usually the first step in variance analysis.

(*b*) In usage variances, if the product involves either a mixing of materials or loss in process or both, then the usage variance can be further analysed into a mixture or a yield variance, or both. These variances are examined below (**19** and **20**).

If mixture and yield variances are involved in an analysis the student is advised *not* to calculate the usage variance directly but to compute the mixture and yield variances and then add them to obtain the usage variance. This advice is given despite the fact that it conflicts with the advice in (**16**), as experience has shown that the direct calculation of the usage variance is something students find difficult and rarely do correctly.

19. Direct materials mixture variance. The *direct materials mixture variance* is the variance arising due to the actual direct materials mixture differing from the standard mixture. Here the word "mixture" refers to the *proportions* in which the different materials involved in making the product are mixed.

Mixture variances occur not only in material variance analyses but also in sales margin variance analyses. In order to reduce the number of formulae the student must learn, the following layout has been designed so that a number of variances and particularly any type of mixture variance can be computed by its use (XX, **5**):

(*a*) *Actual value* £	(*b*) *Actual quantity*	(*c*) *Standard price*	(*d*) *Value* £	(*e*) *Actual quantity in standard proportions*	(*f*) *Standard price*	(*g*) *Value* £	(*h*) *Budget value* £
Not used in material mixture variances			Product of previous two columns	This column is the "X" total *divided into the standard proportions*		Product of previous two columns	Not used in material mixture variances
	Total X			*Total X*			

Mixture variance = difference between (*d*) total and (*g*) total.

The key to this analysis is to remember to take the total *actual* quantity and split it into the *standard proportions* in column (*e*).

To determine the direction of the variance note that the columns move from actual figures to planned, reading from left to right. Consequently, taking any pair of columns, the right-hand column is the more "standard" of the two, and so here column (*g*) is more "standard" than column (*d*). If, then, column (*g*) total is larger than column (*d*) total there has been a saving on the cost and the variance is favourable, and vice versa.

NOTE: Alternatively, remember the rule, for a material mixture variance, "Right larger than left = favourable." However, the student should be warned that this rule reverses for sales margin variances.

EXAMPLE

Data: P, Q and R are mixed in the standard proportions of 1:2:5.

Standard prices per gallon are: P £1
Q £2
R £3

Actual usage of materials are: P 200 gallons
Q 400 ,,
R 600 ,,

Find the mixture variance.

Method:

	(*b*) *Actual quantity*	(*c*) *Standard price*	(*d*) *Value* £	(*e*) *Actual quantity in standard proportions*		(*f*) *Standard price*	(*g*) *Value* £
P	200	£1	200	$\frac{1}{8}$	150	£1	150
Q	400	£2	800	$\frac{2}{8}$	300	£2	600
R	600	£3	1800	$\frac{5}{8}$	750	£3	2250
	1200		£2800		1200		£3000

∴ Mixture variance = £3000 − £2800 = £200 (F)

20. Direct materials yield variance. A *direct materials yield variance* is the variance arising due to the actual direct materials yield differing from the standard yield. This variance must be calculated when there is any loss in process.

Where such loss is inevitable there must be a *standard loss*, *i.e.* a planned loss, and the output which remains after deducting the standard loss is the *standard yield*.

The key to computing a yield variance lies in remembering that the difference between the actual and standard yield (which will be in units of output) is *valued at the standard cost per unit of output*, *i.e.*:

$$\textit{Direct materials yield variance} =$$
$$\left(\begin{array}{c}\textit{Actual}\\ \textit{yield}\end{array} - \begin{array}{c}\textit{Standard yield for}\\ \textit{actual input}\end{array}\right) \times \begin{array}{c}\textit{Standard cost per}\\ \textit{unit of output}\end{array}$$

This standard cost per unit of output is found by dividing the *standard cost of the material input* by the *standard output* (this information can be found on the standard cost card).

For example:

Standard input	= 100 tons at standard price of £9 ton =	£900
Standard loss, 10%	= 10 tons	—
∴ Standard yield	= 90 tons which must be worth	£900

$\therefore$ 1 ton of *output* has a standard cost of $\frac{900}{90} = £10$.

Finding the standard cost per unit of output is the first step in computing the yield variance.

EXAMPLE

Data: Standard: Price of input £4 per gallon.
Standard yield 80%.
Actual: Input 1000 gallons.
Output 770 gallons.

Find the yield variance.

Method:

(*a*) If the standard yield is 80%, then for every gallon of input worth £4, only 0·8 gallons of output are planned.

$\therefore$ Standard cost per unit of output $= \frac{£4}{0{\cdot}8} = £5$ per gallon.

(*b*) Next, the standard yield is 1000 × 80% = 800 gallons
and the actual yield = 770 „

$\therefore$ Yield difference = 30 „

Now 30 gallons at £5 per gallon = £150
$\therefore$ Yield variance = £150 (*A*)

NOTE: Although labour and overheads are also really part of the over-all cost of units of output (*see* XII, 9), by convention only the material costs are usually taken into a yield variance, the labour and overhead losses emerging as efficiency variances.

At this point the student is recommended to attempt Questions 3, 4 and 5 in Progress Test 19 (p. 228).

OVERHEAD VARIANCES

21. Measuring production in standard hours. In standard costing it is necessary to measure production in a common unit, and this may not be easy if the factory manufactures varying quantities of different products. (This is, in fact, our old problem of measuring activity again.) The most generally accepted measure is the number of standard hours of work represented by the actual production achieved. For example, if a standard cost card shows one unit having 4 standard hours, then if 100 units are produced we can measure our production as $4 \times 100 = 400$ standard hours. Thus in order to measure the production for any period it is necessary to:

(*a*) Ascertain the number of units produced of each product.
(*b*) Calculate *standard hours per unit* × *number of units produced* for each product.
(*c*) Add to give a grand total of standard hours, *e.g.*:

Product	*Number of units produced*	*Standard hours per unit*	*Standard hours production*
A	1000	0·1	100
B	200	1·5	300
C	200	2·0	400
Actual production measured in standard hours			800

NOTE: The 800 can be referred to as the *Actual standard hours production*—the word "standard" here being used, not as a "planned" figure but as a "unit measure of production."

22. Overhead absorption in standard costing. In normal absorption costing the overheads absorbed are found by multiplying the overhead rate by the *actual* hours taken. In standard costing, however, it is vital to remember that the overheads absorbed are found by multiplying the overhead rate by the *standard hours production*, *i.e.*:

Overheads absorbed = SHP × *Overhead absorption rate*

Since overheads in standard costing should be absorbed by using both fixed and variable overhead rates this means:

Fixed overheads absorbed = SHP × F.OAR.
and *Variable overheads absorbed* = SHP × V.OAR
and *Total overheads absorbed* = SHP × (F.OAR + V.OAR)

23. Example figures. In order to demonstrate the overhead variances analysed throughout this section, the following figures will be used:

Budget:	Fixed overheads	£1500
	Variable overheads	£750
	Hours	750
Actual:	Fixed overheads	£1520
	Variable overheads	£760
	Worked (clock) hours	700
	Standard hours production	800

Students should note that the budget hours (750) relates to *both* budgeted working hours and also budgeted standard hours production. Clearly, since in the planning stage each hour worked will be expected to produce one standard hour production, then, in the planning stage, these two figures will always be the same. Only *historically* will the hours worked differ from the standard hours production.

Prior to starting our analysis we must compute the standard fixed and variable overhead rates. From the above figures it can be seen these are:

F.OAR = 1500 ÷ 750 = £2 per hour
V.OAR = 750 ÷ 750 = £1 per hour

24. Overhead variance. The *overhead variance* is the variance arising due to the actual overheads incurred differing from the standard overheads absorbed. It is, in fact, simply the under- or over-absorption of overheads. The formula is:

Overhead variance =
Actual overheads − SHP × (F.OAR + V.OAR)

For example: According to the figures given in **23**, 800 standard hours were produced.

∴ Overhead variance = (1520 + 760) − 800 × (£2 + £1)
= 2280 − 2400 = £120 (*F*)

i.e. £120 more was absorbed into production than was incurred, and therefore is an over-absorption.

The overhead variance is clearly the combined effect of the under- or over-absorptions of the fixed and variable overheads. The next step, therefore, is to analyse the fixed and variable overhead variances.

25. Fixed and variable overhead variances. A *fixed (variable) overhead variance* is the variance arising due to the actual fixed (variable) overheads incurred differing from the fixed (variable) overheads absorbed. Again, these variances are simply under- or over-absorptions.

(*a*) *Fixed overhead variance.* The formula here is:

Fixed overhead variance =
Actual fixed overheads – (SHP × F.OAR)

For example: From the figures given in **23**,
Fixed overheads variance = £1520 – 800 × £2 = £80 (*F*).
This variance can be due to either, or a combination of:

(*i*) Actual fixed overheads differing from budgeted overheads, *i.e.* expenditure variance.
(*ii*) Actual production differing from budgeted production, *i.e.* volume variance.

NOTE: An *expenditure variance* is simply a variance due to under- or over-spending relative to an allowed expenditure.

(*b*) *Variable overhead variance.* The formula here is:

Variable overhead variance =
Actual variable overheads – (SHP × V.OAR)

For example: Using the same figures (**23**),
Variable overhead variance = £760 – 800 × £1 = £40 (*F*).
Since variable overheads must always be flexed to the actual level of activity, the original budgeted variable overheads are not relevant here, only the allowed overheads. Under- or over-absorption, then, can be due to either, or a combination of:

(*i*) Actual variable overheads differing from the *allowed* variable overheads, *i.e.* expenditure variance.
(*ii*) Allowed overheads differing from absorbed overheads. Since allowed overheads are usually based on *actual hours worked* (*see* **XVII, 21**) and absorbed overheads on standard hours production, under- or over-absorption will occur if these two figures differ. We have already seen that a difference between worked hours and standard hours production is a measure of efficiency, and so this under- or over-absorption is an *efficiency* variance.

Note that these two overhead variances add to the total overhead variance of £120 (F).

26. Variable overhead expenditure variance. A *variable overhead expenditure variance* is the variance arising due to the actual variable overheads differing from the allowed variable overheads.

As was explained in Chapter XVII (**21**), variable overheads should be flexed on a basis of hours worked, and therefore the allowed overheads are actual hours worked multiplied by the variable overhead rate. Therefore the formula is:

Variable overhead expenditure variance =
Actual variable overheads – (*Hours worked* × V.OAR)

For example: Using the same figures (**23**),
Variable overhead expenditure variance = £760 – (700 × £1) = £60 (*A*).
The variance is an *expenditure* variance, since £60 more was actually spent than was allowed.

27. Variable overhead efficiency variance. A *variable overhead efficiency variance* is the variance arising due to the allowed variable overheads differing from the absorbed variable overheads.

Variable overheads were allowed on 700 hours. However, 800 standard hours were produced. Thus 100 hours of extra overheads were absorbed due to the efficiency of employees. So:

Variable overhead efficiency variance =
(*Hours worked* – SHP) × V.OAR

For example: (*see* **23**),
Variable o'h'd efficiency variance = (700 – 800) × £1 = £100 (*F*).

28. Fixed overhead expenditure variance. The *fixed overhead expenditure variance* is the variance arising due to the actual fixed overheads differing from the allowed fixed overheads.

Since fixed overheads are not flexed, the allowed overheads are the same as the budgeted overheads, and the formula is:

Fixed overhead expenditure variance =
Actual fixed overheads – *Budgeted fixed overheads*

For example: (*see* **23**),
Fixed o'h'd expenditure variance = £1520 – £1500 = £20 (*A*).

29. Volume variance. A *volume variance* is the fixed overhead variance arising due to the actual volume of production differing from the planned volume, volume being measured in standard hours. The planned volume is, of course, the budgeted standard hours production (*see* **23**). The formula is:

$$\textit{Volume variance} = (\text{SHP} - \textit{Budgeted hours}) \times \text{F.OAR}$$

For example: (*see* **23**),
Volume variance = (800 − 750) × £2 = £100 (*F*) (favourable because the extra 50 standard hours production resulted in 50 more £2 lots of overheads being absorbed than planned, so over-absorbing £100 overhead).

A volume variance can itself be analysed, since the difference in volume of production can be due to either, or both:

(*a*) Labour being more or less efficient than planned, *i.e.* efficiency variance.
(*b*) The hours worked being more or less than planned, *i.e.* capacity variance.

30. Volume efficiency variance. A *volume efficiency variance* is the fixed overhead variance arising due to the actual hours worked differing from the standard hours production.

Only 700 hours were worked, yet there were 800 standard hours production owing to the efficiency of labour. Therefore an extra 100 hours more of overhead were absorbed than was expected. The formula therefore is:

$$\textit{Volume efficiency variance} =$$
$$(\textit{Hours worked} - \text{SHP}) \times \text{F.OAR}$$

For example: (*see* **23**),
Volume efficiency variance = (700 − 800) × £2 = £200 (*F*).

31. A note on efficiency variances. It should be noted that all efficiency variances—labour, variable overhead and volume—are based on the difference between the standard hours production and the actual hours worked. In other words:

$$\textit{Any efficiency variance} =$$
$$(\text{SHP} - \textit{Actual hours worked}) \times \textit{Appropriate standard rate}$$

32. Capacity variance. A *capacity variance* is the variance arising due to the actual capacity differing from the planned capacity.

In our example 750 hours were budgeted, but only 700 were worked. If the other 50 hours had been worked, then an extra 50 standard hours production would have been gained (other factors being at standard), and so an extra 50 £2 blocks of overhead absorbed. Failure to work these hours, therefore, gave rise to an under-absorption of £100. The formula then is:

Capacity variance =

(*Hours worked* − *Budgeted hours*) × F.OAR

For example: (*see* **23**),
Capacity variance = (700 − 750) × £2 = £100 (*A*).

33. Calendar variance. A *calendar variance* is the variance arising due to the effect of the calendar.

If the budgeted working hours for a month are based on an average (mean) month, then in months with public holidays, works holidays and five week-ends there will be an under-recovery of overheads due to the shortage of hours. Conversely, in other months there will be above average hours and therefore over-recovery. This over- or under-absorption is the calendar variance.

Since the difference between the budgeted and actual working hours is the basis of the capacity variance, the calendar variance is clearly part of this variance.

Note the following features of a calendar variance:

(*a*) An average month must be determined. Such a month is called a *standard month*. A standard month = Total working days in the year divided by 12.

(*b*) The formula for a calendar variance is:

Calendar variance =

$$\left(\begin{matrix}\textit{Working days in}\\ \textit{actual month}\end{matrix} - \begin{matrix}\textit{Standard}\\ \textit{month}\end{matrix}\right) \times \begin{matrix}\textit{Total no. of work-}\\ \textit{ing hours per day}\end{matrix} \times \text{F.OAR}$$

(*c*) Since the days lost and gained over the year must cancel out, then the calendar variances will cancel out. Such variances should not therefore be written off to profit and loss but transferred to a Calendar Variance Suspense Account, which will naturally end the year in balance.

(*d*) Calendar variances are really not operating variances at all. They can be avoided entirely by either adopting equal budget periods or by the apportionment of fixed overheads to periods in proportion to the lengths of periods.

A worked example of a calendar variance is given below:

EXAMPLE

Data:

Planned working days in a year	240 days
Actual working days in actual month	19 days
Budgeted hours per standard month	10,000 hours
F.OAR	£3

Method:

$$\text{Standard month} = \frac{240}{12} = 20 \text{ days},$$

$$\therefore \text{ Budgeted working hours per day} = \frac{10{,}000}{20} = 500 \text{ hours.}$$

$$\therefore \text{ Calendar variance} = (20 - 19) \times 500 \times £3 = £1500\,(A).$$

Note that this variance is independent of the *actual* hours worked. Indeed, calendar variances can be worked out for the year *in advance.*

34. Capacity usage variance. This variance is that part of the capacity variance that arises due to the actual usage of capacity differing from the planned usage. Usually, however, it is calculated as a series of separate sub-variances that indicate losses and gains due to specific factors (*e.g.* strikes, overtime). The formula is:

$$\textit{Capacity usage variance} = \left(\begin{matrix}\textit{Actual hours}\\ \textit{worked}\end{matrix} - \begin{matrix}\textit{Hours planned for}\\ \textit{actual month}\end{matrix}\right) \times \text{F.OAR}$$

For example, taking the data in the example immediately above and assuming that 9300 hours were actually worked:

$$\text{Capacity usage variance} = \left(9300 - \frac{19}{20} \times 10{,}000\right) \times £3 = £600(A).$$

35. Analysis layout for fixed overhead variances. Students are advised to analyse variances by logical argument as examination questions sometimes include unusual slants that render the mechanical application of formulae impossible. However, where the analysis is straightforward students may find that the application of the following layout will save time:

	Values	*Difference between bracketed values*	*Sum of bracketed variances*		
Fixed overheads	Actual fixed overheads				
		Fixed overhead expenditure variance			
	Budgeted fixed overheads			Fixed overhead variance	
		Capacity variance			
	Actual hours worked × F.OAR		Volume Variance		
		Volume efficiency variance			Overhead variance
	SHP × F.OAR				
Variable overheads	Actual variable overheads				
		Variable overhead expenditure variance			
	Actual hours worked × V.OAR		Variable overhead variance		
		Variable overhead efficiency variance			
	SHP × V.OAR				

At this point the student is recommended to attempt Question 6 in Progress Test 19 (p. 228).

REVISION AND SELLING AND DISTRIBUTION VARIANCES

36. Revision variances. In Chapter XVIII (**15**) it was pointed out that usually standards were only revised at year-ends, but the effect of a changed factor (*e.g.* wages increase) was allowed for in management statements. Such an allowance is made by means of a *revision variance*, which is the variance arising due to the revision of a cost standard when the standard cost itself is *not* to be immediately altered.

To find a revision variance it is simply necessary to calculate what effect the amount of the revision has on the final profit or loss.

EXAMPLE

Data: Standard, 1000 hours at £0·50 per hour.
Actual, 1200 hours for a wages cost of £642.

A £0·02 per hour wage increase had previously been negotiated, but the standard rate was left unchanged. Find the revision variance.

Method: The effect of £0·02 per hour increase would be to decrease the profit by £0·02 for every hour worked.

$\therefore$ Revision variance = £0·02 × 1200 = £24 (*A*).

Note that the wages rate variance would be 1200 × £0·50 − £642 = £42 (*A*), but since the agreed increase accounted for £24 of this, only the £18 adverse balance would be reported to management for their explanation in terms of other reasons, and their control action.

37. Selling and distribution variances. A *selling and distribution variance* is the variance arising due to the actual selling and distribution costs differing from the standard selling and distribution costs. The formula is:

$$\textit{Selling and distribution variance} = \begin{matrix}\textit{Actual selling and} \\ \textit{distribution costs}\end{matrix} - \left(\begin{matrix}\textit{Number of} \\ \textit{units sold}\end{matrix} \times \begin{matrix}\textit{Standard selling and dist-} \\ \textit{ribution cost per unit}\end{matrix}\right)$$

The point to note is that selling and distribution variances are based on *sales*, not on production, as are other cost variances.

In practice, selling and distribution variances are, of course, analysed into sub-variances.

CAUSES OF VARIANCES

So far we have seen how variances can be analysed. However, it is equally important to determine why variances arose. Finding the underlying causes of variances sometimes requires considerable practical skill. The main causes arising in practice are summarised in this section.

38. Wages variances.

(*a*) *Direct wages rate:*

(*i*) General rise in wages rates.
(*ii*) Individual increase in specific wages rates.
(*iii*) "Non-standard" grade of employee.

(*b*) *Direct labour efficiency:*

(*i*) Slow employee.
(*ii*) Employee delayed by factors outside his control (*e.g.* breakdowns; no materials).
(*iii*) Poor working conditions.

(*iv*) Employee restricts output.
(*v*) Abnormal length of run.
(*vi*) Employee handicapped by physical disability (*e.g.* bandaged finger).
(*vii*) Quality of supervision.
(*viii*) Non-standard grade of employee.
(*ix*) Non-standard material used.
(*x*) Non-standard job method used.
(*xi*) Incorrect booking of labour times.

39. Direct materials variances.

(*a*) *Direct materials price:*

(*i*) Change in purchase price.
(*ii*) Change in delivery costs.
(*iii*) Non-standard material purchased.
(*iv*) Bad buying.

(*b*) *Direct materials usage:*

(*i*) Waste or scrap excessive.
(*ii*) Defective material (*e.g.* due to deterioration, poor handling, bad buying).
(*iii*) Rejection of completed work necessitating additional material withdrawals from store.
(*iv*) Pilferage.
(*v*) Non-standard material used.
(*vi*) Incorrect booking of material usage.

40. Overhead variances.

(*a*) *Overhead expenditure:*

(*i*) Excessive or under utilisation of a service (*i.e.* wasteful or economical use of service).
(*ii*) Price change for service units (*e.g.* rate per kWh).
(*iii*) Change in nature of service (*e.g.* using gas in lieu of electricity).

(*b*) *Capacity:*

(*i*) Under or over customer demand.
(*ii*) Breakdowns.
(*iii*) Absenteeism (including lateness).
(*iv*) Labour shortage.
(*v*) Strikes.
(*vi*) Idle time (if not booked as part of time spent on jobs).
(*vii*) Calendar variations (if using a standard month).

(*c*) *Overhead efficiency variance:* this variance arises in conjunction with a labour efficiency variance (*see* **31**), and so will be due to the same reasons.

PROGRESS TEST 19

Practice

1. Given that the cost standards are 20 gallons and £0·25 per gallon, compute the variances when the actuals are:

(*a*) 24 gallons at £0·25 per gallon.
(*b*) 20 gallons at £0·35 per gallon.
(*c*) 24 gallons at £0·35 per gallon.
(*d*) 18 gallons for a total cost of £5.

2. Find the variances where the cost standards are 100 hours and £0·40 per hour and the actuals are:

(*a*) 110 hours at £0·35 per hour.
(*b*) 95 hours for a cost of £36·74.

3. Hydrogen pentoxide is prepared by mixing hydrogen and oxygen in the proportions of 1:5. The standard prices of these gases are £0·50 and £0·05 a cubic foot respectively. During the last production run 10,200 cubic feet of hydrogen was mixed with 57,600 cubic feet of oxygen. Compute the mix variance.

4. Pure wrot is prepared by boiling crude wrot (standard price £0·06 a load) until only 60% of the original input remains. One day last period the process ran too long and a mere 726 loads of pure wrot emerged from an input of 1500 loads of crude. What was the yield variance?

5. MUD is prepared by mixing M, U and D (standard prices £1, £2 and £3 a ton respectively) in the proportions of 1:1:3. A standard loss of 20% is allowed. Last period 1100 tons of M costing £1000, 1000 tons of U costing £2200, and 2900 tons of D costing £8888 were processed to give 3815 tons of MUD. Find the variances.

6. Extract from the following data all overhead variances:

Budgeted production	50 lots
Fixed overhead absorption rate	£3 per hour
Actual and budgeted variable overheads	£7500
Standard hours per lot	100 hours
Actual production	60 lots
Actual fixed overheads	£14,500
Actual hours worked	5600 hours

7. A foundry producing castings of a standard alloy uses standard costs. The standard mixture is as follows:

40% material A at £300 per ton
30% material B at £100 per ton
10% material C at £420 per ton
20% scrap metal of this alloy

It is expected that from each charge there will be a 5% loss in melt, 35% will be returned to scrap stock (runners, heads, etc.) and 60% will be good castings. Scrap is credited and charged at the standard average cost of the metal mixture.

In a certain period the following materials are purchased and used:

380 tons material A at £310 per ton
330 tons material B at £110 per ton
90 tons material C at £420 per ton
200 tons scrap metal at standard price

From this material, 608 tons of good castings are produced, and 340 tons of scrap metal are returned to scrap metal stock.

Present information to management, showing standard metal costs, and variances from standard in respect of this period.

(*I.C.W.A.*)

8. Delaware Ltd has computed the following information for the calendar year, 1962:

Budgeted production	10,000 units
Budgeted fixed overhead	£5000
Budgeted total machine hours	25,000 hours
Budgeted variable overhead	£6000

It is also found that each unit requires 1 lb of raw material at a standard cost of 25p per lb. Labour rates are $33\frac{1}{3}$p per hour and a unit of output requires $1\frac{1}{2}$ standard hours. Labour rates have been stable, but raw material prices have proved to be 5% above standard.

In the present budget period (March 19...) the following information is obtained:

Fixed Expenses	£550
Normal machine hours	2000 hours
Machine hours paid for	1600 hours
(these differ from the standard time because of a strike)	
Idle Time (machine)	60 hours
Actual Production	450 units
Raw Materials	£125
Variable Overhead	£280
Direct wages	£210

You are required to set out the variances under their separate heads for the period March 19... showing precisely how each is calculated; together with variances, summary and analysis.

(*A.C.C.A.* Adapted)

CHAPTER XX

VARIANCE ANALYSIS: SALES MARGIN VARIANCES*

SALES MARGIN VARIANCES

1. Evolution of sales variances. When standard costing and budgetary control first evolved it seemed logical to analyse the difference between actual sales and planned sales. Subsequent reflection, however, revealed that management is not really so much concerned about sales themselves as the *profits from sales.* If, for example, for policy reasons some article was being sold at a small loss the doubling of sales of this article would result more in management concern than management elation.

Unfortunately, by the time this viewpoint became accepted the term "sales variances" had become attached to variances that measured deviations in sales levels. The later type variances have, therefore, been termed "sales margin variances" to distinguish them from the earlier ones.

These variances, then, measure the *effects on profits* of deviations of actual sales from planned sales—not the effect on sales values. The older forms of sales variances will not be illustrated, and in this way it is hoped to avoid the confusion that otherwise arises when students find that there are two different ways of preparing a variance analysis from sales data.

2. Sales margin variance analysis assumes all costs are at standard. Sales margin variance analyses are prepared primarily in connection with the control of sales, and since this function is relatively independent of production from the point of view of control, it is logical to exclude all production (cost) variances and assume that all products are manufactured at standard cost. Sales variance analysis, therefore, assumes that

* Students are warned that at the moment there is little standardisation of the definitions of the variances examined in this chapter. Here the terminology of the Institute of Cost and Works Accountants has been followed as far as possible, although the sales margin mixture and the sales margin units volume variances are not defined in this terminology (*see also* **3** in the Preface).

the cost price of all units sold is the *standard cost*, and actual costs do not enter the analysis at all.

3. Standard sales margin. The standard sales margin was defined in XVIII, **13**. Here it is only necessary to point out that the standard sales margin plays the same part in sales margin variance analysis as standard price in cost variance analysis.

4. Sales margin variances. All the sales margin variances are shown on the right-hand side of the chart in Fig. 26. They are:

(*a*) *Total sales margin variance.* This is the difference between the actual margin from sales (valuing cost of sales at standard) and the budgeted margin (profit). The formula, then, is:

Total sales margin variance =

(*Actual sales* − *Standard cost of sales*) − *Budgeted margin*

(*b*) *Sales margin price variance.* This is an ordinary price variance, and so can be computed from either of the two usual formulae:

Sales margin price variance =

(*Actual margin per unit* − *Standard margin*) × *Units sold*

or alternatively,

Actual margin on sales − (*Actual units sold* × *Standard margin*)

There is, however, a second alternative short cut formula that gives exactly the same answer:

Sales margin price variance =

Actual sales − (*Actual units sold* × *Standard selling price*)

The student may like to discover for himself why these latter two formulae give identical results.

(*c*) *Sales margin quantity variance.* This is an ordinary usage variance, and so can be computed from the formula:

Sales margin quantity variance =

(*Actual units sold* − *Budgeted units*) × *Standard margin per unit*

(*d*) *Sales margin mixture and units volume variances.* These variances arise only where more than one product is sold, and they indicate the effect on the profit of the divergence from standard of the actual sales mixture and units volume. Their value to management is, however, questionable, and there is evidence that they may soon disappear. The method of computation is shown in **5**.

5. Comprehensive layout for computing sales margin variances. When mixture and units volume variances are required it is often worthwhile adopting the layout given previously on p. 215 (with slightly altered headings, as shown in the example below), as this enables a complete analysis of all sales margin variances to be made. The variances are found by comparing pairs of columns as follows:

Sales margin price variance = Column (*a*) — column (*d*)
Sales margin mixture variance = Column (*d*) — column (*g*)
Sales margin units volume variance = Column (*g*) — column (*h*)

The directions of the variances are found by inspection, bearing in mind the remarks below the layout on p. 215, and also the fact that now an actual higher than standard indicates a *favourable* variance.

The sales margin quantity variance and the total sales margin variance can be found by adding the appropriate sub-variances, though the total sales margin variance should be cross-checked by using the formula in **4** (*a*). The following example shows how this comprehensive layout is used:

EXAMPLE

Data:

Budgeted sales: X 5000 units at £10 (Standard margin £4)
Y 4000 units at £5 (Standard margin £2)
Z 3000 units at £3 (Standard margin £1)

Actual sales: X 3000 units for £28,200
Y 5800 units for £25,150
Z 9200 units for £31,000

Method:

	(*a*) *Actual margin**	(*b*) *Actual quantity*	(*c*) *Standard margin*	(*d*) *Value*	(*e*) *Actual quantity in standard proportions*	(*f*) *Standard margin*	(*g*) *Value*	(*h*) *Budgeted margin†*
	£	Units		£	Units		£	£
X	10,200	3,000	£4	12,000	$\frac{5}{12}$ 7,500	£4	30,000	20,000
Y	7,750	5,800	£2	11,600	$\frac{4}{12}$ 6,000	£2	12,000	8,000
Z	12,600	9,200	£1	9,200	$\frac{3}{12}$ 4,500	£1	4,500	3,000
	£30,550	18,000		£32,800	18,000		£46,500	£31,000

* Column (*a*) is found by applying the following formula:

Actual margin = *Actual sales* — (*Actual units* × *Standard cost*)
e.g. Actual margin for X = £28,200 — (3,000 × £6) = £10,200

† Column *h*) is found by the formula:

Budgeted margin = *Budgeted units* × *Standard margin*

Comparing the columns as described above:

Sales margin price variance
= 30,550 − 32,800 = £2,250 (A)

Sales margin mixture variance
= 32,800 − 46,500 = £13,700 (A)

Sales margin units volume variance
= 46,500 − 31,000 = £15,500 (F)

Adding sub-variances to find the remaining variances:

Sales margin quantity variance
= 13,700 (A) + 15,500 (F) = £1800 (F)

Total sales margin variance
= 2250 (A) + 1800 (F) = £450 (A)

This last figure of £450 also equals the difference between the actual margin and the budgeted margin, *i.e.* £30,550 and £31,000, so providing the necessary cross-check.

6. The earlier sales variances (sales value variances). The sales variances which first evolved in cost accounting (*see* **1**) were very similar in method and computation to the variances illustrated above (hence the confusion), except that *sales values and selling prices* were used in lieu of *sales margins.* Students who wish to compute such variances should re-design the layout used in the example in **5**, substituting "sales" or "selling price" for "margin," according to the sense.

It should be explained that these types of variances still have use in practice; they enable the sales manager to see the effects of the various factors on his over-all sales *value* figures. They are, however, rarely called for in examinations.

PROGRESS TEST 20

Practice

1. The Progressive Company budgeted to sell 1000 P, 2000 Q and 3000 R at prices of £10, £8 and £6 respectively. They actually sold 1200 P for £11,500, 1400 Q for £13,200, and 4000 R for £20,000. The standard margin on each product was as follows: P £3; Q £2; R £1.

Compute the sales margin variances.

CHAPTER XXI

STANDARD COST ACCOUNTS

STANDARD ABSORPTION COST ACCOUNTS

1. Basic principles of standard cost book-keeping. The following are the basic principles of standard cost book-keeping:

(*a*) Variances should be accounted for as near as is practical to the moment of occurrence.
(*b*) Variances should be transferred to individual variance accounts.
(*c*) As far as possible, transfers between the main accounts should be at standard. (One should envisage these accounts as having such a distaste for actual figures that they shed the variances as quickly as possible so that actuals are thereby converted into standard figures.)
(*d*) Variances are written off to Profit and Loss at the end of the period.

2. Flow chart for standard absorption cost accounting. A flow chart for standard absorption cost accounting is given in Fig. 27. The following points should be noted:

(*a*) Material standards are usually maintained for production materials only. Consequently, purchases must be segregated into standard materials and non-standard materials, the latter comprising mainly consumable and maintenance stores. Non-standard materials are debited to their stores accounts at actual prices and issued using a non-standard issue price method.
(*b*) The materials price variance on standard materials can be calculated *immediately on receipt of the invoice* by applying to any individual invoice the formula:

Price variance =
Invoice amount – Invoice quantity at Standard price

This enables the price variance to be taken immediately to the Price Variance Account, and the materials

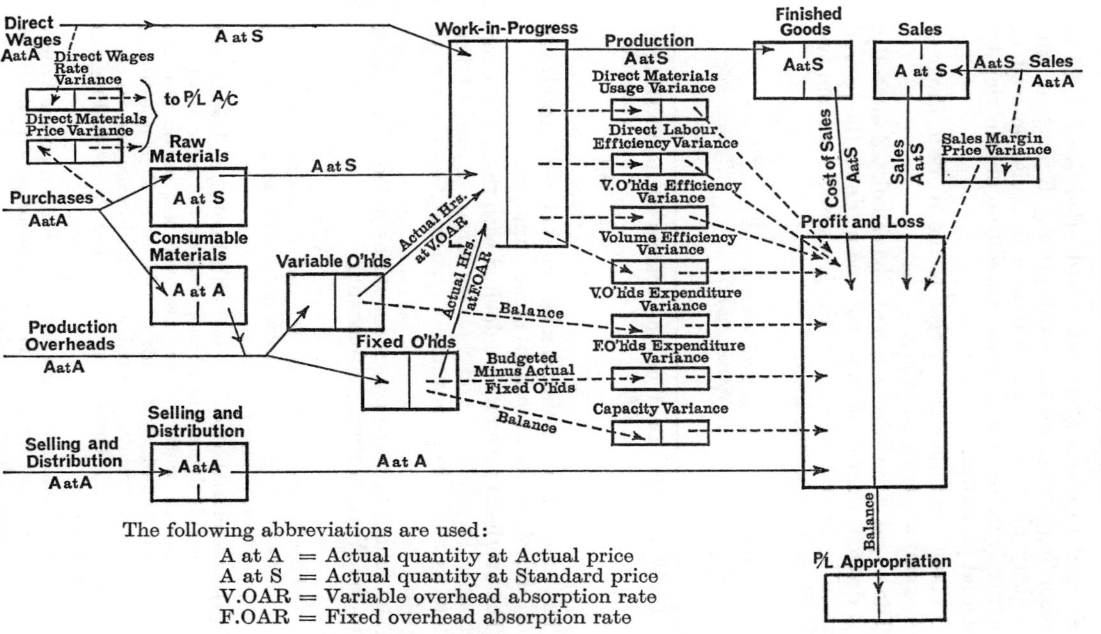

The following abbreviations are used:

A at A = Actual quantity at Actual price
A at S = Actual quantity at Standard price
V.OAR = Variable overhead absorption rate
F.OAR = Fixed overhead absorption rate

FIG. 27.—*Chart of standard absorption cost accounting*

The flow of variances is indicated by broken lines. The main accounts shed the variances as quickly as possible, converting actuals to standard figures, and the variances are written off to profit and loss at the end of the period.

charged to stores at the standard price (*see* III, **20** *re* recording stores at standard price). Note that this slightly alters the price variance formula; instead of multiplying by actual *usage* we will be multiplying by actual *purchases*.

(*c*) On issue, materials are charged to the Work-in-Progress Account at standard prices.

(*d*) The wages rate variance can also be calculated instantly. If desired, the calculation could be made on the payroll itself by inserting alongside the gross wages column two additional columns, thus:

	Gross Wages	*Actual hours at Standard rate*	*Difference: Wages rate variance*
Totals:	Cr. Wages A/c	Dr. Work-in-Progress A/c	Dr. (or Cr.) Wages Rate Variance A/c

The wages rate variance can be found either in total only or, if desired, for each individual employee.

(*e*) The overhead accounts are debited with the actual overheads. Expenditure and capacity variances can be taken out as and when convenient (generally at the month end).

(*f*) The following three points should be noted with regard to the Work-in-Progress Account:

(*i*) The Work-in-Progress Account is credited with the *actual units produced valued at the standard cost* as shown on the standard cost card.

(*ii*) As soon as the total production is known, and remember that this figure will be modified by the increase or decrease in work in progress over the period (though examiners rarely include this factor in their questions), variances relating to efficiency and usage can be computed and transferred from the Work-in-Progress Account.

(*iii*) The balance remaining and carried down on the Work-in-Progress Account is the end-of-period work in progress valued at standard.

(*g*) All finished goods are carried at standard cost. The standard cost value of the finished goods sold is transferred to the Profit and Loss Account as the "Standard cost-of-sales."

(*h*) Selling and distribution variances, though shown on reports, are often not entered into the accounts, the actual costs being transferred direct to the Profit and Loss Account.

(*i*) Sales margin price variances can be computed at the time of invoicing in the same manner as material price variances, and they are taken at once to a sales price variance account.

(*j*) *Budgeted* figures as such do not usually enter the accounts (*e.g.* budgeted sales; budgeted fixed overheads). Incorporating such figures often merely complicates the book-keeping without obtaining any real advantage.

(*k*) The chart, for reasons of clarity, does not show all variances. However, students should have little difficulty with other variances: *e.g.* materials mixture and yield variances merely require a sub-division of the usage variance account.

3. Worked example of standard cost accounts. The cost accounts and accounting entries shown in Fig. 28 relate to the data given in Chapter XIX (**4, 5**) illustrating the computation of variances. It should be appreciated that these accounts are rather more simple than would occur in practice (*e.g.* there are no opening stocks), and that not all the ledger accounts have been shown (*e.g.* there are no fixed assets or capital accounts).

4. Implications of transferring variances to Profit and Loss. It should be noted that when a price variance computed at the time of purchase is transferred to Profit and Loss it may well contain a favourable variance relating to unissued materials, *i.e.* an *unrealised profit* is taken. This may also happen with favourable efficiency and usage variances relating to work in progress or unsold finished goods stock.

To allow for this some accountants, and particularly auditors, hold back favourable variances in the variance accounts until the production to which they relate is sold.

However, we may ask whether there is really anything

MAIN ACCOUNTS

Cash

Sales	£70,700	Wages	£9,900
		Var. o'h'ds	4,100
		Fixed o'h'ds	19,000
		Royalty	1,000
		Selling and Distribution	9,200
		Balance c/d	27,500
Balance c/d	27,500		

Creditors

		Purchases:	
		X	£12,300
		Y	20,900
			33,200

Raw Materials

Purchases:			
X	£12,000	W.I.P.	£34,000
Y	22,000		

Wages

Cash	£9,900	W.I.P. (18,000 hrs at 50p)	£9,000
		Direct Wages Rate Var.	900

Variable Overheads

Cash	£4,100	W.I.P. (18,000 hrs at 25p	£4,500
Var. O'h'd. expenditure	400		

Fixed Overheads

Cash	£19,000	Capacity var. (2000 hrs at £1)	£2,00
Fixed o'h'd. expenditure var.	1,000	W.I.P. (18,000 hrs at £1)	18,00

Royalty

Cash	£1,000	W.I.P. (8,000 cwt at 10p)	£80
		Revision var.	2

Work in Progress

Raw materials	£34,000	F.G. (8,000 cwt at £7·6)	£60,80
Direct wages	9,000		
Var. o'h'ds.	4,500	Mix. var.	72
Fixed o'h'ds.	18,000	Yield var.	1,28
Royalty	800	Direct labour effic. var.	1,00
		V. o'h'd. effic. var.	50
		Volume effic. var.	2,00

Finished Goods

W.I.P.	£60,800	P/L (COS: 7,000 cwt at £7·6)	£53,20
		Balance c/d	7,60
Balance c/d	7,600		

Sales

Sales Margin Price var.	£700	Cash	£70,70
P/L	70,000		

Selling and Distribution Costs

Cash	£9,200	P/L	£9,200

*Alternatively, transfer standard cost and pass variance through a variance account.

FIG. 28.—*Standar*

The cost accounts and accounting entries shown here relate to th variances. It should be appreciated that these accounts have bee accounts have been shown (*e.g.* there are no fixed assets or capita XXII, 4.

VARIANCE ACCOUNTS

Direct Materials Price Variance

rchases X	£300	Purchases Y	£1,100
L	800		

Direct Materials Mixture Variance

W.I.P.	£720	P/L	£720

Direct Wages Rate Variance

ıges	£900	P/L	£900

Direct Materials Yield Variance

W.I.P.	£1,280	P/L	£1,280

Variable Overhead Expenditure Variance

L	£400	Variable O'h'ds	£400

Direct Labour Efficiency Variance

W.I.P.	£1,000	P/L	£1,000

Fixed Overhead Expenditure Variance

L	£1,000	Fixed O'h'ds	£1,000

Variable Overhead Efficiency Variance

W.I.P.	£500	P/L	£500

Capacity Variance

ed O'h'ds	£2,000	P/L	£2,000

Volume Efficiency Variance

W.I.P.	£2,000	P/L	£2,000

Revision (Royalty) Variance

yalty	£200	P/L	£200

Sales Margin Price Variance

P/L	£700	Sales	£700

Profit and Loss

. (Standard COS)	£53,200	Sales	£70,000
ing and Distribution	9,200		
verse Variances:		Favourable Variances:	
irect Wages Rate	900	Sales Margin Price	700
irect Materials Mixture	720	Direct Materials Price	800
irect Materials Yield	1,280	V. O'h'd Expenditure	400
apacity	2,000	F. O'h'd Expenditure	1,000
evision (Royalty)	200		
irect Labour Efficiency	1,000		
. O'h'd Efficiency	500		
olume Efficiency	2,000		
et Profit to Appropriation	1,900		

Profit and Loss Appropriation

		P/L	£1,900

t accounts

a given in Chapter XIX, (**4**, **5**), illustrating the computation of plified (*e.g.* there are no opening stocks) and not all the ledger ounts). The related profit and loss statements are shown in wrong with taking such profit? After all, a favourable variance reflects the efficiency attained during the period that it enters the variance account. Since a primary object of cost accounting is to advise management of their current operating efficiency, it is clear that such favourable variances should be reported for the period *in which they were obtained.*

This difference of treatment is a good example of the need when reporting to keep the *purpose* of a statement clearly in mind. If the purpose is to advise on efficiency, then favourable variances must be taken to the profit and loss statement when they occur; if, however, the purpose is to show the profit available for distribution, then the normal conservative accounting convention applies under which such unrealised profits must *not* be taken (*see also* I, **10**(*c*)).

5. Standard marginal cost accounts. The accounting system discussed in this section relates only to standard absorption costing. If standard marginal costing is employed the accounting is slightly different (*see* XXII, **9**).

PROGRESS TEST 21

Practice

1. The Alpha and Beta Company Ltd budgeted to sell 1000 Sets, but owing to bad trading conditions they only managed to sell 840 for a mere £57,100. Their production, however, was 900 Sets. They had no opening stocks at all, and they had no closing work in progress. During the trading period they suffered breakdowns amounting to 100 hours, during which time normal "direct" wages were paid. To add to their troubles they found 120 MTs broken in the store, apparently due to bad stacking. Other figures relating to the period were as follows:

Purchases (5,000 MTs)	£14,800
Direct wages (17,800 hours)	£9140 (this includes breakdown hours and pay)
Variable overheads	£4580
Fixed overheads	£20,900
Selling and distribution costs	£7000

4550 MTs were issued to production.

The company operate standard costs (a Set standard cost is shown below) and you are to prepare all cost and variance accounts for the period, including the profit and loss.

Standard Cost Card: 1 Set

	£
Direct Materials (5 MTs)	15
Direct Labour (20 hours)	10
Variable overheads (varying with production)	5
Fixed overheads	20
Factory standard cost	50
Selling and distribution (variable)	8
Total Standard Cost	58
Standard Profit (sales margin)	12
Standard selling price	£70

CHAPTER XXII

STANDARD COST AND BUDGETARY CONTROL

Now that we have seen how budgets and standard costs are prepared and variances are computed we will examine certain points involved in the actual use of these techniques for control.

CONTROL AND PERSONNEL

1. Definition of budgetary control. By this time the student should have a good understanding of cost control, and he should therefore reflect upon and learn the following definition: *Budgetary control* is the establishment of budgets relating the responsibilities of executives to the requirements of a policy, and the continuous comparison of actual with budgeted results either to secure by individual action the objective of that policy or to provide a basis for its revision.

Note that this definition involves individuals. It must always be remembered that *control can only be effected through people.*

2. Budgets and standards must be accepted. It is a fundamental principle of good control that the person responsible for maintaining control must *accept the plan*; that is, he must believe it is attainable and agree to be held responsible for those factors within his control in the event of failure. Budgets and standards, therefore, should never be imposed on anyone. If they are, failure is highly probable because the person concerned will:

(*a*) be indifferent to failure, since he will argue he cannot be held responsible for something he said could not succeed from the beginning;

(*b*) have a vested interest in fact, in failure, since success of the plan will prove that his original objections were not valid.

One excellent way of obtaining a man's acceptance of budgets and standards is to allow him to set them himself. Modification resulting from other people's plans is, of course, inevitable, but if such modifications are tactfully made, acceptance is not usually withheld.

3. Responsibility accounting. Clearly, since control can be attained only through individual people, it is necessary that accounting control statements *relate to the operations of individuals*. It is no use presenting two independent managers with a single statement relating to their joint operations, since this fails to pinpoint operating inefficiencies to either manager. A system of accounting that is designed to present managers with information relating to their individual fields of responsibility is termed *responsibility accounting*.

The three major principles of responsibility accounting are:

(*a*) *All data are analysed in terms of budget centres* (*see* XVII, **28**). Variance analyses and reports are all drawn up on a basis of these centres. Needless to say, an organisation chart and manual are invaluable in setting up such a system.

(*b*) *Only controllable costs and their associated variances are charged to budget centres.*

(*c*) *Every cost must be charged to someone*, even if that person's responsibility extends only to explaining the cause of the variance (*e.g.* local government rates are hardly controllable, but somebody should be responsible for ensuring that overpayments due to erroneous assessment are not inadvertently made).

When a manager is responsible for a field that includes the fields of a number of his subordinates (*e.g.* a works manager), then the subordinates have their own individual statements while he has a statement that summarises their performances and also includes data applicable to him alone (*e.g.* costs relating to the works manager's office).

OPERATING STATEMENTS

4. Profit and loss statement. The normal book-keeping profit and loss statement is one that simply lists income and expenditure to arrive at a net profit. Managers, however, are more concerned to know *where their efforts are failing* rather than money totals. Therefore a statement that highlights the place and consequences of these failings is much more valuable. Budgets and standard costs enable this to be done, since the profit and loss statement can start with the budgeted profit and, by incorporating all the variances, end with the actual profit. This budgeted profit is, of course, no new figure to management; they would have debated and agreed it before the period even began.

An example of such a profit and loss statement, using the figures given in XIX, **4** is given below (Example 2). The normal book-keeping statement for these figures is shown first for contrast (Example 1).

EXAMPLE 1: conventional profit and loss statement.

Data: As given in XIX, **4.** In the *conventional profit and loss statement* all figures are actual, though closing finished stock is valued at standard rather than actual cost so that the final net profit agrees with standard costing net profit.

Method:

		£	£
Sales			70,700
Production costs:	Purchases X	12,300	
	Purchases Y	20,900	
	Wages	9,900	
	Variable overheads	4,100	
	Fixed overheads	19,000	
	Royalty	1,000	
		£67,200	
Less closing stock:			
	1000 cwt at £7·60	7,600	59,600
	Gross profit		£11,100
Selling and distribution costs			9,200
	Net profit		£1,900

EXAMPLE 2: control profit and loss statement.

Data: Figures as in XIX, **4** and **5**. The statement begins with *budgeted profit.*

Method:

		£	£
Budgeted profit (10,000 cwt at £1)			10,000
Sales margin variances:			
Favourable:	Price	700	
Adverse:	Quantity	3,000	−2,300
	Actual sales profit		7,700
Cost variances:			
Favourable:	Materials price Y	1,100	
	Variable overhead expenditure	400	
	Fixed overhead expenditure	1,000	
	Selling and distribution	600	+3,100
			10,800
Adverse:	Materials price X	300	
	Materials mixture	720	
	Yield	1,280	
	Revision (royalty)	200	
	Wages rate	900	
	Labour efficiency	1,000	
	Variable overhead efficiency	500	
	Volume efficiency	2,000	
	Capacity	2,000	−8,900
	Actual net profit		£1,900

Some managements prefer the statement to start with budgeted *sales*. This is a doubtful practice, since management's interest should be primarily in profits (sales margins) rather than sales. Moreover, it involves the need to include the standard cost of actual sales, an additional step which otherwise need not be taken. However, for comparative purposes the first part of the Profit and Loss is redrafted in this form in Example 3. Note that the older type sales variances are needed in this method as against the sales variances used in the recommended form in Example 2 (*see* XX, **6**).

DEPARTMENTAL OPERATING STATEMENT

Department ....P3. X Process.. Production ....8,200 Stnd. Hours ....

Foreman ....Mr R. F. Evans.. Working Hours......8,580 ....

Period ....January, 1966.. Budgeted Hours ....8,000 ....

Control Ratios: Activity.........102·5%......... Efficiency.........95·6%......... Capacity.........107%.........

(Note: Overspending +; Saving −; All costs and variances in £'s)

Direct Materials:

Code	Unit	Standard Quantity	Actual Quantity	Difference	Standard Price	Usage Variance	Reason
A	Ft	5300	5650	+350	£0·10 ft	+35	Bad cutting
B	Lb	840	836	−4	£0·50 lb	−2	
Total						+33	
Cr: Excess scrap: A 60 lb at £0·05 lb						− 3	Off-cuts
				Net Variance		+30	

Direct Labour:

Section	Standard Hours	Actual Hours	Difference	Standard Cost	Actual Cost	Total Variance	Analysis		Reason
							Efficiency	Rate	
1	5220	5840	+620	2112	2223	+111	+164	−53	Grade switch
2	2980	2740	−240	1431	1365	−66	−54	−12	Long runs

Overhead	Allowed Cost*	Actual Cost	Expenditure Variance	Reason
Super. and clerical	428	410	−18	Overtime cut
Indirect Labour	762	595	−167	Overtime cut
Indirect Materials	110	122	+12	All-round increase
Maintenance	131	261	+130	P3/11 machine b/down 27/1/66
Power	456	450	−6	
Light and Heat	163	191	+28	Cold snap
Tools	120	133	+13	Excessive use K491
Total	2170	2162	−8	

Variable Overhead Efficiency Variance	Hours	£
Difference between actual hours and standard hours at variable overhead rate of 4*s*. per hour:		
Section 1	+620	+124
Section 2	−240	−48
Variable o'h'd. efficiency variance	+380	+76

* Based on hours worked.

Summary:

Element	Variances	
	This Month	Last Month
Direct materials	+30	+5
Direct labour:		
Efficiency	+110	−34
Rate	−65	+15
Controllable overheads:		
Expenditure	−8	+204
Variable o'h'd. efficiency	+76	−24
Total	+143	+166

Comments: Your new production scheduling is paying off. The reduction of overtime and the long runs resulted in a total saving of £251. Unfortunately it also gave us the £164 and £124 adverse variances on efficiency in Section 1, but now the grade problem has been overcome this should disappear this month.

P3/11. This is the third breakdown in less than a year. In view of the adverse variances resulting, management is considering replacing this machine.

Date.........8/2/66.........

Signed......J. Marshall..........
Cost Accountant

FIG. 29.—*Departmental operating statement*

EXAMPLE 3

Data: Figures as in XIX, 4. This control profit and loss statement opens with *budgeted sales.*

Method:

		£	£
Budgeted sales (10,000 cwt at £10 cwt)			100,000
Sales value variances: (*see* XX, 6)			
Favourable:	Price	700	
Adverse:	Quantity	30,000	−29,300
			70,700
Less standard cost of actual sales:			
7,000 cwt at £9 cwt			63,000
Actual sales profit			£7,700

By deducting the standard cost of actual sales, the figure for the profit on actual sales is reached. The production variances and actual net profit are unaltered (*cf.* Example 2 above).

5. Control ratios. In addition to variances, management often find *control ratios* of assistance in their control work. The most important of these, and their methods of calculation, are as follows:

$$(a)\ \textit{Efficiency ratio} = \frac{\text{SHP}}{\textit{Actual hours worked}} \times 100$$

$$(b)\ \textit{Capacity ratio} = \frac{\textit{Actual hours worked}}{\textit{Budgeted hours}} \times 100$$

$$(c)\ \textit{Activity ratio} = \frac{\text{SHP}}{\textit{Budgeted hours}} \times 100$$

6. Departmental operating statements. A *departmental operating statement* is a statement relating to the operating performance of a departmental manager during a specific period. It is an important statement listing comprehensively all the relevant cost data relating to the operation of the department, and it lies very much at the heart of control accounting.

An example of a simplified departmental operating statement is shown in Fig. 29. The following points should be noted:

(*a*) The *name* of the person responsible is given. Action can only be taken by a person, not by a department or a product, and so the statement names the controlling person. Indeed, every figure on the statement relates to his performance specifically.

(*b*) The *period reported on* and the *date reported* are both vital pieces of information and must be clearly stated.

(*c*) The main body of the statement contains:

(*i*) Production data.
(*ii*) Control ratios.
(*iii*) Material usage.
(*iv*) Labour usage.
(*v*) Controllable overhead expenditure.
(Often some non-controllable data are shown. This type of information, while not strictly necessary, does help the manager to envisage the over-all situation in which he operates.)

(*d*) Variances are clearly shown, individually and in total, together with the reasons where possible. The summary also provides a commentary on over-all performance and on any specific factors relevant to departmental operations.

STANDARD MARGINAL COSTING

7. Suitability of standard marginal costing. It was pointed out in Chapter XVI, (2) that control work could be logically divided so that budgets controlled fixed costs and standard costs controlled variable costs. This indicates that a form of *standard marginal costing* is more suitable for control work than standard absorption costing.

8. Basic features of standard marginal costing. The basic features of standard marginal costing are as follows:

(*a*) Direct materials, wages and expenses, together with variable overheads, are set out on a standard cost card as usual.

(*b*) A *standard contribution* is added to the standard marginal cost to give the standard selling price. This contribution is, of course, the standard sales margin.

(*c*) Budgets are prepared for:

(*i*) Fixed costs.
(*ii*) Sales mixture and volume.

(*d*) In the variance analysis:

(*i*) Volume efficiency and capacity variances no longer appear (the effect of these factors, in so far as they have any effect on the sales margin, appear in the contribution quantity variance).

(*ii*) Contribution variances are a form of sales margin variances and are, of course, calculated in exactly the same way.

9. Standard marginal costing illustrated. A chart depicting the essential features of the accounting flow for standard marginal costing is given in Fig. 30, and a simple worked example of standard marginal costing is given below.

EXAMPLE 4

Data:

(*a*) *Standard cost card*

		£
Product K:	Direct materials	5
	Direct wages	3
	Variable overheads	2
	Standard marginal cost	10
	Standard contribution (margin)	4
	Standard selling price	£14

(*b*) *Budget*

Sales	10,000 Ks. (Production to match sales)
Fixed overheads	£10,000

(*c*) *Actuals*

Production	8,000 Ks
Sales	6,000 Ks for £80,000
Direct materials	£40,000
Direct wages	£24,000
Variable overheads	£15,000
Fixed overheads	£12,000

Method:

(*a*) *Variances*

Materials: Standard cost for 8,000 units = 8,000 × £5
= £40,000.
Actual cost = £40,000. *No variance.*

Wages: Standard cost for 8,000 units = 8,000 × £3
= £24,000.
Actual cost = £24,000. *No variance.*

Variable overheads: Overheads absorbed by 8,000 units
$= 8,000 \times £2 = £16,000.$
Actual overheads = £15,000
∴ *Variable overhead variance* = £1,000 (F)

Fixed overheads: Budget = £10,000. Actual = £12,000.
∴ *Fixed overheads expenditure variance*
= £2,000 (A)

Contribution: (1) Actual sales value of 6,000 units
= £80,000
Standard sales value at £14 each = £84,000
∴ *Contribution price variance* = £4,000 (A)
(2) Also budgeted sales were 10,000 units but actual sales were only 6,000 units.
∴ 4,000 units each carrying a contribution of £4 were lost.
∴ *Contribution quantity variance*
$= 4,000 \times £4 = £16,000$ (A).

(*b*) *Standard marginal cost profit and loss statement*

	£	£
Budgeted profit, $(10,000 \times £4) - £10,000$		30,000
Contribution variances (A): Price	−4,000	
Quantity	−16,000	−20,000
Actual sales profit		10,000
Cost variances:		
Favourable: Variable overheads	1,000	
Adverse: Fixed overheads expenditure	−2,000	−1,000
Actual net profit		£9,000

(*c*) *Conventional accounting profit and loss statement*

	£	£
Sales		80,000
Costs: Direct materials	40,000	
Direct wages	24,000	
Variable overheads	15,000	
Fixed overheads	12,000	
	91,000	
Less Closing stock: 2,000 Ks at £10 each	20,000	71,000
Net profit		£9,000

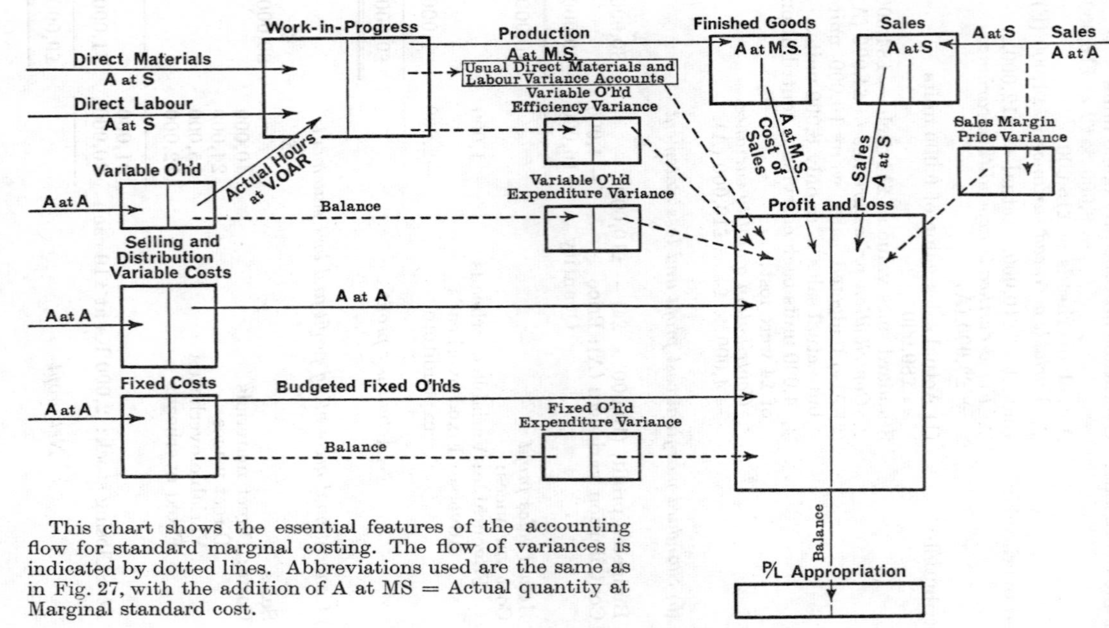

This chart shows the essential features of the accounting flow for standard marginal costing. The flow of variances is indicated by dotted lines. Abbreviations used are the same as in Fig. 27, with the addition of A at MS = Actual quantity at Marginal standard cost.

FIG. 30.—*Chart of standard marginal cost accounting*

PROGRESS TEST 22

Principles

1. What are the features of responsibility accounting? (3)
2. What information should be given in a departmental operating statement? (6)

Practice

3. From the data given in Progress Test 21:

(*a*) Compute the factory control ratios.
(*b*) Prepare a control-type profit and loss statement.

4. Repeat Question 3(*b*) in brief showing the relevant figures that would appear if standard marginal costing was in operation.

PART SIX

THE PRACTICE OF COSTING

CHAPTER XXIII

THE PRACTICE OF COSTING

UNIFORM COSTING

1. Definition. *Uniform costing* is the use by several undertakings of the same costing principles and/or practices. It should be noted that uniform costing is not a separate technique or method—it simply denotes a situation in which a number of undertakings use the same costing principles.

2. Factors requiring consideration under uniform costing. When installing uniform costing a number of factors must be considered. Definitions must be decided upon and methods of treatment selected, after which procedures must be laid down to ensure that the chosen methods are correctly applied. The main factors to which consideration must be given are:

(*a*) Depreciation (*e.g.* straight-line or reducing balance).
(*b*) Pricing stores issues (*e.g.* FIFO; LIFO; Weighted Average).
(*c*) Bases for overhead apportionment.
(*d*) Cost classifications (*e.g.* whether to classify works manager's salary as factory overheads or administration overheads).
(*e*) Overhead absorption rates (*e.g.* direct labour hours; machine hours).
(*f*) Definitions of "capacity" for the purpose of setting fixed overhead rates (*e.g.* whether a machine hour rate will be based on available hours or probable actual working hours).
(*g*) Costing periods (*e.g.* monthly; 4-weekly).
(*h*) Treatment of specific costs such as overtime, interest, charitable donations, etc.
(*i*) Costing statements. (It is clearly very important to have standardised statements if costs of different undertakings are to be compared.)

3. Advantages and disadvantages of uniform costing.

(*a*) The advantages of uniform costing are as follows:

(*i*) *Costs are comparable.* If two undertakings are producing a similar product then higher management may wish to compare their respective costs with the object of assessing relative efficiency. However, if uniform costing is not in operation then a difference between, say, the two factory costs-per-unit may be simply due to using straight-line depreciation in one factory and reducing-balance in the other, and is quite unconnected with efficiency. The prime advantage of uniform costing is that it enables costs to be compared.

(*ii*) *Staff costs may be reduced.* The use of uniform costing often enables the costing in a whole group of undertakings to be done by a single, centralised small team of well-qualified cost accountants, each individual undertaking needing only a competent senior cost clerk capable of applying the cost principles laid down.

(*iii*) *More flexible costing staff.* Where uniform costing is in use cost clerks moved between different undertakings require the minimum of training on transfer.

(*b*) The disadvantages of uniform costing are:

(*i*) *Costing inflexibility.* The imposition of a uniform costing system on an individual undertaking can result in a rigid costing system that may not be as satisfactory as a system tailor-made for the undertaking.

(*ii*) *Poorer cost service for individual undertakings.* The use of less than fully qualified staff in an undertaking can result in the managers not having the quality of cost advice that might otherwise have been available.

(*iii*) *High initial cost.* Setting up a uniform costing system usually entails a high initial cost.

4. Notional charges. It may happen that some of the undertakings have costs that are not incurred by the others (*e.g.* those not owning their own premises must pay rent). In order that costs may be comparable, book charges, called *notional charges*, are raised against those undertakings which are free from such costs and are incorporated in their cost accounts (*see* VIII, **13**).

COST AUDIT

5. Definition. A *cost audit* is the verification of the correctness of cost accounts and of the adherence to the cost accounting plan. Clearly, this will involve checking that:

(*a*) The figures themselves are correct.

(*b*) The cost accounts, cost centres and cost units are correctly charged.

It should be appreciated that the purpose of a cost audit is essentially to check that the various systems can be relied upon to operate in the intended manner rather than to locate and correct individual errors.

6. Cost audit procedure. Cost audits generally follow the same procedure as normal financial audits, *i.e.*:

(*a*) An audit programme is laid down and followed (*see* **7** below).
(*b*) Only a proportion of the day-to-day transactions are checked. Full checking is undertaken only when amounts are large or correct analysis is of considerable importance.
(*c*) Audit note sheets are compiled.
(*d*) Unusual items are examined and queries followed up until the auditor is certain he has the full explanation.

7. A typical cost audit programme. A typical cost audit programme would include:

(*a*) A check to ensure that materials were being correctly charged into store (*e.g.* that freight costs were added to the invoice price).
(*b*) A random check of materials requisitions to ensure the system of recording and pricing stores issues was reliable.
(*c*) An examination of stock discrepancy sheets and a subsequent investigation if something appeared to be amiss with the stores recording system.
(*d*) A random check of employees to ensure that all hours clocked by, and payments made to, individuals were being correctly entered on the wage analysis.
(*e*) A full check of at least one overhead analysis.
(*f*) Both:

(*i*) a follow-through of a number of transactions to ensure that the appropriate cost units were ultimately charged, and,
(*ii*) conversely, a check of a number of cost units to ensure that all costs charged were legitimate.

(*g*) A vouching of most or all cost ledger entries.
(*h*) An investigation of all sources of costs to ensure that no costs were being omitted.
(*i*) A careful appraisal of:

(*i*) The cost profit and loss statement.
(*ii*) Closing stock values, particularly if they are incorporated in the enterprise balance sheet.

OTHER MATTERS

8. Batch costing. *Batch costing* is the method of costing used when a number of identical cost units pass through a process or factory as a distinct and identifiable batch. In this method the batch is costed as a job until such time as it is physically broken up. Then the cost-per-unit of each unit is calculated by dividing the batch cost by the number of good completed units in the batch. Batch costing is most commonly found where small engineering parts are manufactured.

9. Policy costs. There are some costs which are incurred not because of the activity of the enterprise but because management elect to incur them as a matter of policy, *e.g.* costs of public relations office, prestige advertising, charitable donations. Such costs are termed *policy costs*.

10. Treatments of an incurred cost. Students should have appreciated by now that despite the numerous ways of processing data there are basically only five ways of treating an incurred cost:

(*a*) Write off to Profit and Loss: abnormal costs.
(*b*) Charge direct to cost units: direct costs.
(*c*) Charge to overheads and then either absorb into cost units or charge to Profit and Loss: indirect costs.
(*d*) Set off against a planned figure, any balance being taken to Profit and Loss: used when employing pre-determined costs, budgets or standard costs.
(*e*) Capitalise and then charge in period benefiting: pre-paid costs.

11. Cost systems. Every enterprise is in some ways different from other enterprises, and this means that every cost system needs to be different. It is very important to appreciate that a cost system must be *tailor-made to suit the individual enterprise*. Books may supply ideas, but the final detailed system must be the product of the cost accountant's skill, experience and imagination. In this respect cost accountancy makes heavy demands on the creative ability of its practitioners.

As the term "system" is rather vague the following definitions are suggested as an aid to clear thought on this subject:

System—an integrated set of procedures.

Procedure—a formal and organised way of carrying out a task.

12. Presentation of information. As has been repeatedly emphasised, the cost accountant's function is to advise management. Now clearly, if such advice when given is not understood by management, then the cost accountant's time and effort have been completely wasted. It is, therefore, vitally important that cost information is presented in the most comprehensible and effective manner possible. This is really a subject in its own right and one that students should master thoroughly. Here there is only space to list the main points involved in presenting information:

(*a*) Clear and correct English should be used.
(*b*) The person receiving the information—his interests, background knowledge, intellectual capacity (verbal and numerical) and temperament (thorough or impatient)—must be continually borne in mind when deciding the form and detail of the presentation.
(*c*) All the different ways of presenting information should be considered, particularly graphical and diagrammatic forms; (*see Statistics*, W. M. Harper, Macdonald & Evans).
(*d*) Figures should be laid out in a logical, clear and orderly manner with the minimum of crowding. Too many figures may result in mental indigestion. A little, presented and understood, is better than a great deal presented and not understood.
(*e*) Vital information should be in eye-catching positions (*e.g.* first paragraph) and visually emphasised (underlining, etc.).

Finally, never forget it is the responsibility of the cost accountant to make his advice understood; he has the choice of method, words, layout and detail. It is *not* the manager's job to learn to understand the cost accountant; he has plenty of other things to do. The cost accountant who blames management at any level from foreman up for not understanding him is incriminating himself, and any cost accountant who fails to make himself understood is not only wasting his time, but also drawing his salary under false pretences.

13. Comparative figures. When presenting information it is often useful if additional figures are included to enable management to judge, by making comparisons, the extent to which reported figures are satisfactory or otherwise. For instance, a statement of monthly costs, if it is warranted, may have columns for "this month," "last month," "same month last year" and "average monthly costs for year to date" with actual and budgeted figures within the first and last columns.

In examinations, students drafting pro-forma statements should always remember to consider the inclusion of columns for comparative costs.

14. Cost of costing. Costing costs money and is a particularly expensive activity when considerable time is spent recording and analysing data. Indeed, with very small jobs the cost of costing can exceed the factory cost! The cost accountant, therefore, must continually be alert to ensure the cost of costing does not exceed its value to management. This requires considerable skill, for not only must the point of diminishing returns regarding detailed analysis be correctly judged but also ingenious techniques must be devised that enable the maximum information to be obtained for the minimum effort.

When costing costing it is important to include the time spent by shop-floor employees in recording cost data (*e.g.* compiling time sheets).

15. Reliability of cost data. Cost accountants should never forget that their data may not always be reliable. Much of it comes from the shop-floor—time sheets, materials requisitions, materials returned notes, transfer notes, piece-work tickets, scrap returns—and it should be appreciated that many shop-floor employees:

(*a*) Are not clerks, nor are they really paid for clerical accuracy.
(*b*) Rarely have good clerical facilities (either office desks or even proper pencils).
(*c*) Often regard paper-work as an unnecessary obstacle to "getting the job out." (It should be noted, however, that the cost accountant who thinks the paper-work should have priority makes an even graver error.)
(*d*) Often have to record information from memory, because no written reference exists or because it is not at hand.
(*e*) May deliberately falsify the data.

This last possibility may be common where time-sheets are involved, particularly if an incentive scheme is in operation. Two points should be noted here. Firstly, if management use a single record for both computing bonuses and preparing costs, they cannot really complain if the employees use them as instruments to maximise their bonuses in preference to recording accurate cost information. Secondly, attempts to enforce accurate time-recording usually prove abortive; loopholes are almost invariably found unless the scheme is so elaborate that it is uneconomic.

In view of such possible unreliability in their basic data, cost accountants must beware of jumping to conclusions from such data. For instance, when booking time to a mixture of small and large jobs employees may easily forget they worked on some small jobs. Moreover, they are conscious that their excessive time is much more noticeable on a small job than on a large job involving a number of other employees. As a result of either or both these factors small jobs are almost always underbooked and large jobs overbooked and cost accountants should allow for this.

16. The cost accountant and the shop floor. Finally, and perhaps most important of all, we must consider what the cost accountant must know about the shop floor. By now the student should well appreciate that the cost accountant is management's expert on measuring economic performance at all levels and particularly the shop-floor level. It is at this point of manufacturing that profits are made. The most complex set of management services can never be more than an aid to the efficient conversion of materials to products, and sound measurement at this point is vital. However, it is precisely at this point that cost data are most subject to error, distortion, falsification and mis-interpretation. It is absolutely essential therefore, that the cost accountant knows exactly what happens on the shop floor; then he can both judge the quality of his data and assess the implications of his cost statements correctly. But only by *spending time on the shop floor* can he really know what is happening there. Moreover, only by knowing his foremen well can he present information to them in the most meaningful form, and this, too, means he must spend time on the shop floor.

The student must never forget that the real skill of a good cost accountant lies in his ability to marry the theory of this book with his experience of his industry, and of the two the theory is by far and away the easiest to acquire and apply.

PROGRESS TEST 23

Principles

1. What factors must be considered in setting up a system of uniform costing? (2)
2. What are the advantages of uniform costing? (3)
3. What is the purpose of a cost audit? (5)

4. Outline a cost audit programme. (7)

5. In what five basic ways can a cost be treated? (10)

6. What are the main points involved in presenting information? (12)

7. Why are cost data not always reliable? (15)

8. Why is it important for the cost accountant to spend time on the shop floor? (16)

Practice

9. The Thorough Garage finds that the conventional way of job costing small repair and service work on job cards is far too costly. Outline an alternative system.

APPENDIX I

EXAMINATION TECHNIQUE

To pass any examination you must:

1. Have the knowledge.
2. Convince the examiner you have the knowledge.
3. Convince him within the time allowed.

In the book so far we have considered the first of these only. Success in the other two respects will be much more assured if you apply the examination hints given below.

1. Answer the question. Apart from ignorance, *failure to answer the question is undoubtedly the greatest bar to success.* No matter how often students are told, they always seem to be guilty of this fault. If you are asked for a wage analysis, *don't* give a wage sheet; if asked to give the advantages of stores control levels, *don't* detail the steps for computing them. You can write a hundred pages of brilliant exposition, but if it's not in answer to the set question you will be given no more marks than if it had been a paragraph of utter drivel. To ensure you answer the question:

(a) *Read the question carefully.*
(b) *Decide what the examiner wants.*
(c) *Underline the nub of the question.*
(d) *Do just what the examiner asks.*
(e) *Keep referring to the question in your mind as you write.*

2. Put your ideas in logical order. It's quicker, more accurate and gives a greater impression of competence if you follow a predetermined logical path instead of jumping about from place to place as ideas come to you.

3. Maximise the points you make. Examiners are more impressed by a solid mass of points than an unending development of one solitary idea—no matter how sophisticated and exhaustive. Don't allow yourself to become bogged down with your favourite hobby-horse.

4. Allocate your time. Question marks often bear a close relationship to the time needed for an appropriate answer. Consequently the time spent on a question should be in proportion to the marks. Divide the total exam marks into the total exam time (less planning time) to obtain a "minutes per mark" figure, and allow that many minutes per mark of each individual question.

5. Attempt all questions asked for. Always remember that the first 50% of the marks for any question is the easier to earn.

Unless you are working in complete ignorance, you will always earn more marks per minute while answering a new question than while continuing to answer one that is more than half done. So you can earn many more marks by half-completing two answers than by completing either one individually.

6. Don't show your ignorance. Concentrate on displaying your knowledge—not your ignorance. There is almost always one question you need to attempt and are not happy about. In answer to such a question put down all you *do* know—and then devote the unused time to improving some other answer. Certainly you won't get full marks by doing this, but nor will you if you fill your page with nonsense. By spending the saved time on another answer you will at least be gaining the odd mark or so.

7. If time runs out. What should you do if you find time is running out? The following are the recommended tactics:

(*a*) If it is a numerical answer, don't bother to work out the figures. Show the examiner by means of your layout that you know what steps need to be taken and which pieces of data are applicable. He is very much more concerned with this than with your ability to calculate.

(*b*) If it is an essay answer, put down your answer in the form of notes. It is surprising what a large percentage of the question marks can be obtained by a dozen terse, relevant notes.

(*c*) Make sure that every question and question part has some answer —no matter how short—that summarises the key elements.

(*d*) Don't worry. Shortage of time is more often a sign of knowing too much than too little.

8. Avoid panic, but welcome "nerves." "Nerves" are a great aid in examinations. Being nervous enables one to work at a much more concentrated pitch for a longer time without fatigue. Panic, on the other hand, destroys one's judgment. To avoid panic:

(*a*) Know your subject (this is your best "panic-killer").

(*b*) Give yourself a generous time allowance to read the paper. Quick starters are usually poor performers.

(*c*) Take two or three deep breaths.

(*d*) Concentrate simply on maximising your marks. Leave considerations of passing or failing until after.

(*e*) Answer the easiest questions first—it helps to build confidence.

(*f*) Don't let first impressions of the paper upset you. Given a few minutes, it is amazing what one's subconscious will throw up. This, too, is a good reason for answering the easiest question first; it gives your subconscious more time to "crack" the difficult ones.

FORM DESIGN IN EXAMINATIONS

When examiners ask for form designs in examinations they do so to ascertain whether students know what data are relevant to a particular form and also if they can design forms generally.

Rather than memorise typical forms, students should learn to determine for themselves just what data are relevant and then design their own form with the principles detailed below in mind.

NOTE: When it is desired to show a form design with typical entries, the printing on the form should be indicated by using *block letters* and the handwritten data inserted by using normal handwriting.

9. Principles of form design. Forms should be designed so that:

(*a*) There is a clear indication to the person completing the form of the information required.
(*b*) Headings and phrases are unambiguous.
(*c*) The items detailed follow a logical order.
(*d*) The space for insertions is adequate but not excessive.
(*e*) There are no undesignated blank spaces on the form (sometimes a feature of student-designed forms).
(*f*) Handwriting is kept to a minimum.

10. Data common to most forms. The following data should appear or be allowed for on virtually all forms (and the student is strongly advised to memorise this list):

(*a*) *Form title.*
(*b*) *Serial number.* Each individual set of copies should be numbered, these numbers being consecutive and pre-printed so that all issued sets can be accounted for.
(*c*) *Date.*
(*d*) *Units, e.g.* tons, feet, hours, pairs.
(*e*) *Signature,* of the person authorising or reporting the form data.
(*f*) *Distribution of copies, e.g.* "Copy 1 Stores; Copy 2 Production Planning; Copy 3 Retained."
(*g*) *Narrative, e.g.* "Please supply" or "The following orders are outstanding."

11. Single and multiple data. Many forms handle two basic types of data:

(*a*) *Single data.* These are data that are given on a form as a single word, number or phrase, *e.g.* date of form; signature of writer.
(*b*) *Multiple data.* These are data given on the form as a list of words or numbers, *e.g.* materials required for a job; job numbers of finished production.

When *single* data are required the design should allow the information to be written alongside the printing, *e.g.*:

DATE............................ SIGNATURE.........................

If, however, such information requires, or may require, more than one line a horizontal box should be used (*see* Fig. 31).

Where *multiple* data are involved the information should be recorded in columns with printed headings (*see* Fig. 31).

COPY X
Distribution:
1—XXX
2—XXX
3—XXX

TITLE

SERIAL NO.

XXXXX..

XXX.. XXX...............

XXX.. Units...............

Narrative Sentence

XXXX		XXXX		XXX	
XX	XX	XXX	X	X	£

Comments:	Action:

Signature ....

Date.....................

Position...............................

FIG. 31.—*Basic form design*

This skeleton diagram shows the layout pattern which should be followed when designing forms for examination answers.

12. Form layout. Form layout, generally speaking, should comply with the following pattern (reading from top to bottom):

(*a*) Form title (top centre).
(*b*) Serial number and any other reference number or date (top right-hand corner).
(*c*) Single data excluding authorisations, comments and "action" data.
(*d*) Multiple data.
(*e*) Authorisations, comments and "action" data.

NOTE: *Action data* is information relating to action taken as a result of the information on the form, *e.g.* initials of person posting data to accounts; date of subsequent follow-up.

13. Form copies. Form design must take into consideration the number of copies required. Often all copies are printed identically, but on occasions a separate design is warranted for each copy. When designing forms in answer to examination questions students can indicate their knowledge of the use of the form by including details of copy distribution in their design.

14. Forms referred to in this book. All forms referred to in this book are assumed to comply with the above principles. To avoid needless repetition in Chapter II, only the data specifically relevant to the form under discussion are detailed under the heading *Design* (*i.e.* date, etc., is assumed). Under the heading *Copies* a possible distribution is suggested, though in practice this may well be less, since a relatively comprehensive distribution list is aimed at here.

APPENDIX II

EXAMINATION QUESTIONS

1. Discuss and explain the statement "the content of any assessment of cost should always be determined by the use to be made of the resulting figure of cost." (*C.A.*)

2. The price of an article to the public is printed on the outside container.

Detail the main classes of cost which add up to this declared price and against each factor show the unit by which it would be calculated. (*R.S.A.*)

3. As part of a cost audit, you are making a test check of the routine followed, from the raising of a purchase requisition by the stores department to the entries covering the receipt of the goods in the stores and cost ledgers.

Enumerate the documents and entries you would inspect, giving brief details of the main points you would check. (*I.C.W.A.*)

4. Detail fully a system by which orders for materials are initiated and placed on outside suppliers, and list the essential information to be included in such orders. What sections of the organisation should be kept informed and why? (*I.C.W.A.*)

5. List the matters to be considered in deciding the type of stores to be installed in a new branch works and explain the significance of each. (*I.C.W.A.*)

6. The physical contents of a stores bin, the balance on the bin card and the balance on the stores ledger account all show different quantities for a particular item of stock. What steps would you take to find how the discrepancies have arisen? Summarise the causes of a deficiency in the actual stock. (*I.C.W.A.*)

7. Design a material issue requisition suitable for use in a general stores. Outline briefly the procedure for authorising these documents. (*I.C.W.A.*)

8. Tabulate the main features of the following types of store, and of the routines controlling the movements of materials through them:

(*a*) work in progress store;
(*b*) finished goods store;
(*c*) tools store. (*I.C.W.A.*)

9. Briefly describe three distinct methods by which the quantity of material issued or used may be assessed. Give an example in each case. (*I.C.W.A.*)

10. (*a*) Distinguish between slow-moving, dormant and obsolete stocks.

(*b*) What principles would you follow in pricing these stocks for stocktaking purposes?

(*c*) What practical steps should be taken to minimise the losses and costs arising from the existence of these stocks? (*I.C.W.A.*)

11. Your managing director wishes to reduce the investment in stocks and stores as disclosed by a recent balance sheet and asks you to investigate and report. List the type of information you would submit and the factors to which you would draw attention. (*I.C.W.A.*)

12. List, in the form of headings and sub-headings, the factors that affect the amount of stocks carried by a business. (*I.C.W.A.*)

13. Define material control. List the main features of an efficient system of material control. (*I.C.W.A.*)

14. In manufacturing its products, a company uses three raw materials, A, B and C, in respect of which the following apply:

Raw material	*Usage per unit of product, lb*	*Re-order quantity, lb*	*Price, £ per lb*	*Delivery period Weeks* *Min.*	*Av.*	*Max.*	*Re-order level, lb*	*Minimum level, lb*
A	10	10,000	0·1	1	2	3	8,000	
B	4	5,000	0·3	3	4	5	4,750	
C	6	10,000	0·15	2	3	4		2,000

Weekly production varies from 175 to 225 units, averaging 200

(*a*) What do you understand by:

(*i*) minimum stock;
(*ii*) maximum stock;
(*iii*) re-order level?

(*b*) What would you expect the quantities of the following to be:

(*i*) minimum stock of A;
(*ii*) maximum stock of B;
(*iii*) re-order level of C;
(*iv*) average stock level of A? (*I.C.W.A.*)

15. Y. & Co. Ltd manufactures containers for delivering its products to customers.

The average cost of the containers is 50p per unit. They are charged to customers at 75p and on return are credited at 60p. How far, if at all, does this procedure affect: (*a*) the cost records, and (*b*) the financial records of the company?

(*A.C.C.A.* Adapted)

16. To what factors would you direct attention when studying a system of stores accounting with a view to reducing its operating cost? (*I.C.W.A.*)

17. What are the objects of a stores ledger control account? What entries are likely to appear in this account? (*I.C.W.A.*)

18. (*a*) List in classified form the different methods of pricing issues of material. Use the following figures, where appropriate, to illustrate the methods:

Receipt No.	*Date*	*Run No.*	*Price per unit* £	*Quantity (units)*
1	March	101	1·00	20
2	April	102	1·20	15
3	May	103	1·12½	25

On 1st June, there was a first issue of 30 units, at which date the price was £1·05 per unit.

(*b*) What factors affect the choice of method?

(*I.C.W.A.* Adapted)

19. Six units of an item of stores were purchased in the following order:

Lot 1 (3 units) A1, A2, A3 at a price of £*a* each
,, 2 (2 units) B1, B2 at a price of £*b* each
,, 3 (1 unit) C at a price of £*c*

Three issues of two units each are made.

Show formulae for five different methods based on actual prices, for pricing the issues when:

(*a*) all issues are made after the receipt of the third lot; and
(*b*) an issue is made after the receipt of each lot.

Give a brief note with each method stating the main characteristics of that method, with particular reference to production and stock valuations. Indicate when the identity of the unit issued affects the price.

Show basic methods only and exclude elaborations from your answer. (*I.C.W.A.*)

20. (*a*) What bases of remuneration of labour, other than the time basis, are commonly used?

(*b*) What points should be borne in mind in deciding on the basis to be adopted for remuneration of labour in any particular case? (*C.A.*)

21. Piece work is said to be: (*a*) straight; (*b*) progressive; (*c*) regressive. If the total work done is:

Job A 300, Job B 400, Job C 800 and Job D 500

and total wages = £50,400, and the regress rate for the first 500 pieces is 0·23p per piece and the last 500 pieces 0·20p per piece, what is the effective rate per unit of work and how would it be allocated to the respective jobs? (*R.S.A.* Adapted)

22. Using the information given below you are required to:

(*a*) Calculate the amounts earned by each employee under each of the following remuneration methods:

(*i*) piece work (with guaranteed hourly rates);

(*ii*) hourly rates;

(*iii*) bonus system (under which the employee receives $66\frac{2}{3}$% of time savings).

(*b*) Calculate the gross wages paid to each employee under each of the above methods:

	Employee A	Employee B	Employee C
Time allowed: hours per 100 units	23	32	38
Price per unit	6·25p	5p	$7\frac{1}{2}$p
Guaranteed hourly rate	30p	$37\frac{1}{2}$p	25p
Actual time taken: hours	40	42	39
Actual units produced	200	125	150

(*I.C.W.A.* Adapted)

23. In a factory bonus system, bonus hours are credited to the employee in the proportion of time taken which time saved bears to time allowed. Jobs are carried forward from one week to another. No overtime is worked and payment is made in full for all units worked on, including those subsequently rejected.

From the following information you are required to calculate for each employee:

(*a*) the bonus hours and amount of bonus earned;

(*b*) the total wage costs;

(*c*) the wage cost of each good unit produced.

Employee	A	B	C
Basic wage rate, per hour	25p	40p	$37\frac{1}{2}$p
Units issued for production	2500	2200	3600
Time allowed per 100 units	2 hrs 36 min	3 hrs	1 hr 30 min
Time taken	52 hrs	75 hrs	48 hrs
Rejects	100 units	40 units	400 units

(*I.C.W.A.* Adapted)

24. (*a*) Define generally the purpose of incentive schemes.

(*b*) The local managers of a company with numerous selling and service branches are paid a basic salary, with a bonus on turnover. Large and small orders, wholesale and retail, carrying varying rates of profit are handled for a wide range of equipment. Bonus payments vary widely from branch to branch, and complaints from the public of poor service tend to increase.

Enumerate the points which seem to you likely to be applicable to the situation described, and outline your proposals for improvement. (*I.C.W.A.* Adapted)

25. Why would you introduce a bonus system for indirect workers? Discuss the application of such systems and state the alternative bases on which the bonus might be determined. *(I.C.W.A.)*

26. What general principles are involved in remuneration for service? What factors determine wage levels and rates? Give a sub-division of groups of employees which are generally considered separately in assessing wage and salary levels. *(I.C.W.A.)*

27. Tabulate the mechanical aids which are available for wage accounting, and state briefly the purposes for which each may be used. *(I.C.W.A.)*

28. Tabulate the documentation required for wages accounting and state briefly the purpose of each record. *(I.C.W.A.)*

29. Design an employee record card containing all relevant information for use by both the wages and personnel offices. *(I.C.W.A.)*

30. Distinguish between the terms "Research Cost," "Development Cost" and "Pre-production Cost."

Give general examples of each kind of cost and the methods by which they would be absorbed in product costs when reviewing selling prices. *(R.S.A.)*

31. What items would appear in an analysis connected with Advertising?

Draft a form suitable for monthly presentation to the Board of Directors showing debits to specific products and apportionments to other products sold. *(R.S.A.)*

32. Submit a draft form of plant register card suitable for use in an engineering business utilising numerous automatic machines. *(C.A.)*

33. Why is it necessary to provide for depreciation of fixed assets? What method of depreciation would you recommend in each of the following cases? Give reasons.

(*i*) Plant and Machinery;
(*ii*) Leasehold Property;
(*iii*) Freehold Land and Buildings;
(*iv*) Freehold Land purchased for working as a quarry. *(C. of S.)*

34. A large company with many departments and interdependent specialised machinery, consider it economical to employ skilled engineers to:

(*a*) Daily inspect and adjust all machinery.
(*b*) Carry out minor repairs, the materials for which they are authorised to draw from Stores.
(*c*) Report major faults and obtain special works orders for such work from the Chief Engineer's office. These works orders are fully costed.

By what different means could the cost of these maintenance engineers for categories (*a*) and (*b*) be apportioned to the various departments? Describe briefly the procedure adopted to cost the works orders for category (*c*). (*R.S.A.*)

35. A productive department of a manufacturing company has five different groups of machines, for each of which it is desired to establish machine hour rates. A budget for this department for the year ending 30th June, 1963 shows the following overhead:

		£	£
Consumable supplies:	Machine group 1	300	
	2	600	
	3	1,000	
	4	1,200	
	5	1,900	
			5,000
Maintenance:	Machine group 1	700	
	2	800	
	3	1,200	
	4	1,700	
	5	1,000	
			5,400
Power			1,400
Rent and rates			4,800
Heat and light			800
Insurance of buildings			400
Insurance of machinery			1,000
Depreciation of machinery			16,000
Supervision			9,600
General expenses			1,200
			£45,600

Additional operating information is available as follows:

Group	*Effective H.P.*	*Area occupied sq ft*	*Book value of machinery* £	*Machine working hours*
1	10	500	5,000	24,000
2	40	1,500	25,000	40,000
3	20	200	10,000	16,000
4	50	1,000	40,000	20,000
5	80	800	20,000	60,000
	200	4,000	£100,000	160,000

You are required to:

(*a*) calculate a machine hour rate for each of the five groups of machines. Show clearly the bases of apportionment that you use;
(*b*) calculate the overhead that will be absorbed by one unit of product A and one unit of product B on the manufacture of which the following times (in hours) are spent in the machine groups of this department:

Machine group	1	2	3	4	5
Product A (each unit)	2	–	7	1	2
Product B (each unit)	4	1	–	6	1

(*I.C.W.A.*)

36. What is meant by

(*a*) Overheads Incurred;
(*b*) Absorbed Overheads?

How are these costs related at the end of a four-weekly costing period?

What information can be obtained from these costs and what treatment do you recommend should be incorporated in the cost accounts? (*R.S.A.*)

37. You have recently been appointed cost accountant of a company manufacturing a wide range of products in three production departments. Generally, products pass through all departments, but some products may be operated on in one or two departments only.

It has been the practice in past price-fixing to estimate direct material and direct wages cost, adding 100% to prime cost to cover all overheads. To the total so obtained 15% is added as a minimum for net profit.

Accounts for the past year are as follows:

	£
Direct materials	49,545
Direct wages	33,368
Total overheads	81,668
Net profit	10,292
Sales	£174,873

Analysis of the direct wages gives the following figures:

	£	Average wage rate per hour p
Department A	12,241	25
,, B	16,875	30
,, C	4,252	37½

The overheads are analysed as follows:

	£
Factory overhead:	
Department A	12,682
,, B	29,322
,, C	18,290
Selling and distribution costs	20,374

You are asked to prepare figures and present a report on them making recommendations to overcome the unsatisfactory profit position of the company. (*I.C.W.A.* Adapted)

38. During the course of a year your cost accounts indicate that overheads are being under-absorbed. What are the probable reasons?

What steps would you take to deal with the under-absorption, according to the cause? Give reasons. (*I.C.W.A.*)

39. A factory department—B.4—comprises five machines, each of the same type, size and capacity.

Two operators—a mechanic and his assistant—are employed on each of the machines.

A 40-hour week is worked, which includes 3 hours per week for adjustment and set-up time. This work is done jointly by the two machine operators. Their basic wages are: machanic 20p per hour; assistant 10p per hour. The average bonus rate on basic wage is 12½%. The company's year is divided into four 13-week periods.

It is desired to recover both the direct labour cost and the factory overhead by the application of a single machine rate.

Factory overhead

1. Machine set-up time as above.
2. Depreciation at 12½% on machine cost (£800 per machine).
3. Maintenance and repairs: £1·25 per week per machine.
4. Consumable stores: 72½p per week per machine.
5. Electric current: 4 units (at ⅝p per unit) per hour per machine.
6. Allocations to department B.4

Local rates:	£160 per annum.
Heat, light, etc.:	£200 per annum.
Foreman's salary:	£720 per annum.

(*a*) Prepare a summary of the cost of operating *one* machine for a 13-week period; and

(*b*) Compute the hourly rate for operating *one* machine.

(*A.C.C.A.* Adapted)

40. The Earth Moving Company Ltd hire out special equipment on an hourly charge basis. From the following information relating to two machines, you are required to prepare a statement showing the cost per hour which should be charged out for them in order to give a profit of 25% on cost, and the total profit which each machine will earn in a year. Your statement should be constructed in such a way that the effect of any deviations from normal capacity can be readily calculated.

	Machine No. H.E. 123	*Machine No. H.E.* 567
Normal usage in hours	800	800
Fuel and Lubricant costs per 50 hours	£25	£30
Annual Licence	£100	£135
Tyre costs per annum	£55	£65
Wages of driver per annum (weekly contract)	£850	£1000
Wages of driver's assistant per annum (weekly contract)	£650	£750
Depreciation per annum	£900	£1200

In addition to the above, each machine is allocated the following company charges per annum:

Maintenance	£320
Fleet Insurance	100
Management and Administration expenses	134
Rates, Heat, Light, etc.	23
Selling expenses	15

The cost of tyres and depreciation can be assumed to bear a direct relationship to the number of hours which the machines are in use. (*A.C.C.A.*)

41. Blu-Print Ltd are asked to quote for supplying 5000 or 25,000 or 50,000 booklets. They normally expect a profit of 10% on sales.

Costs are reckoned to be:

	£
Paper and other materials, per 1000 copies	3
Wages, per 1000 copies	2
Lay-out cost	50
Variable overhead, 120% of wages	
Fixed overhead	20

Draft a cost computation, showing also selling prices (to the nearest £) that may be quoted per 1000 copies in each of the three cases. (*A.C.C.A.*)

42. The budgeted costs of a manufacturing business for a normal year are as follows:

	£	£
Direct materials		68,273
Direct wages:		
Machine shop (100,000 hours)	27,382	
Assembly (80,000 hours)	22,780	
		50,162
Works overheads:		
Machine shop	33,490	
Assembly	16,237	
		49,727
Administration overheads		12,268
Selling expenses		15,481
Distribution expenses		13,290

The absorption method of costing is in operation.

Prepare a schedule of overhead rates suitable for practical use in this business.

Complete a cost estimate for a job, the technical data for which is as follows:

Material: 20 lb A at $63\frac{3}{4}$p per lb
15 lb B at $8\frac{1}{3}$p per lb
Direct labour: Machine shop: 15 hours at 30p per hour
Assembly: 25 hours at 35p per hour

(*I.C.W.A.* Adapted)

43. The following were some of the balances in the ledger of M. Ltd on December 31, 1959:

	Dr £	*Cr* £
Absorption Accounts:		
40. Direct wages	400	
41. Factory overhead		500
100. Finished stock control	3000	
Work in progress:		
Direct wages:		
110. Metal shop	550	
111. Cabinet shop	300	
Factory overhead:		
112. Metal shop	550	
113. Cabinet shop	200	

The actual direct wages and factory overhead incurred for the three months to 31st March, 1960, were:

	£	£
Direct wages:		
Metal shop	2600	
Cabinet shop	3400	

Factory overhead:		
Rent, rates, heat and light		1000
Depreciation and insurance		800
Factory salaries		1500
Indirect wages:	Metal shop	760
	Cabinet shop	580
Repairs/maintenance:	Metal shop	464
	Cabinet shop	386
Consumable stores:	Metal shop	238
	Cabinet shop	285

The following apportionments are to be made:

	Metal shop	*Cabinet shop*
	On the basis of:	
Rent, rates, etc.	3000 sq ft	2000 sq ft
Depreciation, etc.	£60,000 valuation	£20,000 valuation
Factory salaries	Direct wages	Direct wages

The output of finished units from each cost centre for the three months was:

Metal shop —1300 units at 9 man-hours per unit
Cabinet shop — 800 units at 15 man-hours per unit

The absorption rate per hour for direct wages and factory overhead are:

	Direct wages	*Factory overhead*
Metal shop	25p	100% of direct wages
Cabinet shop	30p	$66\frac{2}{3}$% of direct wages

The work in progress at cost centres on March 31, 1960, was:

Metal shop	2000 man-hours
Cabinet shop	1110 ,,

You are required to write up the appropriate accounts and bring down and schedule the closing balances at March 31, 1960, stating what the absorption account balances represent.

(*I.C.W.A.* Adapted)

44. (*a*) State how you would judge the suitability of a cost unit for the calculation of the cost of a product or service; and (*b*) show how your answer to (*a*) might apply in the cases of: (*i*) gold mining, and (*ii*) road haulage. (*C.A.*)

45. Your company employs three different types of transport vehicle in bringing into the factory heavy steel bars, and delivering to customers finished tubes and fabricated tube products. Detail the procedures necessary to instal satisfactory costing arrangements for the transport, and suggest cost control measures which might be introduced. (*I.C.W.A.*)

46. XYZ Ltd manufacture one mineral water product of uniform quality and size. From the following information prepare a Cost Sheet for the month of June 1948 showing the output in cases, total cost under the appropriate headings and the cost per case produced (in detail and total).

	No. of cases of Minerals	*Ingredients* £	*Bottles and packing* £
Stocks, June 1, 1948	3000	600	360
Purchases	—	795	690
Stocks, June 30, 1948	1500	420	625
Sales	8000	—	—

Other expenditure:	Total, June 1948. £	
Water consumed	150	(90% used in product, 10% for ordinary cleaning, etc.)
Factory expenses	450	
Factory wages	1000	
Administration expenses	250	

(*C. of S.*)

47. A special printing process is performed at infrequent intervals, the costs of four runs (material cost excluded) are:

	Cost	*Articles processed*
1st run	£7·50	1500
2nd run	£9·00	2400
3rd run	£11·00	4400
4th run	£7·00	700

(*a*) Arrange these runs in order of costliness.
(*b*) What factors contributed to these results?
(*c*) What further information is required to enable one to judge the efficiency of the respective runs? (*R.S.A.* Adapted)

48. After several processes, a certain by-product is yielded, saleable at 25p per lb. Augmented by material K, followed by further processing, the by-product commands a higher price.

The main product sells at £1 per lb. There are three processes A, B and C. Department D bottles and packages.

Materials X, Y and Z are carefully weighed and issued, under laboratory control, to process A for mixing, before passing to process B, where a 10% loss in weight by evaporation occurs. The remainder then passes to process C. Further loss occurs, so that 80% of the process input weight is the maximum transferable to department D as main product.

Without strict control in process C, as much as 35% of the process input weight may emerge as by-product.

The alternative to selling the by-product at 25p per lb is to add 50% to its weight by adding material K, and to process further in another department. The process loss here is 40%, but the resultant product has a sales value of £2·75 per lb. The costs of this last process are:

Material K:	15p per lb
Variable cost	32½p per lb of mixture at commencement
Fixed cost	£800 per month

The other relevant figures are:

Issues to process A:

Material	X	7500 lb at 27½p per lb
,,	Y	2800 ,, ,, 25p ,, ,,
,,	Z	900 ,, ,, 20p ,, ,,

Variable costs:

Process A:	9p per lb of material introduced
,, B:	10p ,, ,, ,, part processed product introduced
,, C:	12½p ,, ,, ,, part processed product introduced
Dept. D:	11p ,, ,, ,, part processed product introduced

The processes are fully occupied.

Tabulate a cost statement to give total manufacturing cost and profit:

(*a*) when 20% of C input is produced as by-product;
(*b*) when material K is added to the by-product:

(*i*) where this is 20% of C input; and
(*ii*) where this is 35% of C input. (*I.C.W.A.* Adapted)

49. A company operates process plant to produce a single product from one process. At the month-end, work in process, consisting of 1700 units of product completed but not passed to stores, was valued as follows:

	£
Direct material	12,750
Direct wages	5,100
Overhead	5,100 (100% of direct wages)

During the next month 18,500 further units were put into process, the cost figures used being £138,750 for direct materials, £55,500 for direct wages, and, using 100% of direct wages,

£55,500 for overhead. 18,000 units were completed and transferred to finished stock, and 2200 remained at the month end as work in process, complete as to material and half completed as to wages and overhead. The average method of valuing work in process is used.

Compile a process cost and production sheet to show total and unit process costs for each cost element, effective units of output and the apportionment of production cost as between completed product and closing work in process for the month. (*I.C.W.A.*)

50. A system of job order costing is operated at a small engineering works where part of the production is defective but capable of rectification.

Design a sheet to record an item of defective production, and the necessary variable cost additions for rectification. Show how the figures obtainable from the record would be journalised. (*I.C.W.A.*)

51. What do you understand by the term joint costs?

Give *one* example from any business with which you are familiar, and discuss briefly some of the considerations involved in cost allocation. (*A.C.C.A.*)

52. How should by-products be dealt with in Costing?

(*a*) Where they are of small total value.
(*b*) Where they are of considerable total value.
(*c*) Where they require further processing.

The yield of a certain process is 80% as to the main product, 15% as to by-product and process loss 5%. The material put in process (500 units) cost £3 per unit and all other charges £1000, of which power is £230. It is ascertained that power is chargeable as to by-product and main product in the ratio of 2:1.

Draw up a statement showing the cost of the by-product. (*A.C.C.A.*)

53. A textile company has a department which concentrates upon one style of garment which is redesigned annually. Since high-grade production is aimed at, a proportion of the output, usually 20%, is sold without the brand name, being sub-standard. A further 2% has no value except for certain pieces of salvaged material, usable for trimming.

The figures for a batch of 100 were as follows:

	£	
Direct materials	3·00	per garment
Direct wages	1·50	,, ,,
Variable overhead	2·00	,, ,,
Fixed overhead	150·00	(total)

Output:				£	
First grade	78	garments:	sales value	15·00	each
Sub-standard	20	,,	sales value	8·00	,,
Scrap	2	,,	value	0·50	,,

No difficulty is experienced in using salvaged material from scrap up to 5%, but beyond this level scrap is virtually of no value.

Sickness and holiday absence make the engagement of temporary staff necessary. The employment of temporary staff increases sub-standard output to 30% and scrap to 7%. Fixed overhead is unaffected.

Using the figures given, show how the joint costs would be allocated.

Determine profits on first grade and sub-standard output in (*a*) normal conditions, and (*b*) where the use of temporary staff has produced 7% scrap and 30% sub-standard garments.

What advice would you give to management?

(*I.C.W.A.* Adapted)

54. The present sales turnover is 1000 articles at £55 each. By reason of a price reduction of 10% the size of orders has increased by 50%, although the number of orders has remained practically constant.

Present a comparative statement of the influence on the total profit arising out of this increase in sales income.

Base your statement on a present cost structure of:

	%
Materials	40
Variable wages and expenses	30
Fixed overhead	15
Profit	15
	100

Show the new cost structure. (*R.S.A.*)

55. The following figures apply to a manufacturing company producing a wide range of products which may be classified into three main groups:

Product group	*Annual sales* £	*Variable costs* £
A	3,000,000	1,000,000
B	3,000,000	2,000,000
C	3,500,000	3,000,000

The fixed costs total £2,500,000.

Plot on a graph the marginal income slopes for the three product groups in alphabetical order to enable you to plot the average marginal income slope for the total output.

What information may be derived from the graph? What conclusions can it be used to illustrate? (*I.C.W.A.*)

56. Joe Banger contemplates starting a workshop for production of metal stampings of uniform pattern and has supplied the following technical and financial information:

(1) Sales will be made on a long-term contract requiring delivery of a regular number of stampings per week.

(2) The rent of the workshop, inclusive of general and water rates, heating, lighting and all services, will be £4 per week.

(3) He will install as many stamping presses as are required to produce the number of stampings sold. Each press will involve depreciation and maintenance of the rate of £8 per week and electrical power costing 5p per productive hour worked.

(4) For each press installed he will employ an operative whose wages (including national insurance and holiday pay) will cost £12 for a guaranteed 42-hour week. No overtime will be worked.

(5) The maximum productive hours for a press will be 40 hours per week and each press will produce stampings of the sale value of £1·75 per productive hour. Two hours weekly will be required for maintenance of each press and, if necessary, output will be restricted to the number of stampings to be delivered in each week.

(6) In addition to operatives he will employ one labourer whose wages, together with other fixed overhead expenses, will cost £16 per week.

(7) Each press will require to be fed with strip metal costing 92½p per operating hour, and sale of scrap will realise 4% of the cost of strip metal processed.

(8) Use and maintenance of tools will be allowed for at the rate of 10p per press per productive hour.

You are required:

(*a*) to submit a break-even chart based on weekly operations covering sales up to £250 per week, and

(*b*) to state the level of sales at which a profit of £16 per week could be expected. (*C.A.* Adapted)

57. A cost accountant is asked to examine a proposal to supplement an existing product which is showing a declining profit margin.

Give an outline of the considerations on which the new proposition would be examined from a costing point of view. (*R.S.A.*)

58. A business consisting of two departments, A and B, makes

two products, X and Z, each of which passes through both departments. Standard cost, etc., information is as follows:

	Product X	Product Z
Direct materials	65p per unit	25p per unit
Direct labour times:		
Dept. A	30 minutes per unit	60 minutes per unit
,, B	40 ,, ,, ,,	30 ,, ,, ,,
Selling price	£2·20 per unit	£1·80 per unit

Direct labour hour rates are:

Dept. A	20p per hour
,, B	30p ,, ,,

Variable overhead rates are:

Dept. A	20p per direct labour hour
,, B	60p ,, ,, ,, ,,

Fixed overheads amount to £1500 per month, and are exactly equal to the normal variable overheads. They are apportioned to the two departments on the same basis as variable overheads.

In a month in which 1000 units of product X and 2000 units of product Z were produced and sold at standard selling prices, the actual costs were as follows:

		£
Direct materials		1150
Direct wages	Dept. A	550
,, ,,	,, B	575
Variable overheads	Dept. A	550
,, ,,	,, B	1150
Fixed overheads		1500

Present information to management in order to show: (*a*) profitability; (*b*) efficiency. (*I.C.W.A.* Adapted)

59. A company making a single product has a factory in the South, and distributes its production through three depots situated in the South, Midlands and North.

It is estimated that during the coming year 100,000 units will be manufactured and sold at a price of £20 per unit, the sales being spread as follows:

South	70,000 units
Midlands	20,000 ,,
North	10,000 ,,

Standard costs of production are:

Direct materials	£4·80 per unit
Direct wages	£3 ,, ,,
Factory variable overheads	140% on direct wages
Factory fixed overheads	£400,000 per annum

The costs of selling and distribution incurred by the depots are estimated as follows:

Fixed costs	South	£80,000 per annum
,,	Midlands	£50,000 ,,
,,	North	£30,000 ,,
Variable costs	South	5% of sales value
,,	Midlands	8% ,,
,,	North	10% ,,

From the budget for the business prepared from these figures, management is considering the desirability of closing the depots and selling organisations in the Midlands and/or North. If this is done it is expected that all sales in these areas will be lost, but that sales in the South will remain unaffected.

Prepare a budget for the business from the figures provided, indicating why management is thinking of closing the depots in the Midlands and/or North. Present additional information to help management make a decision in regard to this problem, and make recommendations from your figures. (*I.C.W.A.* Adapted)

60. R.I.S. Ltd is a contracting company. In December 1959 the company was invited to undertake two contracts, one in Southampton and one in Norwich, but the company's resources do not permit the acceptance of both. Both jobs would commence on January 1, 1960, and would take a year to complete.

On December 20, 1959, the directors held a meeting to consider the alternatives and the following financial statement was submitted:

	Southampton contract £	*Norwich contract* £
Materials: In stock, at December 20, 1959 (at cost) Type A	15,000	
Type B		6,600
To be purchased at estimated prices ruling in 1960	16,000	20,400
Direct labour	33,000	49,000
Depreciation of plant on site	2,400	3,200
Total of direct charges	66,400	79,200
Office and administration oncost, 6% of direct charges	3,984	4,752
	70,384	83,952
Contract price	80,000	96,000
Profit	9,616	12,048

If the Southampton contract is accepted, the stock of type B materials, which have recently risen in price, can be sold for £12,500. If the Norwich contract is accepted, the stock of type A materials can be sold for £14,950. It is assumed that, whichever contract is accepted, the stocks not required will be sold.

Depreciation of plant, charged in the financial accounts, calculated by the straight line method, is £3200 a year.

The company owns 25 units of plant, of which 20 would be used on the Southampton contract, while all 25 would be used on the Norwich contract. If the Southampton contract is accepted, 5 units will be hired out to other contractors at a rental of £300 each for the year 1960.

Office and administration expenses are expected to amount to £4600 for the year 1960, whichever contract is accepted.

You are required to produce a revised financial statement designed to show which contract should, in your opinion, be accepted. (*C.I.S. Final*)

61. A manufacturing concern has multi-purpose plant capable of operating at full capacity at 5000 machine hours per monthly production period. It may produce three products interchangeably, for which the output and cost details are as follows:

Product A: 500 units per machine hour.
Material cost, £4·25 per thousand units.
Product B: 250 units per machine hour.
Material cost, £1·75 per thousand units.
Product C: 1000 units per machine hour.
Material cost, £3 per thousand units.

Labour costs per machine hour	£1·50
Variable costs ,, ,, ,,	£0·50

The fixed costs of the department are £10,000 per monthly production period.

The fixed assets involved are valued at £28,940 and the current assets in use amount on average to 33⅓% of a month's sales.

The management of the company estimates from past experience that the full capacity can be used at all times if machine time can be freely moved from one product to another as dictated by demand, and is anxious to establish suitable product selling prices (per 1000 units). The three price-fixing proposals which are being considered are:

(*a*) to fix selling prices at product costs plus 20%;
(*b*) to fix prices so as to give a contribution of £3·50 per machine hour; and
(*c*) to fix the prices arbitrarily (per 1000 units) at product A—£15, product B—£23 and product C—£9.

Calculate the prices which would be charged under these three proposals and prepare a comparative schedule. Would you be prepared to select one of these methods of pricing? Explain your choice. What additional information might aid you in your choice? (*I.C.W.A.* Adapted)

62. On a farm of 200 acres the farmer plans to sow 100 acres of barley, 20 acres of kale and to use 80 acres on which to graze milk cattle.

For the barley, seed will cost £2·50 per acre, and fertilisers £3·50 per acre. It is expected that the yield will be 30 cwt per acre, which will be sold at £25 per ton.

The kale will cost £2 per acre for seed and £5 per acre for fertilisers. The kale produced will be fed to the cattle.

On the 80 acres, 40 milking cows will be kept, and in addition to the kale, other feeding stuffs will cost £1000 in all for the year. Each cow should produce one calf which will be sold at £10 each, together with an annual milk yield sold at £120. Cows will "depreciate" at the rate of £10 per annum.

Other farm costs (which are unlikely to change, however the farm is worked) are, per annum:

	£
Farmworkers' wages	1800
Rent, rates, etc.	1200
General charges	3000

A suggestion is made that kale should be purchased instead of grown: if this is done it is estimated that kale will cost £12·50 per cow, per annum.

Prepare figures to indicate to the farmer whether the kale should be purchased or grown. If the kale is purchased, show how the 20 acres could be used to best advantage. (*I.C.W.A.* Adapted)

63. A manufacturing company produces three products X, Y and Z, by passing materials through two departments, A and B. In a time of expanding trade, the management accountant is asked to provide information to illustrate the relative profitability of products.

The company has adequate finance, materials can be obtained well in excess of maximum requirements and plant and machinery are available for additional work in both departments.

Standards per unit are as follows:

Product	X	Y	Z
Material costs	£2·80	£2·40	£2·75
Labour hours:			
Department A	2	3	1
Department B	2	1	3
Selling price	£9·00	£7·50	£10·00

Other budget figures are:

Department	A	B
Direct labour wage rates (per hour)	25p	30p
Direct labour hours per annum	80,000	120,000
Overhead costs per annum:		
Variable	£24,000	£60,000
Fixed	£24,000	£120,000

Present information, and make recommendations to management.
(*I.C.W.A.* Adapted)

64. What do you understand by "Principal Budget Factor?"
Describe the items and circumstances to which this term can be applied. How does the Principal Budget Factor influence the policy of a Company when considering: (*a*) products; (*b*) selling prices; (*c*) markets? (*R.S.A.*)

65. It has been suggested that budgets are impracticable and of small value for a business in which sales are largely dependent on some factor over which the management has no control, *e.g.* the weather.

Discuss this suggestion. (*C.A.*)

66. Itemise a procedure for scheduling the material requirements of a production budget. (*I.C.W.A.*)

67. Distinguish between overhead allowance and overhead absorption. Where the standard departmental overhead rate is £1·50 per hour, calculate the level on which it has been fixed, given the following figures:

Activity level	*Overhead allowance*
4,000 hours	£6,300
7,000 hours	£9,900
10,000 hours	£13,500

(*I.C.W.A.* Adapted)

68. The following budgeted information is available for one period in a factory which produces three products:

	Selling price	COSTS *Direct materials*	*Direct wages*	*Variable over-heads*	*Pro-duction*	*Sales*
	p	*p*	*p*	*p*	*units*	*units*
X	300	70	80	10	16,000	13,600
Y	250	55	70	5	10,000	9,600
Z	200	$23\frac{1}{3}$	60	$6\frac{2}{3}$	8,000	7,200

There is no stock at the beginning of the period. Fixed overhead is absorbed on the basis of direct wages. Budgeted total costs are £70,400 for the period.

You are required to:

(*a*) prepare a statement showing budgeted profit for the period;
(*b*) show the value of the budgeted stock of each product at the end of the period. (*I.C.W.A.* Adapted)

69. A company manufactures two models of a machine and distributes them in three sales areas. The budgeted Profit and Loss Account for the year ended December 31, 1965, is:

Sales:

	Large	*Small*	*Total*
	£	£	£
Area			
A	12,500	25,000	37,500
B	25,000	37,500	62,500
C	37,500	62,500	100,000
	£75,000	£125,000	200,000

	£	£
Production cost of sales:		
Large (60% of sales)	45,000	
Small (70% „ „)	87,500	
		132,500
Gross profit		67,500

Direct selling and distribution costs:

Area	*A*	*B*	*C*	*Total*
	£	£	£	£
Salesmen's salaries	3,625	4,000	1,875	9,500
„ expenses	1,125	750	625	2,500
Sales office costs	1,750	1,550	1,200	4,500
Advertising	350	850	400	1,600
Carriage	675	600	725	2,000

Indirect selling and distribution costs:

	£		
Advertising	6,000		
Carriage	1,100		
Warehousing	3,850		
Credit control	2,200		
General administration	4,000		
		17,150	
			37,250
Budgeted net profit			£30,250

The budgeted analysis of sales is:

	LARGE		SMALL	
Sales area	*Sales volume (machines)*	*No. of orders*	*Sales volume (machines)*	*No. of orders*
A	2000	300	2000	400
B	4000	500	3000	500
C	6000	200	5000	300

The cost manual of the company states that:

(1) Indirect selling and distribution costs are to be apportioned to sales areas as follows:

	On basis of:
Advertising and general administration:	Sales values
Carriage and warehousing:	Sales volume
Credit control:	Number of orders

(2) Selling and distribution costs of sales areas are to be apportioned to models on the basis of sales values.

You are required to:

(*a*) prepare a comparative statement showing an analysis of budgeted selling and distribution costs by sales areas;
(*b*) prepare a comparative budgeted profit and loss statement for each model by sales areas;
(*c*) show the budgeted average net profit per unit for each model in each sales area. (*I.C.W.A.*)

70. The accounts of a company for the year ended March 31, 1964, were as follows:

	£
Direct materials	96,000
Direct wages	48,000
Variable overheads	24,000
Fixed overheads	48,000
Profit	24,000
Sales	240,000

The balance sheet as at March 31, 1964, appeared as follows:

	£		£
Share capital	50,000	Freehold land and buildings	20,000
Capital reserves	20,000	Plant and machinery	40,000
Profit and loss A/c.	20,000	Stocks	40,000
Taxation reserve	10,000	Debtors	40,000
Trade creditors	16,000		
Bank overdraft	24,000		
	£140,000		£140,000

Experience shows that creditors can be maintained at the equivalent of two months' purchases of direct materials, whilst stock and debtors should each continue to be kept at the value of two months' sales.

The budget for the year commencing April 1, 1964, gives quarterly sales as follows:

	£
Quarter 1	60,000
2	66,000
3	72,000
4	78,000

It is expected that all variable costs will be incurred at the same relative prices and efficiencies as in the year to March 31, 1964. Fixed overheads will remain at £48,000 paid evenly over the year.

Taxation (£10,000) will be paid in January, 1965. Plant and machinery costing £10,000 will be purchased and paid for in March 1965, but will not be subject to depreciation during the budget year. Other plant and machinery will be depreciated at 10% per annum.

Prepare a forecast of the accounts, with balance sheets as at the end of each quarter of the budget year. (*I.C.W.A.*)

71. (*a*) How does a flexible budget differ from a fixed budget?

(*b*) From the following selected data of a department whose normal and expected work load is 3000 hours per month:

(*i*) compile a flexible budget for 2000, 2800 and 3600 hours of work;

(*ii*) compile a fixed budget;

(*iii*) calculate the departmental hourly overhead rate for the total of the following items.

Expense heading	*Behaviour of expense*
Supervision	£250 up to 2000 hours
	An extra £60 for steps of 400 hours above 2000
	A further £30 from 3600 hours upward
Depreciation	£400 up to 3000 hours
	£550 above 3000 hours and up to 4200 hours
Consumable supplies	£12 per 100 hours
Heat and light	£45 from 1200 to 2000 hours inclusive
	£55 above 2000 hours and up to 3000 hours
	£60 above 3000 hours
Power	£15 per 100 hours up to 3200 hours
	£12 per 100 hours for hours above 3200

Cleaning	£30 up to 2800 hours
	£40 above 2800 hours
Repairs	£75 up to 1600 hours
	Additional £25 for steps of 400 hours up to 3200 hours
	Additional £40 above 3200 hours
Indirect wages	£20 per 100 hours
Rent and rates	£180

(*I.C.W.A.*)

72. You are involved in the operation of a standard cost scheme and are responsible for the preparation of cost standards in respect of (*a*) direct labour, and (*b*) indirect labour, for the production sections of the factory. What information would you require to prepare these standards, and from what sources would you seek to obtain it? Give one example of the calculation required for each of these standards. (*I.C.W.A.*)

73. The standard mix of a compound of four materials is as follows:

Material	"A"	"B"	"C"	"D"
% by weight	30%	40%	20%	10%
Price per lb	$6\frac{2}{3}$p	$7\frac{1}{2}$p	$17\frac{1}{2}$p	15p

This compound should be used at the rate of 4 lb per cu ft of production. During a period in which 1000 cu ft of finished product was made, actual usage was:

Lb used	1180	1580	830	440
Price per lb	$6\frac{1}{4}$p	$8\frac{1}{3}$p	$16\frac{2}{3}$p	15p

Present appropriate figures to management of an undertaking where standard costing is used. (*R.S.A.* Adapted)

74. The AB Company Ltd budget to sell in the month of January 2500 lb of product A at £3 per lb, 1200 lb of product B at £2 per lb and 2000 lb of product C at £2·50 per lb. During the month, actual sales were 2000 lb of product A for £5500, 1800 lb of product B for £4050 and 2200 lb of product C for £4950. Budgeted costs of A—£2 per unit, B—£1·50 per unit and C—£2 per unit were in line with actual. You are required to calculate the effect of sales variances (price, quantity and mix) on budgeted profit and to prepare a statement showing how each product has contributed to the increase or decrease in budgeted profit. (*A.C.C.A.* Adapted)

75. By journal entries, without financial details, trace the material accounting procedure from the receipt of raw material, direct and indirect, to the production of finished goods, when standard costing obtains. (*I.C.W.A.*)

76. Explain the different uses of (*a*) standard costs, (*b*) flexible budgets, (*c*) fixed expense budgets, with particular reference to the control of costs. (*I.C.W.A.*)

77. The XY Chemical Company manufactures one basic product which passes through several processes during manufacture. You are given the following information, which relates to Process No. 2 for the month of May 1961, and you are required to prepare the process account for the period and to write a brief report on the variances disclosed and their meaning.

The company uses the direct cost method, *i.e.* overheads are not allocated to processes. Output is transferred to the next process and finished stock is valued at direct standard cost.

The standard cost sheet for Process 2 is as follows:

Direct standard cost per gallon				£
Material: 1 gallon of A from Process I				2·37½
Labour:	Grade I	2 hours × 45p hour	90p	
	Grade II	1 hour × 40p hour	40p	
				1·30
				£3·67½
Normal loss during process no scrap value: 2 gallons per 100 = 2%				·07½
∴ Direct Standard Cost per Gallon =				£3·75

During the period 500 gallons were received from Process I; 90 gallons completely processed were in stock at the beginning of the period and 80 gallons at the end; 470 gallons were transferred to Process 3 and there was no work in progress at the beginning or end of the period. Actual labour charges were Grade I: 1100 hours at a total cost of £495 and Grade II: 550 hours at a total cost of £233·75. (*A.C.C.A.* Adapted)

78. During the first period of four weeks a company had standard costs based on 10 men working 160 hours each at 30p per hour, with a standard production of 160 articles each employee. This cost was met in practice.

In the second period a wage increase to 35p per hour was negotiated, but production fell to 140 articles each employee.

What variances in cost would have arisen during the two periods? What purposes would have been served by the calculations? Show the relative formulae. (*R.S.A.* Adapted)

79. The Alpha Production Company budget to produce in the month of June 23,400 units. This will require an input of 26,000 units as the expected waste rate is 10%. Production is to be carried on evenly on the twenty working days in the month. For this period budgeted fixed overheads are £1170. During the month actual input was 25,500 units which resulted in an output of 24,000 units. Due to a power cut the factory was closed for one day which was partially offset by working one additional half day, *i.e.*

Saturday morning. The actual amount spent on fixed overheads was £1000. Prepare a statement disclosing the variances in fixed overhead expenses indicating, by a brief note, the significance of each. (*A.C.C.A.*)

80. What are the features of any good system for control of the expenditure of an industrial concern? (*C.A.*)

81. Shapers Ltd manufacture a single product which is sold direct to a retail organisation under a long term contract. The budget for the week ended May 22, 1965, was as follows:

	Per unit	*Per week*
	p	£
Sales—1200 units at standard price	57½	690·00
Standard cost of sales:		
Materials 48 cwt at £2·50 per cwt	10	120·00
Direct wages:		
(10 men: 40 hour week: 60p per hour)	20	240·00
Variable expenses	7½	90·00
Fixed expenses	10	120·00
	47½	570·00
Standard profit	10	£120·00

The Trading and Profit and Loss Account for that week, prepared in conventional form, showed the following position:

	£		£
Materials purchased:		Sales (at standard	
46 cwt at £2·55	117·30	price)	632·50
Wages	240·00		
Variable expenses	80·70		
Fixed expenses	120·00		
	558·00		
Net profit	74·50		
	£632·50		£632·50

There were no opening or closing stocks nor any work in progress. The week's actual production (all of which was sold) was achieved in 36 hours.

You are required to prepare a Trading and Profit and Loss Statement for the week on standard costing lines showing the breakdown, into the appropriate variances, of the difference between the standard profit and the actual profit. (*C.A.* Adapted)

82. R.K.D. Ltd. commenced business on January 1, 1962. The company manufactures one product of a standard type. The following trial balance was extracted from the books as on December 31, 1962:

Trial Balance

Issued share capital (70,000 shares of £1 each)		£70,000
Balance at bank	£16,450	
Debtors and creditors	9,000	10,000
Freehold property	10,500	
Machinery, at cost, less depreciation to December 31, 1962	32,000	
Purchases of materials (34,000 lb)	54,400	
Sales (1800 units)		162,000
Manufacturing wages	48,300	
Depreciation of machinery	7,000	
Factory expenses	34,750	
Administration and selling expenses	29,600	
	£242,000	£242,000

The stock of materials at December 31, 1962, was 3000 lb.

The stock of finished products at December 31, 1962, was 300 units. There was no loss or wastage of materials or finished products and there was no work in progress at the end of the year.

Manufacturing wages were paid at a piece-work rate of £23 per unit of the finished product.

There are ten machines, of uniform type, in the factory.

The standard cost per unit of the finished product has been calculated on the following basis:

(*i*) Standard quantity of materials: 14 lb per unit.
(*ii*) Standard price of materials: £1·50 per lb.
(*iii*) Standard manufacturing wages: £23 per unit.
(*iv*) Budgeted factory expenses for the year 1962 (including depreciation of machinery): £40,000.
(*v*) Standard operating time per unit: 8 machine-hours.
(*vi*) Normal operating time for the factory with all machines in use: 2000 hours per year.

The actual operating time in 1962 was 1900 hours, during which all machines were in use.

You are required:

(*a*) to prepare a manufacturing account and a trading and profit and loss account for the year 1962;

(*b*) to prepare a summary of the balance sheet as on 31st December, 1962; and

(*c*) to state the total variance (if any) under the following heads: (*i*) materials, (*ii*) manufacturing wages and (*iii*) factory overheads.

The output of finished products is to be transferred from the manufacturing account to the trading account at standard factory cost, and the stock of finished products is to be shown in the balance sheet at standard factory cost.

Ignore taxation. (*C.I.S. Final* Adapted)

83. The following summarised details relate to a company which makes two main products:

Sales:

Product X : 500 at £2000 each
,, Y : 600 at £3000 each

The marginal cost of sales at standard is as follows:

	Material	*Factory wages and variable overhead*	*Variable selling and distribution overhead*
	£	£	£
Product X	400,000	160,000	40,000
,, Y	800,000	440,000	60,000

In the period under review, the following variances occurred:

		Product X	*Product Y*
		£	£
Factory wages, etc.	Gain		6,000
	Loss	34,000	
Material usage	Gain	6,000	
	Loss		2,000
Material price	Gain	2,000	6,000

The period costs (fixed) were budgeted at £180,000 for product X and £220,000 for product Y, and favourable variances occurred amounting to £3000 (product X) and £5000 (product Y).

(*a*) Using the above data, tabulate an income and expense statement, individually for the two products, and in total. At the appropriate points in the tabulation insert the following:

A1 margin at standard
A2 margin at standard as per cent of sales
B1 margin at actual
B2 margin at actual as per cent of sales
C net fixed costs
D net operating profit or loss
E profit or loss percentage of sales

(*b*) Calculate from the figures in your tabulation: (*i*) the break-even point; (*ii*) the margin of safety. (*I.C.W.A.*)

84. In drafting a uniform costing system it is necessary to lay down certain instructions regarding overhead. Enumerate three of the overhead topics that you would cover, stating why each requires special instructions. (*I.C.W.A.*)

85. Set out the major features of Batch Costing. Sketch the general outline of the costing procedures involved to ensure the orderly compilation of product costs. (*R.S.A.*)

86. In order to reduce cost it is necessary to instil a "cost consciousness" into the minds of foremen and charge-hands. In what ways can this be done? (*I.C.W.A.*)

87. Draft a monthly cost statement for a small works producing one product only (figures are not required). State briefly the source of each type of information shown. (*I.C.W.A.*)

88. A Company sells many different products to the public through a large number of individual retailers by the employment of a closely organised body of travellers, supported by advertising and sales inducement offers. Under what headings would you report the cost of such marketing so that the efficiency of each selling section may be reviewed? Give brief details of items under each heading. (*R.S.A.*)

89. Outline a costing system which could be applied to a professional office, *e.g.* an architect or an accountant or a solicitor. (*A.C.C.A.*)

90. Write a brief outline report to the general manager on a manual costing system required for non-standard jobs in a small works. There are no selling expenses. Mention the basic documentation necessary to arrive at the final invoice price. (*I.C.W.A.*)

APPENDIX III

SUGGESTED ANSWERS

Progress Test 3

10. Steps taken from reaching a re-order level to charging material to a job:

(*a*) Purchase requisition made out and sent to purchase office.
(*b*) Buyer selects a supplier and raises purchase order.
(*c*) Purchase order sent to supplier.
(*d*) Supplier forwards goods and invoice.
(*e*) Receipt of goods recorded on a goods received note.
(*f*) Goods inspected and result recorded on an inspection note.
(*g*) Goods passed into store and details recorded on stores record card.
(*h*) Supplier's invoice checked and passed for payment. (Ultimately supplier is paid.)
(*i*) Foreman writes out materials requisition for the material stating the job number.
(*j*) Requisition exchanged for material at the store.
(*k*) Requisition passed to stores record office where issue details are entered on, and requisition priced from, the stores record card.
(*l*) Requisition passed to cost office.
(*m*) Cost office enters material value on the materials analysis.
(*n*) Materials analysis figure posted to the job card.

11.

Level	*A*	*B*
(*a*) Re-order	$300 + 50 \times 5 = 550$	$150 + 50 \times 3 = 300$
(*b*) Minimum	$75 \times 4 = 300$	$75 \times 2 = 150$
(*c*) Maximum	$550 - 4 \times 25 + 300 = 750$	$300 - 2 \times 25 + 500 = 750$
(*d*) Average stock	$(550 - 50 \times 5) + \frac{300}{2} = 450$	$(300 - 50 \times 3) + \frac{500}{2} = 400$

The lower levels for B reflect the shorter re-order period. In the case of the maximum level this factor is compensated for by the larger re-order quantity.

NOTE

(*a*) Minimum level plus normal usage for average delivery period. In practice, the level would probably be a little higher, as this level would result in the minimum level being reached too often for optimum efficiency.
(*b*) Minimum period for getting supplies (assumed emergency delivery time) times maximum usage possible during this period.
(*c*) Re-order level less minimum usage during quickest delivery period: then add new delivery.
(*d*) If order put in at re-order level the stock will on average drop to *re-order less average use during average delivery period*. At this point the new order will be received pushing the stock to an average high level from which it will steadily fall to the re-order point. The average stock, then, will be the mid-point of these average high and low points.

12. A continuous stocktaking could be organised as follows:
(*a*) The stores items are reviewed and a decision made regarding the number of times an item should be checked during the year.
(*b*) A schedule is drawn up detailing which items are to be checked during each week of the year.
(*c*) Blanks are duplicated as follows:

Continuous Stocktaking

Store.................................Week ending.................................

Date	*Description*	*Code*	*Location*	*Units*	*Quantity*			*Checked by*	*Discrepancy*	*Comments*
					Count	*Bin card*	*SRC**			

* SRC = Stores record card.

(*d*) Separate blanks are used for each week-ending and each store.
(*e*) Blanks are pre-written with: week-ending; store; description; code; location; units.
(*f*) Stocktaker (who is not part of stores personnel) is given appropriate blank. During the week he works through the items listed.
(*g*) To allow for requisitions to pass through the stores record office, the SRC figure is inserted on the day after the count and bin card figures are inserted. Bin card and SRC are marked to show point of audit.

(*h*) Discrepancies are examined and the comments column filled in.

(*i*) Shortages are signed for by a responsible person, and then priced and valued, the amount being written off in the Stores Account.

(*j*) Correct figures are entered on bin cards and SRC, these being marked to show that recorded figures agree with physical quantities.

(*k*) An element of surprise is maintained by keeping secret which items are about to be checked.

13. (*a*) FIFO: (40 at £25 + 40 at £30) − (30 at £25 + 10 at £25 + 20 at £30) = £600. Alternatively 20 at £30.

(*b*) LIFO: (40 at £25 + 40 at £30) − (30 at £25 + 30 at £30) = £550. Alternatively 10 at £25 + 10 at £30.

(*c*) Weighted average: Receipts 1/6/.... = 40 × £25 = £1000
Issues 2/6/.... = 30 × £25 = 750

Balance in stock:	10 units for	250
Receipts 8/6/.... =	40 units for	1200
	50	£1450

$$\therefore \text{ New average price} = \frac{£1450}{50} = £29$$

∴ Value of 20 units closing stock = 20 at £29 = £580

Progress Test 4

14.

	X	*Y*
(*a*) Total time allowance	189 × $\frac{1}{3}$ = 63 hrs	204 × $\frac{1}{4}$ = 51 hrs
Less Time taken	45 hrs	39 hrs
Time saved	18 hrs	12 hrs
∴ Bonus payable	18 × $\frac{1}{2}$ × 50p = £4$\frac{1}{2}$	12 × $\frac{1}{2}$ × 50p = £3
(*b*) Basic week's pay	42 × 50p = £21	42 × 50p = £21
Overtime	3 × 1$\frac{1}{2}$ × 50p = £2$\frac{1}{4}$	*Nil*
∴ Gross wage payable	4$\frac{1}{2}$ + 21 + 2$\frac{1}{4}$ = £27$\frac{3}{4}$	3 + 21 = £24
(*c*) Good units made	189 − 6 = 183	204 − 4 = 200
∴ Wage cost per good unit	$\frac{£27\frac{3}{4}}{183} \simeq$ 15p	$\frac{£(24 - 1\frac{1}{2})^*}{200}$ = 11$\frac{1}{4}$p

* Assume 3 hours at 50p per hour booked to dayrate work.

Progress Test 8

15. (*a*) Charge to overheads of the department in which the shop-steward operates.

(*b*) Capitalise and then:

(*i*) In the event of the experiments being a failure, write-off to Profit and Loss.*

(*ii*) If the experiments are successful, charge a small proportion of the cost to each unit bearing the improved surface quality until the whole of the cost has been absorbed.

(*c*) This is an abnormal cost and should be written off direct to Profit and Loss.

(*d*) Charge direct to contract.

* The cost cannot be charged to overheads, since if it had been capitalised it would not relate to the current period, and past costs cannot be charged to later periods. If, however, a regular charge is made to overheads for unsuccessful experiments the cost could be then set against such charges.

Progress Test 9

Question 7. Overhead Analysis and

Overhead	*Basis of apportionment*	*Total*		
		£	*Units*	*Rate per unit*
Indirect wages and supervision	Allocation	20,400		
Maintenance wages	Allocation	5,200		
Indirect materials	Allocation	12,775		
Power	Effective H.P.	6,000	*100*	£60
Rent and rates	Area (000 sq ft)	8,000	*50*	£160
Lighting and heating	Area (000 sq ft)	2,000	*50*	£40
Insurance	Book values (£000's)	1,000	*100*	£10
Depreciation	Book values (£000's)	20,000	*100*	£200
Total		75,375		
Services:				
Maintenance	Allocation (wages)			
	Maintenance wages (balance)		*4,000*	£2
			*	†
Stores	Direct labour hours (000's)		*300*	£12
General	Direct labour hours (000's)		*300*	£14
Total	£	75,375		

* Wages allocated to departments sharing apportionment.
† *I.e.* £2 maintenance overhead per £1 maintenance wages.

8. (*a*) Labour hour rate:

Total direct labour hours = $(5 \times 2000) + (25 \times 800) =$ 30,000 hrs

$$\therefore \text{ Labour hour rate} = \frac{£12{,}000}{30{,}000} = £0{\cdot}40 \text{ hr}$$

$\therefore$ Overhead for: Alpha = $£0{\cdot}40 \times 5 = £2{\cdot}00$

Beta = $£0{\cdot}40 \times 25 = £10{\cdot}00$

(*b*) Machine hour rate:*

Total machine hours = $(2 \times 2000) + (10 \times 800) =$ 12,000 hrs

$$\therefore \text{ Machine hour rate} = \frac{£12{,}000}{12{,}000} = £1 \text{ hr}$$

$\therefore$ Overhead for: Alpha = $£1 \times 2 = £2$

Beta = $£1 \times 10 = £10$

* A machine hour rate is permissible here, since there are only two products, and both are worked on by machines.

Overhead Absorption Rate

Services						*Productive department*							
aintenance		*Stores*		*General*		*Machine X*		*Machine Y*		*Assembly*		*Packing*	
nits	£	*Units*	£	*Units*	£	*Units*	£	*Units*	£	*Units*	£	*Units*	£
	2,250		1,150		2,425		3,800		4,350		4,125		2,300
	5,200		—		—		—		—		—		—
	900		675		400		2,700		3,600		1,800		2,700
'0	600	—	—	—	—	*40*	2,400	*40*	2,400	—	—	*10*	600
3	480	*5*	800	*2*	320	*10*	1,600	*7½*	1,200	*15*	2,400	*7½*	1,200
3	120	*5*	200	*2*	80	*10*	400	*7½*	300	*15*	600	*7½*	300
5	150	*2½*	25	*2½*	25	*30*	300	*40*	400	*5*	50	*5*	50
5	3,000	*2½*	500	*2½*	500	*30*	6,000	*40*	8,000	*5*	1,000	*5*	1,000
	12,700		3,350		3,750		17,200		20,250		9,975		8,150
	−4,700		250		450		1,000		2,000		500		500
	−8,000		—		—	*1,000*	2,000	*2,000*	4,000	*500*	1,000	*500*	1,000
	Nil		3,600		4,200								
			−3,600			*100*	1,200	*75*	900	*75*	900	*50*	600
					−4,200	*100*	1,400	*75*	1,050	*75*	1,050	*50*	700
	Nil		*Nil*		*Nil*		22,800		28,200		13,425		10,950
rs (machine/labour)						50,000		60,000		75,000		50,000	
head absorption rate er machine/direct labour hour)						£0·456		£0·470		£0·179		£0·219	

(c) Wages percentage rate:

Total direct wages £(2 × 2000) + £(5 × 800) = £8000

$$\therefore \text{ Wage percentage rate} = \frac{£12{,}000}{£8000} \times 100 = 150\%$$

$$\therefore \text{ Overhead for: Alpha} = 150\% \text{ of } £2 = £3{\cdot}00$$
$$\text{Beta} = 150\% \text{ of } £5 = £7{\cdot}50$$

Progress Test 10

4. Job A. 8473:

			£
Direct materials:	14 cwt 2 qr 12 lb at £2·37½ cwt		34·69
Direct wages:	X: 18 hrs at 35p hr		6·30
	Y: 32 hrs at 30p hr		9·60
Overheads: Variable:	X: 18 hrs at 66⅔p hr*		12·00
	Y: 32 hrs at 80p hr*		25·60
Fixed:	50 hrs at 75p hr*		37·50
(a) *Total Cost*			£125·69
(b) *Profit:* 19½% on cost			£24·31
Selling price			£150·00

* *Overhead rates:*

$$\text{Variable: X} = \frac{£6000}{9000 \text{ hrs}} = 66\tfrac{2}{3}\text{p per direct labour hour}$$

$$\text{Y} = \frac{£8000}{10{,}000 \text{ hrs}} = 80\text{p per direct labour hour}$$

$$\text{Fixed} = \frac{£16{,}500}{22{,}000 \text{ hrs}} = 75\text{p per direct labour hour}$$

Progress Test 11

4. Accounts and Trial Balance for the Simplas ABC Co. Ltd.

FINANCIAL LEDGER

Creditors Control

Cash	1,500	Balance	2,000
Discounts	100	Purchases	
Balance c/d	2,400	(Cost control)	2,000
	4,000		4,000
		Balance	2,400

Debtors Control

Balance	1,000	Cash	2,000
Sales		Discounts	150
(Cost Control)	2,500	Balance c/d	1,350
	3,500		3,500
Balance	1,350		

FINANCIAL LEDGER (*continued*)

Bank

Balance	1,000	Creditors	1,500
Debtors	2,000	Wages (Cost Control)	1,000
Balance c/d	500	Gen. operating expenses (Cost Control)	1,000
	3,500		3,500
		Balance	500

Cost Control

Balance	7,000	Debtors	2,500
Creditors	2,000		
Wages	1,000	Fixed assets	500
Gen. Operating Expenses	1,000	Balance c/d	8,630
Depreciation	30		
Notional Rent (P/L)	100		
Profit (P/L)	500		
	11,630		11,630
Balance:			
R.M.	1,000		
W.I.P.	2,630		
F.G.	5,000		
	8,630		

Fixed Assets

Balance	3,000	Depreciation	30
Additions (Cost Control)	500	Balance c/d	3,470
	3,500		3,500
Balance	3,470		

Financial P/L

Discounts Allowed	150	Cost Profit (Cost Control)	500
Net Profit to Appropriation	550	Notional Rent written back	100
		Discounts Received	100
	700		700

Capital

		Balance	10,000

Discounts Allowed

Debtors	150	P/L	150

Discounts Received

P/L	100	Creditors	100

P/L Appropriation

		P/L	550

COST LEDGER

Raw Material

Balance	2,000	W.I.P.	3,000
Purchases	2,000	Balance c/d	1,000
	4,000		4,000
Balance	1,000		

Work in Progress

Balance	2,000	Finished Goods	4,000
Raw Materials	3,000	Capital Expenditure	500
Wages	1,000	Balance c/d	2,630
Overheads	1,130		
	7,130		7,130
Balance	2,630		

Overhead Control

Gen. Operating Expenses	1,000	W.I.P.	1,130
Notional Rent	100		
Depreciation	30		
	1,130		1,130

Notional Rent

Financial P/L	100	Overheads	100

COST LEDGER (*continued*)

Capital Expenditure

W.I.P.	500	Fixed Assets	500

Finished Goods

Balance	3,000	Cost of Sales (P/L)	2,000
W.I.P.	4,000	Balance c/d	5,000
	7,000		7,000
Balance c/d	5,000		

Sales

P/L	2,500	Debtors	2,500

Trial Balance—Simplas ABC Ltd as at 31/1/.........

Capital		10,000
Creditors		2,400
Debtors	1,350	
Bank		500
Cost Control:		
R.M. 1,000		
W.I.P. 2,630		
F.G. 5,000	8,630	
Fixed Assets	3,470	
P/L Appropriation		550
	£ 13,450	13,450

Cost P/L

Finished Goods	2,000	Sales	2,500
Cost Profit c/d	500		
	2,500		2,500
Financial P/L	500	Cost Profit	500

5. *Reconciliation Statement:*

	£	£
Profit as per cost accounts:		19,770
Add:		
Selling expenses difference £(7500 − 7100)	400	
Discounts received (not in cost accounts)	260	
Profit on sale of land (not in cost accounts)	2,340	3,000
		22,770
Subtract:		
Closing stock difference £(4280 − 4080)	200	
Works expenses difference £(12,130 − 10,500)	1,630	
Administration expenses difference £(5340 − 5000)	340	
Depreciation difference £(1100 − 800)	300	2,470
Profit as per financial accounts		£20,300

Progress Test 12

4.

	Process A	Process B
	£	£
Material input	5,221	9,331
Process labour and overheads	4,650	10,480
	9,871	19,811
Less scrap value	540	890
Value of good production	£9,331*	£18,921

$\therefore$ Cost per unit of good finished production $= \frac{18,921}{1802} = £10{\cdot}50$

5.

Cost element	Opening W.I.P.	Period cost	Total cost	Complete units	Work in Progress			Total Eff. units	CPU	W.I.P. Value
					Units	%	Eff.			
	£	£	£						£	£
Material	29,600	112,400	142,000	28,000	12,000	100	12,000	40,000	3·550	42,600
Wages	6,600	33,400	40,000	28,000	12,000	33⅓	4,000	32,000	1·250	5,000
Overhead	5,800	30,200	36,000	28,000	12,000	33⅓	4,000	32,000	1·125	4,500
Total	42,000	176,000	218,000						5·925	52,100

Total value completed output = 28,000 at £5·925 = £165,900

6. From the information in the answer to Question 5 above, the 8000 units lost can only affect the completed units.

Now value of 8000 units = 8000 × £5·925 = £47,400

$\therefore$ Extra cost per unit to be charged to remaining completed good units $= \frac{£47,400}{20,000} = £2{\cdot}370$

$\therefore$ Complete cost per unit = £5·925 + £2·370 = £8·295

The work-in-progress value remains the same, as such work has not reached the rejection point and cannot, therefore, carry any of the costs of such losses.

NOTE: Cross check: £165,900 + £52,100 = £218,000.

* As Question 4 asks for the *finished* cost only, the cost per unit at this point has not been computed.

Progress Test 13

6. Total joint cost = £31,200 + £13,800 = £45,000

	Product A	*Product* B
Sales	£38,000	£42,000
Selling costs	5,000	20,000
"Effective" sales value	33,000	22,000
Joint cost apportionment (ratio of 3:2)	27,000	18,000
Profit	£6,000	£4,000

Progress Test 14

5. From the break-even chart shown below it will be seen that:

(*a*) The break-even point is at sales of £72,000.
(*b*) The margin of safety is £84,000 − £72,000 = £12,000 = 14%.
(*c*) The gap between the sales and total cost curves (*i.e.* the profit) extends to £10,000 when the sales are £102,000.

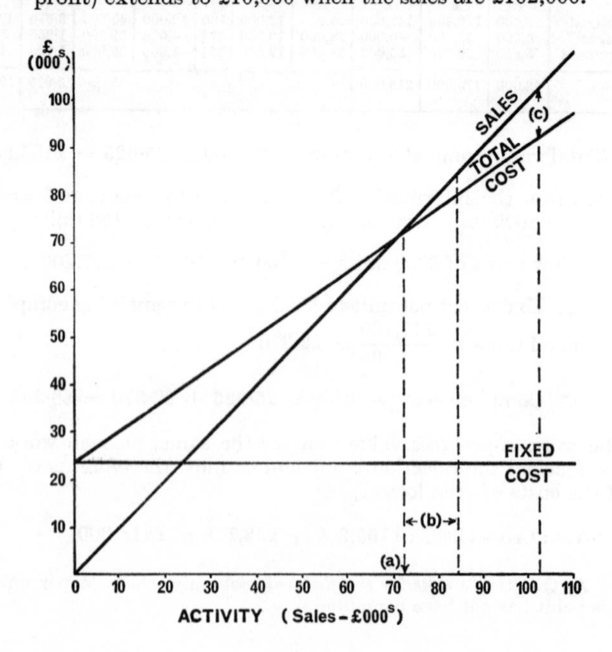

Progress Test 15

1. Contribution = £5 − £3 = £2 unit.

∴ No. of units to give contribution equal to fixed costs

$$= \frac{10,000}{2} = 5000 \text{ units} = \text{B/E point.}$$

£40,000 sales must come from $\frac{40,000}{5} = 8000$ units.

∴ Contribution, 8000 × £2 = £16,000
Less fixed costs = £10,000

Profit £6,000

2. Contribution = £80,000 − £60,000 = £20,000

∴ P/V ratio $= \frac{20,000}{80,000} = 25\%$

∴ Contribution from B/E sales = 25% × 60,000 = £15,000
∴ Fixed cost = £15,000
∴ Profit = Contribution − Fixed costs = £20,000 − £15,000
= £5,000

3. The variable and fixed costs are first computed. For the sake of mathematical simplicity costs per 6000 pallets are taken:

	Variable Cost 6000 *Pallets*		*Fixed Costs per week*
	Manual	*Machine*	*Machine only*
	£	£	£
Wages*	52	—	16
Expendable supplies	12	12	—
Maintenance	—	—	3
Operating costs	—	6	—
Depreciation	—	—	4
Total	£64	£18	£23

These figures show that by using the equipment there will be a saving of £64 − £18 = £46 variable costs per 6000 pallets. However, fixed costs of £23 per week will be incurred, which means there must be a minimum of $\frac{23}{46} \times 6000 = 3000$ pallets moved per week if the variable cost savings are not to be less than the

* It is assumed that the pallet-movers under the manual method could do other work if not engaged on moving pallets, and therefore their wages are variable. The equipment operator, however, is assumed to work only on his equipment, and therefore his wage is fixed.

extra fixed cost. Above this level the savings are obviously greater than the additional fixed costs.

NOTE: This type of problem is fairly common. The method of solution can be summarised so:

Find the variable cost *savings* per unit obtained under the scheme and then compute how many units must be involved so that the variable cost savings exactly equal the extra fixed cost. This is the minimum level that justifies operation of the scheme.

4. Trading and Profit and Loss accounts: (*a*) fixed overhead is absorbed; (*b*) it is charged against sales. (Stock details would normally have been omitted from the marginal cost statement and the marginal cost of sales calculated directly, but are included here for comparative purposes.)

	Per Unit (£)	*Quarter 3*			*Quarter 4*		
		Units	£	£	*Units*	£	£
(*a*) Sales	1·00	28,000		28,000	32,000		32,000
Production costs:							
Variable	0·65	34,000	22,100		28,000	18,200	
Fixed	0·20	34,000	6,800		28,000	5,600	
		34,000	28,900		28,000	23,800	
Plus Opening Stock	0·85	*Nil*	—		6,000	5,100	
		34,000	28,900		34,000	28,900	
Less Closing Stock	0·85	6,000	5,100		2,000	1,700	
Cost of sales	0·85	28,000	23,800	23,800	32,000	27,200	27,200
Gross profit	0·15	28,000		4,200	32,000		4,800
Selling and Administration costs			2,100			2,100	
U/o absorption of fixed production costs			800 Cr	1,300		400 Dr	2,500
Net profit				£2,900			£2,300
(*b*) Sales	1·00	28,000		28,000	32,000		32,000
Production costs:							
Variable	0·65	34,000	22,100		28,000	18,200	
Plus Opening Stock	0·65	*Nil*	—		6,000	3,900	
		34,000	22,100		34,000	22,100	
Less Closing Stock	0·65	6,000	3,900		2,000	1,300	
Marginal cost of sales	0·65	28,000	18,200	18,200	32,000	20,800	20,800
Contribution	0·35	28,000		9,800	32,000		11,200
Fixed costs:							
Production			6,000			6,000	
Selling and Administration			2,100	8,100		2,100	8,100
Net profit				£1,700			£3,100

5. This is essentially a differential cost problem.

(*a*) Under these circumstances 10,000 lb of A which would have been sold for 10p lb will be sold for 95p lb, *i.e.* the extra income will be 95p − 10p = 85p lb. However, the order will require extra direct costs being incurred of £5 + £5 + £5 = £15 per 50 lb of A = 30p lb.

∴ Net gain per lb = 85p − 30p = 55p lb.

∴ *Order should be accepted.*

Additional profit resulting will be 10,000 × 55p = £5500. The minimum price would be direct costs plus loss of "scrap" sales income = 30p + 10p = 40p. lb.

(*b*) Under these circumstances the 10,000 lb of A will need to come from extra processing.

Now a batch of 150 lb input gives 50 lb of A.

$\therefore \frac{10{,}000}{50}$ = 200 batches will need to be processed.

Production schedule:

Product	*Lb per batch*	*Output from 200 batches*
A	50	10,000 lb
B	45	9,000
C	45	9,000
Scrap	10	2,000
		20,000 lb

And the extra joint cost incurred will be:*

Per batch:	Material 150 lb at $33\frac{1}{3}$p lb	= £50
	Labour £(12·5 + 11·25 + 11·25)	= £35
		£85

For 200 batches: 200 × £85 = £17,000

∴ Total extra cost = £17,000 + Direct costs of 10,000 lb at 30p lb = £20,000

However, extra income is only:

From sales of A: 10,000 lb at 95p	£9,500
From sales of B, C and Scrap: 20,000 lb at 10p =	£2,000
	£11,500

* Since the costs are joint, if one is incurred all are incurred. As we are only interested in *extra* costs, there is no point in apportioning the joint cost.

Now this £11,500 extra income is less than the extra cost.
∴ *Order should not be accepted.*

If the order were accepted the minimum price would need to exceed the 95p offered by an amount that would just allow the "loss" at 95p to be recovered.

Now "loss" is £20,000 − £11,500 = £8500

Over 10,000 lb, this is $\frac{£8500}{10,000}$ = 85p lb

∴ Minimum price: 95p + 85p = £1·80 lb

(c) Again, the 10,000 lb of A will need to come from extra processing and production, and total extra joint costs will be as in (b). However, all C and 6750 lb of B can be sold at the standard selling prices. Therefore:

Extra income:	A 10,000 lb at 95p lb	=	£9,500
	B 6,750 lb at £$\frac{55}{45}$ lb	=	8,250
	B 2,250 lb at 10p lb	=	225
	C 9,000 lb at £$\frac{35}{45}$ lb	=	7,000
	Scrap: 2,000 lb at 10p lb	=	200
			£25,175
Extra costs: Joint		=	£17,000
Direct:	A 10,000 lb at 30p lb	=	3,000
	B 6,750 lb at £$\frac{14}{45}$ lb	=	2,100
	C 9,000 lb at £$\frac{10}{45}$ lb	=	2,000
			£24,100

The extra income is therefore greater than the extra costs.
∴ *Order should be accepted.*

Additional profit resulting = £25,175 − £24,100 = £1075

Minimum price: In these circumstances the price could only be lowered until the £1075 vanished. Over 10,000 lb of A this is £1075 ÷ 10,000 = 10·75p per lb
∴ Minimum price would be 95p − 10·75p = 84·25p lb.

6. First, find the selling price:

	£
Last period (9,000 units sold):	
Variable costs at £5 each	45,000
Fixed costs	20,000
	65,000
Loss	2,000
∴ Sales	£63,000

$$\therefore \textit{Selling price} = \frac{£63{,}000}{9{,}000} = \quad £7 \text{ unit}$$

Next, the basic planned contribution:

Fixed cost	£20,000
Planned profit	£4,000
Planned contribution	£24,000

Proposal A. This proposal will increase variable cost per unit by £0·50

∴ Contribution per unit: up to 12,000 = £7 − £5·50 = £1·50
over 12,000 = £7 − £6·50 = £0·50

∴ First 12,000 units will give a contribution of 12,000 × £1·50 = £18,000

This leaves £6000 to be found, and at £0·50 per unit this means an additional $\frac{£6000}{0{\cdot}50}$ = 12,000 units must be sold, *i.e.* a total of 24,000 units.

∴ Increase is 24,000 − 9000 = 15,000 units, *i.e.* $\frac{15{,}000}{9000} \times 100$ = $166\frac{2}{3}\%$ increase in sales.

Proposal B. This proposal, through the increase in fixed costs, will increase planned contribution by £2000 to £26,000

Now contribution per unit: up to 12,000 = £7 − 5 = £2
over 12,000 = £7 − 6 = £1

∴ First 12,000 units will give a contribution of 12,000 × £2 = £24,000

This leaves £2000 to be found, and at £1 per unit this means an additional 2000 units must be sold, *i.e.* a total of 14,000 units.

∴ Increase is 14,000 − 9000 = 5000 units, *i.e.* $\frac{5000}{9000} \times 100 \simeq$ $55\frac{1}{2}\%$ increase in sales.

Proposal C. Dropping selling price by £0·50 results in contribution per unit dropping £0·50 at all levels. This, of course, is equivalent to increasing variable cost by £0·50, *i.e.* the consequences are the same as in A.

∴ Increase in sales = $166\frac{2}{3}\%$.

Proposal D. New contribution per unit (below 12,000) = £7 − £4 = £3

∴ Contribution from sales of 9000 units = £27,000

This is £3000 above planned contribution.

∴ Fixed machine costs can rise by a maximum of £3000.

Progress Test 17

11. (*a*) *4-week profit forecast:*

	A	B
	£	£
Sales at £5 unit	250,000	500,000
Less total costs:		
Direct materials, 50% sales	125,000	250,000
Direct labour at £25 for 50 units	25,000	50,000
Indirect wages at £25 a week	8,000	14,000
Power	5,000	10,000
Maintenance	15,000	25,000
Distribution	10,400	14,800
Selling costs $2\frac{1}{2}\%$ sales	6,250	12,500
Depreciation	5,000	5,000
Other fixed costs	15,000	15,000
Total costs	£214,650	£396,300
Forecasted profit	£35,350	£103,700

(*b*) (*i*) All figures in £'s. Production: 60,000; Sales: 40,000 units.

Element	*Cost 50,000 units*	*Cost 100,000 units*	*Increase = Variable cost of 50,000 units*	*Variable cost per 10,000 units*	*Fixed cost**	*Variable cost for actual activity*	*Total allowed cost*
Known variables:							
Direct materials, £2½ unit					—	150,000	150,000
Direct labour, £25 for 50 units					—	30,000	30,000
Selling costs, 2½% sales					—	5,000	5,000
Known Fixed:							
Depreciation					5,000	—	5,000
Other fixed costs					15,000	—	15,000
Other costs:							
Indirect wages	8,000	14,000	6,000	1,200	2,000	7,200	9,200
Power	5,000	10,000	5,000	1,000	Nil	6,000	6,000
Maintenance	15,000	25,000	10,000	2,000	5,000	12,000	17,000
Distribution	10,400	14,800	4,400	880	6,000	3,520†	9,520
						Total allowed cost for period	£246,720

* Fixed cost = Total cost of 50,000 units less variable cost of 50,000 units. † Based on *sales* of 40,000 units.

(*b*) (*ii*) Total allowed cost		£246,720
Less: Depreciation	5,000	
Materials on credit 10%	15,000	20,000
Total cash payments		226,720
Total cash receipts: Sales 40,000 at £5		200,000
Net reduction in bank balance		26,720

∴ Closing bank balance should be £31,850 − £26,720 = £5,130 (Cr.)

12. (*a*) *Standard cost statements for* 1,000 *gm:*

	C 100			C 300		
	Usage	*Price*	£	*Usage*	*Price*	£
Direct materials						
XY	110 gm	10p per 10	1·10	60 gm	10p per 10	0·60
DR	900 gm	15p per 10	13·50	1000 gm	15p per 10	15·00
Direct labour:						
Process 1	1 hr	30p	0·30	1⅓ hr	30p	0·40
Process 2	½ hr	40p	0·20	½ hr	40p	0·20
Energy			4·00			5·00
Total standard direct cost			£19·10			£21·20

(*b*) *Profit forecast:*

	£	£
C 100: Sales, 1800 batches at £24 each	43,200	
Less marginal cost of sales, 1800 at £19·1 each	34,380	
Contribution		8,820
C 300: Sales, 1000 batches at £26 each	26,000	
Less marginal cost of sales, 1000 at £21·2 each	21,200	
Contribution		4,800
Total Contribution		13,620
Less fixed costs: Manufacturing overheads	4,500	
Administration overheads	3,800	8,300
Forecasted Profit		£5,320

(*c*) *Cash forecast:*

Required functional budgets:

(*i*) Stock budgets:

Code	*Units*	*Opening stock*	*Closing stock*	*Stock change*
C 100	Batches	60	260	Increase 200
C 300	,,	35	135	,, 100
XY	1000 gm	22	12	Decrease 10
DR	,, ,,	145	125	,, 20

(*ii*) Production budget:

Product	*Units*	*For sales*	*For stock*	*Production*
C 100	Batches	1800	200	2000
C 300	,,	1000	100	1100

(*iii*) Purchase budget:

		XY 1000 gm		DR 1000 gm	
	Batches	*Per batch*	*Total*	*Per batch*	*Total*
Production requirements:					
C 100	2000	0·11	220	0·9	1800
C 300	1100	0·06	66	1·0	1100
			286		2900
Less stock run-down			10		20
Purchases			276		2880

		£
Purchase values:	XY 276 × 1000 at 10p per 10 gm =	2,760
	DR 2880 × 1000 at 15p per 10 gm =	43,200
		£45,960

(*iv*) Labour budget:

Process	C 100 2000 batches		C 300 1100 batches		*Total hrs*	*Rate*	*Cost* £
	Hrs per batch	*Total hrs*	*Hrs per batch*	*Total hrs*			
1	1	2000	$1\frac{1}{3}$	$1466\frac{2}{3}$	$3466\frac{2}{3}$	30p	1040
2	$\frac{1}{2}$	1000	$\frac{1}{2}$	550	1550	40p	620
Total wages							£1660

Cash forecast:

	£	£	£
Opening balance (Balance Sheet)			2,300
Add Receipts:			
From old debtors (Balance sheet)		6,200	
From sales: C 100	43,200		
C 300	26,000		
	69,200		
Less new debtors ($\frac{1}{12}$)	5,767	63,433	69,633
			71,933
Deduct payments:			
To old creditors (Balance sheet)		2,920	
Purchases (Budget)	45,960		
Less new creditors ($\frac{1}{12}$)	3,830	42,130	
Energy: C 100 2000 batches at £4	8,000		
C 300 1100 batches at £5	5,500	13,500	
Wages (Budget)		1,660	
Manufacturing overheads (excluding depreciation)		3,900	
Administration overheads (excluding depreciation)		3,700	
Capital expenditure		2,200	70,010
Forecasted closing balance			£1,923

(*d*) *Estimated balance sheet:*

Balance Sheet *as at year end*

	£	£		£	£
Share capital		50,000	Equipment:		
			Cost: Opening value	62,000	
Profit and Loss	13,863		Plus Additions	2,200	64,200
Plus Forecasted profit	5,320	19,183	Depreciation:		
Net Worth ...		69,183	Opening balance	8,000	
			For the year: 600 + 100	700	8,700
Creditors		3,830			55,500
			Stock*	9,823	
			Debtors	5,767	
			Cash	1,923	17,513
		£73,013			£73,013

* Budgeted closing stock of £9823 is found thus:

		£
C 100	260 batches at £19·1 per batch	4966
C 300	135 ,, at £21·2 ,, ,,	2862
XY	12,000 gm 10p per 10 gm	120
DR	125,000 ,, at 15p ,, ,, ,,	1875
		£9823

Progress Test 19

1. Standard cost £5.

(*a*) Total variance = £5 − (24 × £0·25) = £1 (A)
Usage variance = (20 − 24) at £0·25 = £1 (A)
No price variance.

(*b*) Total variance = £5 − (20 × £0·35) = £2 (A)
Price variance = £(0·25 − 0·35) × 20 = £2 (A)
No usage variance.

(*c*) Total variance = £5 − (24 × £0·35) = £3·40 (A)
Usage variance = (20 − 24) at £0·25 = £1 (A)
Price variance = £(0·25 − 0·35) × 24 = £2·40 (A)

(*d*) Total variance = £(5 − 5) = *Nil*
Usage variance = (20 − 18) at £0·25 = £0·50 (F)
Price variance = (£0·25 × 18) − £5 = £0·50 (A)

2. (*a*) Wages variance = (100 × £0·40) − (110 × £0·35)
= £1·50 (F)
Labour efficiency variance = (110 − 100) × £0·40
= £4·00 (A)
Wages rate variance = £(0·40 − 0·35) × 110 = £5·5 (F)
(*b*) Wages variance = (100 × £0·40) − £36·74 = £3·26 (F)
Labour efficiency variance = (100 − 95) × £0·40
= £2 (F)
Wages rate variance = (95 × £0·40) − £36·74 = £1·26 (F)

3.

	Actual quantity	*Standard price*	*Value £*		*Actual quantity in standard proportions*	*Standard price*	*Value £*
H	10,200	£0·50	5,100	$\frac{1}{6}$	11,300	£0·50	5,650
O	57,600	£0·05	2,880	$\frac{5}{6}$	56,500	£0·05	2,825
	67,800		£7,980		67,800		£8,475

∴ Mixture variance = £7980 − £8475 = £495 (F).

NOTE

(*i*) Cross-check: Standard cost of 6 cubic feet HO_5 =
(1 × £0·50) + (5 × £0·05) = £0·75

$$\therefore \text{ Standard cost of } 67{,}800 = \frac{67{,}800}{6} \times £0{\cdot}75 \qquad = £8475$$

And actual cost (at standard prices) = £7980

Excess value of output over value of input £495

(*ii*) Favourable mixture variances should not really be allowed to occur; they do not so much indicate a saving as an adulterated product (since an excessive quantity of the cheaper component has been allowed into the final product).

4. From an input of 1 load of crude costing £0·06 there is a standard output of only 0·6 load.

$$\therefore \text{ Standard cost per unit of output} = \frac{£0{\cdot}06}{0{\cdot}6} = £0{\cdot}10 \text{ per load}$$

Now standard yield from 1500 loads = 60% of 1500 = 900
Actual yield = 726
∴ Difference = 174
∴ Yield variance = 174 at £0·10 = £17·40 (A)

			£
NOTE: Cross-check:	Cost of input 1500 at £0·06	=	90·00
	Value of output 726 at £0·10	=	72·60
	Excess value of input over output		£17·40

5. Standard cost card for MUD:

	£
10 tons M at £1	10
10 tons U at £2	20
30 tons D at £3	90
50 tons	120
−10 20% loss	—
40 tons MUD	£120

∴ 1 ton MUD has standard cost of £3

			£
Price variances:	M = (1100 × £1) − £1000	=	100 (F)
	U = (1000 × £2) − £2200	=	200 (A)
	D = (2900 × £3) − £8888	=	188 (A)
			£288 (A)

	Actual Quantity	*Standard price*	*Value* £	*Actual quantity in standard proportions*		*Standard price*	*Value* £
M	1,100	£1	1,100	$\frac{1}{5}$	1,000	£1	1,000
U	1,000	£2	2,000	$\frac{1}{5}$	1,000	£2	2,000
D	2,900	£3	8,700	$\frac{3}{5}$	3,000	£3	9,000
	5,000		£11,800		5,000		£12,000

∴ Mixture variance = £11,800 − £12,000 = £200 (F)

Standard yield from input of 5000 tons = 4000 tons
Actual yield = 3815 ,,
Difference 185 ,,

∴ Yield variance = 185 × £3 = £555 (A)
Usage variance = £200 (F) + £555 (A) = £355 (A)
Total material variance = £355 + £288 = £643 (A)

NOTE: Cross-check: Total actual cost = £1000 + £2200 + £8888
= £12,088
Standard cost of actual output = 3815 × £3 = £11,445

Total variance £643(A)

6. (*a*) If budgeted production = 50 lots, and 1 lot = 100 standard hours, then budgeted hours were $50 \times 100 = 5000$ hours.

(*b*) Also, if F.OAR = £3 per hour, then the budgeted fixed overheads must have been $5000 \times £3 = £15{,}000$.

(*c*) Also V.OAR must be $\frac{£7500}{5000} = £1{\cdot}50$ hour.

(*d*) Finally, SHP = $60 \times 100 = 600$ hours.

So: Overhead variance

$= 6000 \times (3 + £1{\cdot}50) - £(7500 + 14{,}500) = £5000$ (F)

Fixed overhead variance = $(6000 \times £3) - £14{,}500 = £3500$ (F)

Variable overhead variance = $(6000 \times £1{\cdot}50) - £7500$ $= £1500$ (F)

Variable overhead expenditure variance

$= (5600 \times £1{\cdot}50)$* $- £7500 = £900$ (F)

Variable overhead efficiency variance

$= (6000 - 5600)$ at $£1{\cdot}50 = £600$ (F)

Fixed overhead expenditure variance = $£15{,}000 - £14{,}500$ $= £500$ (F)

Volume variance = $(60 - 50) \times 100 \times £3$ $= £3000$ (F)

Volume efficiency variance = $(6000 - 5600)$ at £3 $= £1200$ (F)

Capacity variance = $(5000 - 5600)$ at £3 $= £1800$ (F)

7. *Standard cost card for input of* 100 *tons:*

		£
A	40 tons at £300 ton	12,000
B	30 tons at £100 ,,	3,000
C	10 tons at £420 ,,	4,200
Scrap	20 tons at £240 ton	4,800
	100 tons (at £240)	24,000
	– 5 5% loss	—
	95	24,000
Scrap –	35 tons return at £240 ton	8,400
	60 tons	£15,600

Standard cost per ton of good casting = $\frac{£15{,}600}{60} = £260$

NOTE: To find scrap price per ton, let x = average alloy price.

$\therefore$ Total cost = $(12{,}000 + 3000 + 4200 + 20x) = 19{,}200 + 20x$

$\therefore$ Average alloy price = $(19{,}200 + 20x) \div 100 = 192 + 0{\cdot}2x$

$\therefore x = 192 + 0{\cdot}2x \qquad \therefore 0{\cdot}8x = 192 \qquad \therefore x = 240.$

* The variable overheads allowed for 5600 actual hours worked.

Variances: £

Price A = 380 × £(300 − 310) = 3800 (A)
B = 330 × £(100 − 110) = 3300 (A)
C = Nil

£7100 (A)

Mixture:

	Actual Quantity	*Standard price*	*Value* £	*Actual quantity in standard proportions*		*Standard price*	*Value* £
A	380	£300	114,000	40%	400	£300	120,000
B	330	£100	33,000	30%	300	£100	30,000
C	90	£420	37,800	10%	100	£420	42,000
Scrap	200	£240	48,000	20%	200	£240	48,000
	1,000		£232,800		1,000		£240,000

∴ Mixture variance = £232,800 − £240,000 = £7200 (F)

NOTE: If there is a standard cost card the total of the final column (£240,000) can be found simply by this formula:

$$\text{Required value} = \frac{\text{Actual quantity}}{\text{Cost card quantity}} \times \text{Cost card cost}$$

$$e.g.\ \frac{1000}{100} \times £24{,}000 = £240{,}000$$

This eliminates the entire right-hand half of the layout. (Note that figures are those *prior* to losses.)

Yield variance:

From 1000 tons input a total output of 950 tons is expected. Actual good castings and scrap amount to 948 tons.

∴ Yield variance (950 − 948) at £260* = £520 (A).

Scrap variance:

From 1000 tons input 350 tons of scrap was expected, but only 340 tons obtained. However, if 350 tons *had* been obtained, then since the total output was 948 tons, only 598 tons of good castings would have been produced. Since there was 608 tons of good castings, then the 10 tons scrap lost was lost because *it went into good production.*

* It has been assumed the additional loss affected the good production. Alternatively, it could be regarded as affecting the scrap (in which case £240 would be used) or even affecting scrap and good production in the proportions of 35:60.

∴ Scrap variance = 10 tons at scrap and good differential, *i.e.* 10 at £(260 − 240) = £200 (F).

Summary: (for presentation to management)

	£	£	£
Standard cost of production, 608 tons at £260			158,080
Variances: Favourable Mixture	7,200		
Scrap	200	7,400	
Adverse Price A	3,800		
,, B	3,300		
Yield	520	7,620	
Total material variance		£220 (A)	+220
Actual cost			£158,300*

8. *Material variances:*

Standard material cost = 450 × 1 × 25p = £112·5

∴ Material variance = £112·5 − £125 = £12·50 (A)

Now price increase = 5% = 1·25p lb

$$\therefore \text{Usage } \frac{\pounds 125}{26{\cdot}25\text{p}} = 476{\cdot}2 \text{ lb}$$

∴ Price variance = 476·2 at 1·25p = £5·95 (A)

Usage variance = (476·2 − 450) at 25p = £6·55 (A)

Labour variances:

Standard direct wage cost = 450 × $1\frac{1}{2}$ × $33\frac{1}{3}$p = £225

∴ Wages variance = £225 − £210 = £15 (F)

And since rates have remained stable the whole amount must be attributed to the *labour efficiency variance.*

Overhead variances:

$$\text{Note: Standard } \textit{machine} \text{ hours per unit} = \frac{25{,}000}{10{,}000} = 2{\cdot}5$$

* This can be checked against the actual cost computed from "actuals" in the question.

This differs from standard direct labour hours. The question implies *overheads are to be related to machine hours.*

$$\therefore \text{ F.OAR} = \frac{5000}{25{,}000} = £0{\cdot}20 \text{ hr}$$

$$\text{V.OAR} = \frac{6000}{25{,}000} = £0{\cdot}24 \text{ hr}$$

$$\text{and SHP} = 450 \times 2{\cdot}5 = 1125 \text{ hrs}$$

Overhead variance

$$= 1125 \times £(0{\cdot}20 + 0{\cdot}24) - £(550 + 280) = £335 \text{ (A)}$$

Fixed overhead variance

$$= (1125 \times £0{\cdot}20) - £550 = £325 \text{ (A)}$$

Variable overhead variance

$$= (1125 \times £0{\cdot}24) - £280 = £10 \text{ (A)}$$

Variable overhead expenditure variance

$$= (1540^{*} \times £0{\cdot}24) - £280 = £89{\cdot}6 \text{ (F)}$$

Variable overhead efficiency variance

$$= (1125 - 1540) \times £0{\cdot}24 = £99{\cdot}6 \text{ (A)}$$

Fixed overhead expenditure variance

$$= \left(\frac{2000}{25{,}000} \times £5000\right)\dagger - £550 = £150 \text{ (A)}$$

Volume variance $= (2000 - 1125) \times £0{\cdot}20 = £175$ (A)

Volume efficiency variance

$$= (1125 - 1540) \times £0{\cdot}20 = £83 \text{ (A)}$$

Capacity variance $= (2000 - 1540) \times £0{\cdot}20 = £92$ (A)

Idle time variance $= 60$ hrs at $£0{\cdot}20 = £12$ (A)

Strike variance $= (2000 - 1600) \times £0{\cdot}20 = £80$ (A)

Summary: (All variances *adverse* unless otherwise shown)

	£	£
Direct materials cost:		
Material price	5.95	
Usage	6.55	12·50
Direct wages:		
Labour efficiency		15·00 (F)
Variable overheads:		
Variable overhead efficiency	99·60	
Variable overhead expenditure	89·60 (F)	10·00

NOTE: The *A.C.C.A.* examiners often regard variable overheads as varying with production. This leaves only an expenditure variance for variable overheads (*e.g.* in this case a variance of £10 (A)).

* Actual machine hours spent on production.

† Budgeted fixed overheads for a month of 2000 hours.

Brought forward			£7·50
Fixed overheads:			
Idle time		12·00	
Strike		80·00	
Capacity		92·00	
Volume efficiency		83·00	
Volume		175·00	
Fixed overhead expenditure		150·00	325·00
Total cost variance			£332·50 (A)

NOTE: This answer is rather long for an examination. By simply computing overhead expenditure and efficiency variances and also the capacity sub-variances, some of the work can be cut out.

Progress Test 20

1. *Sales margin variances:*

	Actual margin £	*Actual quantity*	*Standard margin*	*Value* £	*Actual quantities in standard proportions*	*Standard margin*	*Value* £	*Budgeted margin* £
P	3,100	1,200	£3	3,600	$\frac{1}{6}$ 1,100	£3	3,300	3,000
Q	4,800	1,400	£2	2,800	$\frac{2}{6}$ 2,200	£2	4,400	4,000
R	*Nil*	4,000	£1	4,000	$\frac{3}{6}$ 3,300	£1	3,300	3,000
	7,900	6,600		10,400	6,600		11,000	10,000

NOTE: Actual margin is found by taking actual sales less standard cost of sales: *i.e.* P = £11,500 − (1200 × £7) = £3100; Q = £13,200 − (1400 × £6) = £4800; R = £20,000 − (4000 × £5) = Nil.

Summary of Sales Margin Variances:

			£
Price:*	P:	£3100 − 3600	= 500 (A)
	Q:	£4800 − 2800	= 2000 (F)
	R:	£Nil − 4000	= 4000 (A)
	£(7900 − 10,400)		= 2500 (A)

* It is generally preferable to analyse the price variance to products, since selling prices are relatively independent, whereas mixtures and unit volumes are inter-dependent.

Mixture:	£10,400 − 11,000 =	600 (A)
Units volume:	£11,000 − 10,000 =	1000 (F)
Quantity:		£400 (F)

Total sales margin: £(2500 − 400) = £2100 (A)

Progress Test 21

1. The cost and variance accounts in answer to this question are continued on the following pages. The letters in brackets refer to the explanatory notes given on pp. 325–26.

MAIN ACCOUNTS

Raw Material Stores

Purchases[a]	£14,800	W.I.P.[b]	£13,650
Price var.	200	Breakages	360
		Balance c/d	990
	£15,000		£15,000
Balance	990		

Finished Goods

W.I.P.	£45,000	P/L[j]	£42,000
		Balance c/d	3,000
	£45,000		£45,000
Balance	3,000		

Direct Wages

Cash	£9,140	Wages Rate var.[c]	£240
		Breakdowns[d]	50
		W.I.P.[e]	£8,850

Fixed Overheads

Cash	£20,900	W.I.P.[k]	£17,700
		Expenditure var.[l]	900
		Capacity var.[m]	2,300

Variable Overheads

Cash	£4,580	W.I.P.[f]	£4,500
		Expenditure var.	80

Selling and Distribution Costs

Cash	£7,000	P/L[n]	£6,720
		Selling and distribution var.	280

Work in Progress

Materials	£13,650	Finished Goods[g]	£45,000
Direct Wages	8,850	Materials Usage Var.[h]	150
Variable o'h'ds	4,500		
Fixed o'h'ds	17,700		
Efficiency vars.[i]			
Labour	150		
Volume	300		

Sales

P/L	£58,800	Cash	£57,100
		Price var.[o]	1,700

VARIANCE ACCOUNTS

Direct Materials Price

P/L	£200	R.M. Stores	£200

Breakages

R.M. Stores	£360	P/L	£360

Direct Wages Rate

Direct Wages	£240	P/L	£240

Breakdowns

Direct Wages	£50	P/L	£150
Capacity var.	100		

Capacity

Fixed o'h'ds	£2,300	Breakdowns(p)	£100
		P/L	2,200

Fixed Overhead Expenditure

Fixed o'h'ds	£900	P/L	£900

Variable Overhead Expenditure

Variable o'h'ds	£80	P/L	£80

Direct Labour Efficiency

P/L	£150	W.I.P.	£150

Volume Efficiency

P/L	£300	W.I.P.	£300

Direct Materials Usage

W.I.P.	£150	P/L	£150

Selling and Distribution

Selling and distribution Costs	£280	P/L	£280

Sales Margin Price

Sales	£1,700	P/L	£1,700

Profit and Loss Account

Cost of Sales:		Sales	£58,800
F.G.	£42,000		
Selling and Distribution	6,720		
Adverse variances:		Favourable variances:	
Breakages(q)	360	Direct Materials Price	200
Direct Wages Rate	240	Direct Labour Efficiency	150
Breakdowns(q)	150	Volume Efficiency	300
Capacity	2,200		
F. O'h'd Expenditure	900		
V. O'h'd. Expenditure	80		
Direct Material Usage	150		
Selling and Distribution	280		
Sales Margin Price	1,700		
Net Profit to Appropriation	4,670		

Profit and Loss Appropriation

		P/L	£4,670

The following explanatory notes are given for the benefit of the student checking his answer.

(a) "Actual" figures shown here for clarity.
(b) 4550 at £3.
(c) £9140 − 17,800 at £0·50.
(d) 100 hrs at £0·50.
(e) 17,700 at £0·50.

(*f*) 900 at £5. (The allowance here is not based on hours but on production in accordance with the note on the standard cost card.)
(*g*) 900 at £50.
(*h*) Standard usage (900 × 5) − 4550 = 50 at £3.
(*i*) SHP (900 × 20) − 17,700 = 300 hours at appropriate rate.
(*j*) Standard cost of sales, *i.e.* 840 at £50.
(*k*) From the standard cost card F.OAR is clearly £1 per hour. Therefore since 17,800 − 100 hours breakdowns = 17,700 hours went to production, the W.I.P. charge is 17,700 at £1.
(*l*) Budgeted fixed overheads clearly must have been 1000 × £20 = £20,000 (*i.e.* budgeted Sets × overheads per Set). Therefore expenditure variance = £20,000 − £20,900.
(*m*) 20,000 Budgeted hours − 17,700 Hours spent on production, at £1.
(*n*) 840 at £8.
(*o*) £57,100 − (840 at £70).
(*p*) Fixed overheads chargeable to breakdowns: 100 at £1. (This step is optional.)
(*q*) Since no breakages or breakdowns were planned these costs are, in effect, variances and so have been included among the variances.

Progress Test 22

3. (*a*) *Efficiency ratio* $= \frac{(900 \times 20)}{17{,}700} \times 100 = 101{\cdot}7\%$

Capacity ratio $= \frac{17{,}700}{(1000 \times 20)} \times 100 = 88{\cdot}5\%$

Activity ratio $= \frac{900}{1000} \times 100 = 90\%$

(*b*) *Profit and loss statement*

	£	£
Budgeted profit (1000 at £12)		12,000
Sales margin variances:		
Adverse: Price	1700	
Quantity (1000 − 840) at £12	1920	−3,620
		8,380
Selling and distribution variance:		
Adverse: Expenditure		−280
		8,100

Brought forward			£8,100
Purchase variance:			
Favourable: Material price			+200
			8,300
Production variances:			
Favourable: Efficiency:	Labour	150	
	Volume	300	+450
			8,750
Adverse:	Variable overhead expenditure	80	
	Fixed overhead expenditure	900	
	Capacity	2200	
	Wages rate	240	
	Material usage	150	
	Material breakages	360	
	Machine breakdowns	150	−4,080
Actual net profit			£4,670

4. Direct cost of 1 Set:

Direct materials, direct wages, variable overheads, and selling and distribution costs = £38

∴ Standard contribution = £70 − £38 = £32

∴ *Profit and loss statement:*

		£	£
Budgeted profit			12,000
Contribution variances:			
Adverse:	Sales price*	1700	
	Sales quantity: (1000 − 840) at £32	5120	−6,820
			5,180
Less net of other relevant variances†			−1,710
Actual net profit			£3,470

NOTE: The difference between the actual net profit here and the profit figure in 3(*b*) (£4670 − £3470 = £1200) is due to difference in stock valuations, *i.e.*

60 Sets at £50	= 3000
60 Sets at £30 (factory marginal cost)	= 1800
Difference	£1200

* As before in Question 3(*b*).

† All other variances except volume efficiency, capacity and fixed overhead part of breakdown cost.

Progress Test 23

9. The following is an alternative system of job costing for the Thorough Garage:

(*a*) The service manager is given permission to quote the price of all minor work, either on the basis of a set of standard charges or his own estimate.

(*b*) A single standing order number is raised for *all* such work.

(*c*) Employees are instructed to book all time and materials on such work to this order number. This will simplify workshop recording and analysis, since any employee who spends all his time on a succession of minor jobs will simply book the whole of his time (and materials used) to the one order number by means of a single entry.

(*d*) An account is opened for this order number and all materials, labour and direct expenses booked against the number, together with the appropriate overheads, are debited to this account. Also all sales are credited.

(*e*) At the end of each costing period the balance on this account (apart from any work in progress, which should be insignificant) is the over-all profit or loss on minor work. As long as this balance figure is reasonable, there is no real need for further details of individual jobs, since the service manager is ensuring that all costs are covered and a reasonable profit is being obtained on this work as a whole.

INDEX